M. Wozniak 6/2015

D1328228

Constantinople

Nicaea

Anatolia

DETAILED AREA

Edessa

Antioch

Aleppo

Rhodes

🏰 *Krak des Chevaliers*

Cyprus

Tripoli

Mediterranean Sea

Tyre

•Damascus

Acre

Nazareth

Sea of Galilee

Tiberias

Jaffa

Ascalon

Jerusalem

Bethlehem

Egypt

Damietta

200 mi.

N
W   E
S

The Glory
of the Crusades

STEVE WEIDENKOPF

The Glory
of the Crusades

Catholic
Answers
Press

Published by Catholic Answers, Inc.
2020 Gillespie Way
El Cajon, California 92020
1-888-291-8000 orders
619-387-0042 fax
catholic.com

Printed in the United States of America

Cover design by Devin Schadt
Interior design by Sherry Russell

ISBN 978-1-941663-00-4 hardcover
ISBN 978-1-941663-01-1 paperback
ISBN 978-1-941663-02-8 Kindle
ISBN 978-1-941663-03-5 ePub

To my beloved and devoted wife Kasey

If it's half as good as the half we've known,
here's Hail! to the rest of the road.

Contents

Acknowledgments

I deeply thank my beautiful and wonderful wife Kasey who supported me in various ways throughout the completion of this work. I also sincerely thank my patient children, Maddie, Maximilian, Thérèse, Luke, Jeb, and Martin.

Thanks also to Todd Aglialoro for approaching me to write this book. Dan Lord's editorial effort improved this book greatly. Dr. Kris Burns graciously allowed me to utilize space at the Notre Dame Graduate School of Christendom College—without that sanctuary this work would not have been completed. I wish to give a hearty thanks to my friends who read and commented on the manuscript throughout this process and for their unwavering support and encouragement: for my dear friend, Joe Burns, thanks for being my wingman; and Greg Erkens, thank you for your honest critique and thoughtful discussions. I also wish to remember the work of Dr. Warren H. Carroll (1932–2011), Catholic historian and founder of Christendom College. His many works of Catholic history are inspiring.

Lastly, I give thanks to the Blessed Virgin Mary and to the great St. Bernard of Clairvaux whose intercession throughout this project enabled its completion.

The men of Normandy had faith that what they were doing was right, faith that they fought for all humanity, faith that a just God would grant them mercy on this beachhead or on the next.
It was the deep knowledge—and pray God we have not lost it— that there is a profound, moral difference between the use of force for liberation and the use of force for conquest. You were here to liberate, not to conquer, and so you and those others did not doubt your cause. And you were right not to doubt.

Ronald Reagan, Pointe de Hoc,
Normandy, June 6, 1984

crusades
begins 1090

Author Preface

We have returned to the Levant, we have returned apparently
more as masters than ever we were during the struggle of
the Crusades—but we have returned bankrupt in that spiritual
wealth which was the glory of the Crusades.

Hilaire Belloc, *The Crusades*, 1937

In our age the Crusades are described as barbaric, wasteful, shameful, and even sinful. Rarely are they called glorious. This is because the modern world embraces a false narrative about the Crusades. This false story, however much discredited by authentic modern scholarship, remains entrenched in the minds of the masses.

Yet it was not always so. During the Crusading movement these military events were mostly seen in a positive light throughout Christendom, with popes and saints exhorting Catholic warriors to engage in them. Warriors who participated in these armed pilgrimages did so for a multitude of reasons but primarily for the sake of their own salvation. The Crusades emerged from a feudal society that stressed personal relationships founded on honor, loyalty, and service to one's vassal. Crusading knights invoked those virtues as they fought for Christ and the Church to recover ancient Christian territory stolen by Muslim conquerors.

The Crusades also emerged from an age in which faith permeated all aspects of society. This does not mean medieval Europe was heaven on earth or that Christendom was some idyllic utopia. But it was nonetheless an era in which people made radical life decisions because of their faith in Jesus Christ and his Church. Accordingly, the Crusading movement was a Catholic movement. Popes called for them, clerics (and saints) preached them, and Catholic warriors fought them for spiritual benefits. The Crusades cannot be properly understood apart from this Catholic reality.

Sadly, though, too many Catholics today seem more inclined to apologize for the Crusades rather than to embrace their glory.

Perhaps this is because the meaning of glory is not properly understood. The Old Testament can help provide us a proper understanding of glory. After Moses had led the Israelites out of Egypt, they sinned against God by worshipping the golden calf. God wanted to destroy the Israelites for their idolatry but Moses interceded for the people and the Lord relented. Moses' special relationship with God included the gift of being in the presence of the Lord in the meeting tent where Moses spoke to God face to face. Moses pleaded with God for his presence to remain with the Israelites on their journey to the Promised Land so that the other nations would see their uniqueness.

Moses also begged the Lord to show him his glory (Ex. 33:18). The Hebrew word for "glory" used most often in the Old Testament is *kabod*, which means "heavy in weight." To recognize the glory of something, therefore, means to acknowledge its importance or "weight." Moses wanted the Lord's glory to shine for the people in order that they would recognize the important act of their deliverance from bondage. To recognize the glory of the Crusades means not to whitewash what was ignoble about them, but to call due attention to their import in the life of the Church.

Perhaps by reclaiming the true Catholic narrative of the Crusades we may be emboldened to honor our Lord by proudly bearing the cross against modern enemies that threaten his Church no less than did the followers of Mohammed a millennium ago.

I

An Attack on the Crusades and the Church

*The Roman pontiffs and the European princes were engaged at
first in these crusades by a principle of superstition only, but when
in the process of time they learnt by experience that these holy wars
contributed much to increase their opulence and to extend their
authority . . . [then] ambition and avarice seconded and enforced the
dictates of fanaticism and superstition.*

Johann Lorenz von Mosheim (1693–1755),
German Lutheran historian[1]

Criticizing the Church is not a new phenomenon—it is almost
as old as the Church itself. Attacks on the Church's teachings
and the persecution of its faithful are a mainstay of its history.
However, what is relatively new is the misuse of historical events
to undermine the Church and its teachings. This "historical attack" began in the fires of the Protestant Revolution but in the
modern world has become a trite, overused tactic against the
Church. Nonetheless, it has proven quite effective, as many people in today's society (including, unfortunately, many Catholics) believe the false history presented by critics. Influenced by
the media, Hollywood, and other outlets, popular perception of
historical events reigns supreme even when that perception is
completely at odds with historical reality.

The Importance of Learning Church History

The historical attack is largely successful because Catholics do
not know their own history. This is not to fault the individual
Catholic, since Church history is not often a subject taught in

schools and universities—or, at least, it is not often well-taught.
Still, knowing our history well helps us know who we are.
Knowing our history badly will negatively influence our world-
view and cloud our relationship with the Church.

It is also important to learn Church history in order to defend the Church against its critics. The accepted historical narrative presented in the English-speaking world is centered on
a predominantly Protestant perspective. This perspective is not
amenable to an authentic understanding of Catholic history. As
a result, most Catholics throughout their educational careers
are provided an English Protestant interpretation of historical
events that warps and dismisses the Catholic story.[2] It is the necessary work of Catholic historians to undo the false aspects of
this Protestant view as well as provide an authentic Catholic
narrative in order to assist the faithful in defending the Church.

The Crusades

The Crusades are among the most misused and, by far, the most
misunderstood endeavors in all Church history. In the minds of
most modern people the very word "Crusade" conjures negative images of blood-thirsty, barbaric, and greedy European nobles setting out to conquer peaceful Muslims living in the Holy
Land. These images are reinforced by the media, both in print
and film. Hollywood last addressed the Crusades in the 2005
movie *Kingdom of Heaven*, which purports to tell the story of
the Kingdom of Jerusalem during the reign of Baldwin IV, the
"Leper King." The film's storyline includes the dramatic Battle
of Hattin and the siege and loss of Jerusalem to the Muslim general Saladin. Provided with such dramatic and engaging story
arcs, the movie had the potential to be a true masterpiece and an
example of authentic history on screen.

Unfortunately, the director and producers decided to rely on
faulty and even damaging popular imaginations of the Crusades
rather than on historical fact. Jonathan Riley-Smith, one of the
foremost authorities on the Crusades today, remarked the film was

"Osama bin Laden's version of history."[3] Although the film was highly anticipated, it did not do very well at the domestic US box office, taking in a mere $47 million (it cost $130 million to make).[4]

It is extremely frustrating for serious scholars of the Crusades to witness these events thoroughly maligned and misrepresented in the media. However, the fact is "Crusading was always controversial,"[5] and there were many critics even throughout the Crusading movement itself. What is particularly aggravating about modern criticism is that despite the significant amount of serious scholarship over the last forty years, popular perception remains shaped by outdated and false images. As one modern Crusades historian recently remarked, "The Crusades remain one of the few subjects of professional history that carry wide popular recognition even if little serious understanding."[6]

A survey of this landscape of popular misconceptions about the Crusades reveals seven main myths, which this book will refute:

Popular Misconceptions

1. The Crusades were wars of unprovoked aggression.
2. The Crusaders were motivated primarily by greed and the prospect for plunder and riches.
3. When Jerusalem was liberated in 1099, the Crusaders killed all the inhabitants of the city—so much blood was spilled that it ran ankle deep.
4. The Crusades were colonial enterprises.
5. The Crusades were also wars against the Jews and should be seen as the first Holocaust.
6. The Crusades were wars of conversion.
7. The Crusades are the source of the modern tension between Islam and the West.

Seeds of the Myths

The creation of these myths began in the sixteenth century when Protestant authors used the still-ongoing Crusades to attack the Church and, principally, the papacy. Most Protestant critics of that time viewed the Crusades as the creation of the anti-Christ (the pope) to increase Church wealth. Crusaders were portrayed as ignorant followers of superstition who participated in holy wars, which were nothing more than examples of Catholic bigotry and cruelty. Protestant teaching was completely opposed to the Crusading movement because it necessitated obedience to the papacy, preserved the unity of Christendom, and provided spiritual benefits (indulgences).[7]

Martin Luther set the stage for the Protestant interpretation of the Crusades by seeing the Ottoman Turkish threat to Europe in the early sixteenth century as part of God's plan for divine retribution against the evils of the Catholic Church. At the height of his revolution against the Church, Luther wrote, "to fight against the Turks is to oppose the judgment God visits upon our iniquities through them."[8] After a Turkish invasion force reached the gates of Vienna in 1529, Luther reconsidered his anti-Crusade stance and actually encouraged Christian princes (Catholic and Protestant alike) to join together to fight the Turkish horde. Of course, Luther did not actually call for a Crusade, nor did he desire a religious war resembling the Crusades. He steadfastly rejected any such notion by writing, "If in my turn I were a soldier and saw in the battlefield a priest's banner or cross, even if it were the very crucifix, I should want to run away as though the devil were chasing me!"[9]

Watering the Myths

If these Reformation-era writers were the first to view the Crusades through the lens of anti-papal rhetoric, seeing the entire effort as nothing other than a vast waste of European resources undertaken by barbaric, superstitious warriors, these themes received increasing nourishment once combined with the new anti-Church hostility of the Enlightenment.

Centered in France and occupying the seventeenth and eighteenth centuries, the philosophical movement known as the Enlightenment sought to weaken the influence of the Church in European society. Enlightenment thinking affected most areas of life, including the study and presentation of history. Crusade history was used by intellectuals "not as a historical study in its own right but as a tool in conceptual arguments about religion and the progress of civilization."[10] The Crusades would continue to be used in this way by future generations to further their own agenda against society and the Church.[11]

The main Enlightenment critics of the Crusades were the Frenchmen Voltaire and Denis Diderot, and England's David Hume and Edward Gibbon. Voltaire (1694–1778) waged a fierce campaign of satire and ridicule against the Catholic Church. In 1751 he published an essay on the Crusades in which he described them as an "epidemic of fury which lasted for 200 years and which was always marked by every cruelty, every perfidy, every debauchery, and every folly of which human nature is capable."[12] He further opined that the Crusades were "wasteful, pointless, ruined by excessive papal ambition for worldly power, an example of the corrosive fanaticism of the middle ages."[13]

Diderot (1713–1784) also saw the Crusades in a wholly negative light and criticized them for the despoliation of Europe. Diderot wrote that the consequences of these "horrible wars" were "the depopulation of its nations, the enrichment of monasteries, the impoverishment of the nobility, the ruin of ecclesiastical discipline, contempt for agriculture, scarcity of cash and an infinity of vexations."[14] Diderot also complained that the Crusades were worthless enterprises of savagery in which European knights were sent by the Church to "cut the inhabitant's throats and seize a rocky peak [Jerusalem] which was not worth one drop of blood."[15]

Hume (1711–1776) believed the Muslim world was superior in "science and humanity" and the Crusades were "the most signal and most durable monument to human folly that has yet appeared in any age or nation."[16]

The reflections of Edward Gibbon (1737–1794) on the Crusades mimicked the writings of his fellow "enlightened" thinkers principally in the thought that the Crusades brought nothing but negative consequences to Europe. In Gibbon's mind, the

Crusaders were ignorant and superstitious criminals manipulated by the Church:

> At the voice of their pastor, the robber, the incendiary, the homicide, arose by their thousands to redeem their souls by repeating on the infidels the same deeds which they exercised against their Christian brethren; and the terms of atonement were eagerly embraced by offenders of every rank and denomination. None were pure; none were exempt from the guilt and penalty of sin; and those who were the least amenable to the justice of God and the Church were the best entitled to the temporal and eternal recompense of their pious courage.[17]

Gibbon also believed that the primary motivation of the Crusaders was greed, with Western warriors bent on the pursuit of "mines of treasures, of gold and diamonds, of palaces of marble and jasper, and of odoriferous groves of cinnamon and frankincense."[18] This erroneous view of Crusader motivations, still commonly held, may be Gibbon's enduring mark on the popular history of the Crusades.

Modern Scholarship

In the early twentieth century, the Crusades were brushed with a colonial color which later greatly influenced (and still influences) modern Islamic understanding of the movement. The dissolution of the Ottoman Turkish Empire after its defeat in the First World War produced colonial mandates for the British and French in the Middle East. These European powers used Crusading imagery to describe their overseas colonies. A London magazine published a cartoon of King Richard I watching the British marching into Jerusalem with the words, "At last my dream come true."[19] The French commander of Syria, General Henri Gouraud, was reported to have remarked, "Behold, Saladin, we have returned."[20] The main author who contributed to this colonial interpretation of the Crusades was the Frenchman

Rene Grousset (1858–1952). However, within a half-century of the publication of his *History of the Crusades*,[21] most scholars had thoroughly rebuked Grousset's colonial view.

As the twentieth century reached its midpoint, another group of historians would interpret the Crusades through the lens of economics. For these Marxist scholars, the Crusades were colonial endeavors motivated by economic factors impacted by the growth in medieval population and the shortage of resources in Europe.

Additionally, most historians of the early to mid twentieth century viewed the Crusades in a wholly negative light because of a personal animus against religion as a whole. These scholars could not fathom the idea of warriors with actual faith engaging in warfare for primarily religious reasons. Instead these critics believed the "medieval crusades were evil precisely because they were wars of religion."[22]

More recent Crusades scholarship has been shaped by the writings of two historians who had vastly different careers. Carl Erdmann (1898–1945) was a brilliant scholar whose work, *The Origins of the Idea of Crusading* (1935) examined the Crusades as an outgrowth of the papal reform movement in the eleventh century, which primarily sought to ensure the independence of the papacy and Church against secular interference. He also expanded the scope of the Crusades to any area where Christian warriors, motivated by spiritual incentives, engaged in armed conflict. Unfortunately, Erdmann would die relatively young at the age of forty-seven while serving in the German *Wehrmacht* in the Balkans.[23]

More than any other historian, Steven Runciman (1903–2000) shaped modern popular understanding of the Crusades, and his interpretation continues to influence Hollywood and the media.[24] Runciman specialized in Byzantine history, and in his still-influential three-volume *History of the Crusades* (1951–1954) viewed the Crusades through that prism. Most modern Crusades scholars are highly critical of Runciman's work, for although it is well written and engaging it is more literature than history, and is colored by Runciman's Byzantine leanings. Christopher Tyerman wrote, "The scholarship is wide but not deep; the literary technique effective in short stretches but taken in large doses tends to indigestion."[25] Runciman was another historian, in a long line, who failed to view the Crusades from a contemporary point of view, making his work "dated in technique, style and content; derivative, misleading, tendentious; a polemic, masquerading as epic."[26]

Nonetheless, Runciman shaped modern popular perception of the Crusades, Crusaders, and medieval Muslims by illustrating Western warriors as simple barbarians bent on the destruction of a peaceful and sophisticated Islamic culture. He saw Western Europe as over-populated, violent, and economically stagnant; the Crusades were thus "great barbarian invasions."[27] In contrast to the barbaric and ruthless Western warriors, the Muslim general Saladin was presented as the perfect ruler who was merciful, considerate, tolerant, modest, and intellectual. In essence, Saladin was reduced by Runciman "to a catalogue of nineteenth-century English upper-class virtues."[28] Ultimately, Runciman condemned the Crusades as sins against the Holy Spirit:

> In the long sequence of interaction and fusion between Orient and Occident out of which our civilization has grown, the Crusades were a tragic and destructive episode. The historian as he gazes back across the centuries at their gallant story must find his admiration overcast by sorrow as the witness that it bears to the limitations of human nature. There was so much courage and so little honor, so much devotion and so little understanding. High ideals were besmirched by cruelty and greed, enterprise and endurance by a blind and narrow self-righteousness; and the Holy War itself was nothing more than a long act of intolerance in the name of God, which is a sin against the Holy Ghost.[29]

Happily, Crusades scholarship over the last generation has greatly enhanced our understanding of the Crusading movement and overturned much of the erroneous interpretations and fanciful tales of the agenda-driven authors of the past. Modern scholars are focused on studying the Crusades from the perspective of the participants and understanding what motivated people to participate in them.[30] Yet despite the work of these excellent scholars, popular perception of the Crusades remains fixated in a Protestant/ Enlightened/Runciman orientation.

Catholic Misunderstandings

Even good Catholic writers can find themselves relying on old stereotypes when discussing the Crusades. Fr. Robert Barron's popular video series and companion book, *Catholicism*, strikes a condemnatory tone when discussing the Crusades. Referencing the four marks of the Church, Fr. Barron addresses the criticism leveled against the Church's holiness and remarks, "How could one possibly declare as holy a church that has been implicated in so many atrocities and outrages over the centuries? How could a holy church have supported the Crusades, the Inquisition and its attendant tortures, slavery, the persecution of Galileo... and the burning of innocent women as witches?"[31] In Father Barron's assessment, the Crusades are one example in a long "litany of crimes" in which even high-ranking clergy did "cruel, stupid and wicked things."[32] He even suggests that the saintly Bernard of Clairvaux was probably "wrong, even sinful, to preach the Second Crusade."[33]

Fr. Barron's work in this area betrays a lack of awareness of the recent and authentic scholarship on the Crusades (as well as the Inquisition) and instead relies on old, formulated, and erroneous criticisms of the Church's historical past. Regrettably, the popularity of his (otherwise excellent) series ensures that these false narratives continue to influence the understanding of Catholics today.

Critics of the Church and even those within the Church argue that Pope St. John Paul II addressed the Crusades when during the Great Jubilee of 2000 he "apologized" for the sins of the Church; therefore, Catholics should not view these events in a positive light.

This view is not supported by the facts. John Paul II did not apologize for the Crusades; in fact, he never even mentioned the word during the Day of Pardon on March 12, 2000. In order to set the Church on a renewed footing as it entered the Third Millennium of the Faith, the pope tasked the International Theological Commission[34] to study the concept of a purification of memory that aimed "at liberating personal and communal conscience from all forms of resentment and violence that are the legacy of past faults, through a renewed historical and theological evaluation."[35] On the Day of Pardon, John Paul II requested forgiveness from God for the faults and failings of our brothers and sisters who have gone before us in the Faith. His desire was born from a love of God and the Church in order for it to enter the third millennium free from the sins of Church members in the past. The pope not only asked God for forgiveness for the failings of past members of the Church but also called the Church to forgive those who have trespassed against it.

John Paul also recognized the importance of understanding the historical context in which the events of the past were lived, and he had no desire to pass judgment on our Catholic predecessors.[36] He did not reject the Church's historical past, which is replete with examples of mercy, forgiveness, holiness, and grand achievement. In his September 1, 1999 general audience he expressly said that the Church's "request for pardon must not be understood as an expression of false humility or as a denial of her 2,000-year history . . . instead, she responds to the necessary requirement of the truth, which, in addition to the positive aspects, recognizes the human limitations and weaknesses of the various generations of Christ's disciples."[37]

The Church has *not* apologized for the Crusades because an apology is not necessary. On the contrary, for centuries the Crusading movement was integral to the lived expression of the Faith.

An authentic presentation of the Crusades thus centers on viewing them through a contemporary perspective. The Catholic historian Hilaire Belloc understood this truism and illustrated it throughout his historical books. In his work on the history of the great heresies in Christendom, Belloc wrote that "the most difficult thing in the world in connection with history, and the rarest of achievement, is the seeing of events as contemporaries saw them, instead of seeing them through the distorting medium of our later knowledge."[38]

An authentic understanding of historical events begins not with the present time of the historical author, but with the contemporary time of the participant. Failure to adhere to that premise falsifies history and produces a "reading into" rather than a "learning from" historical events.[39] Critics of the Crusades and the Church usually fall into the trap of believing that their own opinion or society is superior to those that came before them.

The International Theological Commission recognized this trap and encouraged those who would presume to judge the actions of Catholics in the past to keep "in mind that the historical periods are different, that the sociological and cultural times within which the Church acts are different, and so, the paradigms and judgments proper to one society and to one era might be applied erroneously in the evaluations of other periods of history, producing many misunderstandings."[40] Understanding the Crusades from the perspective of those who lived during and participated in them is vital. The movement must also be understood as the lived expression of the vibrant Catholicism of medieval people.

Abandoning the Defensive

The purpose of this work is to present a restored narrative of the Crusades, utilizing modern scholarship in order to give Catholics today the tools to answer the critics and defend the Church and its history.

Most people associate the Crusades with armed expeditions by Western warriors against the Muslims in the Holy Land. Although that association is not incorrect, it is incomplete. Because the Crusading movement evolved over time, there were many types of Crusades over the centuries, including those against heretics, pagans, and enemies of the Church. Regardless, this book will concentrate on the major Crusades against the Muslims in the Holy Land, Egypt, the Mediterranean Sea, and Europe, precisely because the major misunderstandings about the Crusades centers on these expeditions. Only an authentic presentation of the Crusading movement and its campaigns against Islam can equip Catholics to defend the Church, countering the false historical narrative prevalent in society today with a proper understanding.

At the same time, as the Church progresses through its third millennium and in light of the call by recent pontiffs for a New Evangelization, the time is ripe for a reinvigorated sense of Catholic identity. Catholics must know the authentic history of the Church in order to defend it from the many critics in the modern world; however, for a truly vibrant Catholic identity to flourish once more, defending the Church is not enough. We must go on the attack and present the story of our Catholic family with vigor, courage, and resolve.

In the words of Walter Cardinal Brandmüller, president emeritus of the Pontifical Committee for the Historical Sciences, "[W]e should finally stop being like the frightened rabbit that stares at the snake before it is swallowed by it. This defeatist attitude, this whining self-pity that has gained so much ground . . . in Catholic circles, is an insult to God. What is needed is a new, forceful consciousness of being Catholic."[41]

2

Birth of the Crusades

The Lord is a warrior; the Lord is His name!

Exodus 15:3

The Crusading movement occupied a central place in European and Church history for nearly 700 years and was a unique cultural and religious phenomenon. Despite its longevity and influence, defining what the Crusades actually were has proven problematic for historians.[42] The very nature of the Crusading movement, its evolution throughout its history, and its appeal to contemporaries contribute to the difficulty in definition. During the movement people of all social backgrounds supported the Crusades, and sifting through their views presents "a range of ideas from the most cerebral to the most primitive."[43]

One area of agreement concerns the very word "Crusade": Those who participated in these expeditions did not use it. "Crusade" is a modern word, not a medieval one. It is a hybrid, derived from Spanish, French, and Latin and first used in 1706, passing into popular usage through the writings of David Hume and Edward Gibbon.[44] Crusading contemporaries used the term *passagia*, among others, meaning an "exceptionally large military expedition declared against unbelievers."[45] Those who undertook the *passagia* were known as *crucesignati*, or "those signed with the cross."

In essence, "a Crusade was fought against those perceived to be the external or internal foes of Christendom for the recovery of Christian property or in defense of the Church or Christian people."[46] Those who participated in the Crusades were seen as pilgrims and their journey was an armed pilgrimage, which

was a revolutionary idea since to that point pilgrims had been
obliged to leave their weapons at home.[47]

Essential Ingredients of the Crusades

Although historians disagree over exact definitions, there were
several essential ingredients necessary for an armed expedition
to be considered a Crusade.[48]

The first ingredient was called "taking the cross," which included a public ecclesiastical vow that bound the aspirant to undertake
the *passagia*. The vow was made to God (not to the pope, a bishop,
or any secular lord) and was legally binding; to abandon it was to
risk excommunication. Those who took the vow were marked by
the wearing of a cloth cross on their garments that was only removed upon successful completion of their journey. In the beginning of the Crusading movement, the vow was also accompanied
by the bestowal of the pilgrim's purse and staff.[49] This act illustrates
the penitential nature of the Crusades and the view by contemporaries that Crusaders were fundamentally armed pilgrims.

The second basic element consisted of papal approval of the
expedition. Those who took the cross were granted special privileges as well. One of the major concerns for warriors was the
protection of their family and property while they were away.
Since the Crusading movement developed in a feudal society,
warriors were afraid that while overseas fighting for Christ their
neighbor might invade and take their land. In order to allay that
fear, the Church promised protection of a Crusader's property
through the threat of excommunication for violators. Crusaders
received secular as well as spiritual privileges. They could demand and receive hospitality from the Church on their journey.
They were exempt from taxes and tolls, and held immunity from
arrest. But the main motivator for participation was the granting
of an indulgence—the remission of the temporal punishment
due to sins already forgiven in the sacrament of penance.

Crusading was an integral part of the lived expression of
the Faith for multiple centuries and cannot be considered an

aberration in Church history.[50] It was the teaching of the Church for nearly 700 years that men had a moral obligation to take the cross in order to liberate and defend Christian territory. Popes from Bl. Urban II to Bl. Innocent XI exhorted the faithful to participate in these armed expeditions, providing spiritual benefits to encourage participation.

Indeed, participation in Crusades was not limited to laymen, for even bishops, abbots, papal legates, and even popes (Pius II) took the cross. St. Bernard of Clairvaux, St. Hildegard of Bingen, St. Francis of Assisi, St. Catherine of Siena and other saints supported the Crusades and encouraged warriors to take the cross.

The Crusades were even a topic at six of the twenty-one ecumenical councils. These six councils either called for Crusades or spent considerable time planning expeditions. In fact, the Fourth Lateran Council (1215) and the Second Council of Lyons (1274) crafted two of the Crusades' main documents.[51]

The Rise and Expansion of Islam

While it is vital to recognize the Crusades as integral events in the life of the Church, it is at least equally important to understand *why* they were undertaken. The seventh-century rise of the militaristic and imperialistic movement known as Islam, and its subsequent conquest of ancient Christian territory, was the prime cause for the creation of the Crusading movement and the reason for its longevity.

Islam's entrance onto the world stage is steeped in mystery. The standard historical narrative presents the story of a solitary Arab receiving alleged divine inspiration and revelations, which spontaneously produced a radically new civilization in the seventh century. Recent scholarship challenges this narrative and posits that Islam instead grew by reshaping elements of existing surrounding civilizations into a new community: "The puzzle of Islam's origins might be viewed . . . as a black hole sucking in a great spiraling swirl of influences before casting them back out in a radically different form."[52] Over the last generation, much of what has traditionally been known about the origins of Islam and its founder Mohammed has come into question; modern studies have even led some historians to question the very existence of Mohammed.[53] The first recorded public reference to Mohammed occurred sixty years after his death and the first biographies were not written until 150 years later.[54]

The traditional Muslim narrative of Mohammed describes a man born in the city of Mecca in the Arabian Peninsula in the late sixth century. He was the member of an important and wealthy tribe that generated its wealth from lucrative trade with pilgrims coming to Mecca to worship the pantheon of Arabian gods in the Kaaba shrine. At this time the Arabian Peninsula contained various nomadic tribes that were "the most superstitious and ignorant in the world."[55] They were also vicious and ruthless warriors who found employment in the Roman Empire as auxiliary troops, augmenting the Roman legions when the need arose.[56] In A.D. 610, while in a cave near Mecca, Mohammed allegedly experienced "history's most epochal mid-life crisis."[57] Later Muslim tradition (the story is not recounted in the Qur'an), related that Mohammed was awoken from a deep sleep by the voice of a heavenly messenger, later identified as the Archangel Gabriel, which informed him of his calling as the messenger of God.

Mohammed's initial reaction to this voice was terror, and belief that he was possessed of an evil spirit. Distraught, he contemplated suicide: "I will go to the top of the mountain and throw myself down that I may kill myself and gain rest."[58] The messenger consoled Mohammed and ordered him to recite the words of God. Mohammed continued to receive private revelations for the following three years. Finally, in 613, Mohammed was ordered to make his revelations public.

Mohammed revealed the contents of his private revelations in Mecca, but initially met indifference. However, the frequency and urgency of his teachings eventually drew heightened responses. His teachings were radical and revolutionary. He claimed there was only one God and it did not have an idol in the Kaaba. Mohammed demanded also total submission (*islam*) to the will of God. His most revolutionary teaching, and the one that most influenced future events, was the call to abandon tribal relationships. This was "the most stomach-churning prospect imaginable for any Arab."[59] Those who submitted to the will of God joined a unique community (*umma*) where all were considered equal. The formation of this community created a sharp distinction between Muslims and non-believers. Those in the community lived in the House of Islam; those without lived in the House of War. This relationship presupposed a permanent state of war between the two houses. The unity of the *umma*, in theory, prevented infighting and led to outward expansion from the beginnings of Islam.

After fleeing Mecca for fear of his life in 622, Mohammed and his initial followers settled in Medina, which later became known as the "City of the Prophet." Medina was the site of Mohammed's militant revelations and the base of combat operations. According to a later biographer, Mohammed personally led nine combat raids from Medina wielding his favorite sword known as "the Cleaver of Vertebrae."[60] Another biographer quotes Mohammed as saying, "[T]he gates of Paradise lie in the shadow of the sword."[61]

Mohammed laid the foundation for the Crusades when, at the end of his life, he instructed his followers to "fight all men until they say there is no God but Allah."[62] This statement was later written into the Qur'an as "fight those who believe not in God."[63] During his life, Mohammed embodied these words in his campaigns against his fellow Arabs as well as against Jews. Mohammed's militaristic teachings and actions set the example for his followers who sought to emulate the *jihad* undertaken by the prophet. *Jihad* and imperial expansion of the *umma* promised not only material but also spiritual riches for the Muslim, as heaven awaited him if he died on *jihad* and hell awaited those who fought against him.[64]

Mohammed's teachings on the *umma* and *jihad* oriented Islam toward imperialistic expansion. The conflict between the

Sunni's based in Bagdad
Shites based in Egypt

House of Islam and the House of War began during Mohammed's lifetime when Islamic forces raided Palestine and Syria.
Within a decade of his death in 632, Muslim armies conquered
the Christian areas of Syria (635), Jerusalem (638), and Egypt
(642). In 674, Muslim forces even laid siege to the capital city of
the Byzantine Empire, Constantinople, but were repulsed. Islam
also expanded westward through North Africa, sweeping away
all resistance so that by 700 the last Christian stronghold fell.
Former pagan nomads from the Arabian Peninsula now ruled
the ancient Roman provinces, which had once converted to the
Catholic Faith by the blood of the martyrs.

Mohammed's focus on building a community united in political and military purpose through religion was tested mightily after his death, as competing families engaged in a game of
thrones. The pursuit of power produced conquered territories
which, although originally provinces of a united Muslim empire, soon became independent territories in competition with
one another. In the century before the Crusades, the Muslim
world was united by language and religion but broken into regional centers of power: the Abbasid (Sunni) caliphate in Baghdad, the Fatimid (Shi'ite) caliphate in Egypt, and the Umayyad
caliphate of Cordoba in Spain.

The early eleventh century witnessed a destructive event that
shook Europe to its core. Egypt was controlled by the demented
caliph al-Hakim who, in 1009, ordered the destruction of the
Church of the Holy Sepulchre, known at the time in the Islamic world as the "church of the dung heap."[65] Al-Hakim's reign
was marked by bizarre regulations against his Muslim subjects
and persecution against the *dhimmi* (non-Muslims). He mandated
Muslim women wear a veil in public but then ordered them to not
leave their homes.[66] He required all Christians and Jews to wear
a black turban and either a cross or a block of wood in public.[67]
Edicts passed in 1011 and 1012 prohibited the use of wine even in
the celebration of the Eucharist, required the removal of all exte-
rior crosses and destruction of all missals.[68] The persecution came
to an end when al-Hakim was murdered in 1021. Al-Hakim's

destruction of one of the most important churches in Christendom and his persecution of indigenous Christians were horrific events that left a lasting imprint on the people of Europe.

The danger grew for native Holy Land Christians and the Byzantine Empire in the middle of the eleventh century with the arrival of a new group of people onto the world stage: the Seljuk Turks. The Seljuks were nomadic people from the Asian steppes who converted to Sunni Islam and consolidated their power in the Abbasid caliphate based in Baghdad. The Seljuks mistreated indigenous Christians by destroying churches, killing priests, and harassing European pilgrims to the Holy Land. One example of Seljuk brutality is found in the story of Günther, bishop of Bamberg, who led a group of 12,000 pilgrims to the Holy Land in 1065. The group managed to survive great trials in Hungary, mistreatment by the Byzantines, and the general discomfort and hardship involved in such a journey, but they were not to survive their encounter with the Seljuks, who massacred the entire group on Good Friday, only two days march from Jerusalem.[69]

The Seljuks were not content to control Armenia, Syria, and Palestine, and soon set their sights on Anatolia (modern-day Turkey), a very important province of the Byzantine Empire. Unfortunately, the arrival of the Seljuks occurred at the worst possible time for the Byzantines, who were ruled in the later eleventh century by a series of incompetent emperors who allowed the army to decline. This decline in readiness was manifested in the result of the Battle of Manzikert on August 19, 1071. The news of the Seljuk invasion of Anatolia reached Emperor Romanus IV Diogenes (r. 1068–1071), who gathered a force of 60,000, including Western mercenaries, to fight the Turks. The fighting was intense but the numerically superior Seljuks were victorious when they succeeded in wounding and capturing Emperor Romanus.

Manzikert was a disaster for the Byzantines. The imperial army was in shambles, the emperor had been captured, and the province that provided the bulk of military recruitment and economic prosperity was in enemy hands. The Seljuks would consolidate their power in Anatolia, establishing it as the Sultanate of Rum with its capital in the ancient Christian city of Nicaea—site of the first ecumenical council in 325 and within striking distance of Constantinople. By all accounts, the disaster of Manzikert was the "shock that launched the Crusades."[70]

The Byzantine Empire began to recover under the vital leadership of Emperor Alexius I Comnenus (r. 1081–1118). Alexius knew the threat posed to Byzantium by the Seljuk Turks was so dire that it required extreme measures and more manpower than he could raise or afford, so he decided to seek help from the West. He sent ambassadors to the pope, the one person with the universal authority required to organize and recruit a rescue effort of such immensity.

The Call to Arms

Many men give speeches; some are memorable, others are forgotten; few speeches are world changing. The speech given by Bl. Urban II at the council of Clermont in November 1095 changed the world.

Urban was born into a northern French noble family and, although he entered the service of the Church, he understood the martial class and how to motivate it.[71] He used this knowledge to great effect at Clermont. The main event of the council occurred on November 27 when Urban spoke to a large assembly in the open air.

Urban's speech, which inaugurated the Crusading movement, focused on three main themes: the liberation of the Holy City of Jerusalem, the violent activities of the Turks, and an exhortation to Western warriors to take up arms.[72] The central element in his speech was the cross, and it is clear that Urban intended the journey to the east to be penitential.

The liberation of Jerusalem was paramount for Urban and he knew this focus would resonate with the assembled French nobility and knights. There was much devotion to the Holy City in France, which spread due to the influence of the great monastery of Cluny, and pilgrimages were very popular even among the nobles, many of whom had taken to naming their daughters "Jerusalem."[73] The Holy City was considered the center of the world, and its occupation by the Muslims was distasteful to the citizens of Christendom. Urban's call was focused on rousing warriors from their slumber and their selfish interests, to valiantly march to the East to restore ancient Christian lands, most importantly Jerusalem, to Christ and the Church:

> This royal city, therefore, situated at the center of the world, is now held captive by his enemies, and is in subjection to those who do not know God... She seeks therefore and desires to be liberated, and does not cease to implore you to come to her aid.[74]

Urban's preaching also focused on the plight of Christians in the Holy Land, who were subject to cruel tortures and punishments at the hands of the Turks. His graphic description of Turkish atrocities was designed to elicit a visceral response from his hearers in order that they might take up their arms to liberate their Christian brothers and sisters.

Since participation in the Crusades was voluntary, it was necessary for Urban to find ways to motivate the assembled warriors at Clermont to travel thousands of miles from home and risk certain death. Urban knew that few knights would undertake the arduous journey simply to help the Byzantine Christians, since they were schismatics who rejected the universal jurisdiction of the Roman pontiff. So, Urban appealed to the military adventures of the great warriors in French history in order to exhort his listeners to join the Crusade:

> Let the deeds of your ancestors move you and incite your minds to manly achievements; Oh, most valiant soldiers and descendants of invincible ancestors, be not degenerate, but recall the valor of your progenitors.[75]

Finally, Urban offered the spiritual incentive of a plenary indulgence, which was unique and provided the main motivator for those who undertook the journey. Through the power and authority of the Petrine Office, Urban decreed: "Whoever goes on the journey to free the church of God in Jerusalem out of devotion alone, and not for the gaining of glory or money, can substitute the journey for all penance for sin."[76] Urban repeated this spiritual incentive in his letter to the clergy and people of Bologna where many were considering taking the cross. Urban exhorted them to do so: "[I]f any among you travel, not for the desire of the goods of this world, but only those who go for the good of their souls and the liberty of the churches, they will be relieved of the penance for all of their sins, for which they have made a full and perfect confession."[77]

Urban announced the departure for what came to be known later as the First Crusade for the Feast of the Assumption of Mary: August 15, 1096. He appointed Bishop Adhemar de Monteil as leader of the expedition and the official papal representative.

The Church and War

Pope Bl. Urban II asked soldiers to volunteer to utilize their martial skills, and this call to arms is one thing many modern-day Catholics and secularists find distasteful about the Crusades. Critics believe the Crusades highlight the hypocrisy of Christians, who, on the one hand, profess to follow Jesus who willingly accepted his passion and death, and on the other participated in and supported an armed expedition to violently recover the Holy Land.

Ignoring the historical context of the Crusades or applying modern-day sensibilities and political conditions to events in the past produces a gross misunderstanding of the Crusades and those who participated in them. The answer to this objection, then, lies in understanding the Church's teaching on warfare and its application in various historical periods.

The Church's teaching on violence is a combination of the understanding and purpose of warfare from two traditions: the Jewish and the Greco-Roman, with both influenced by the teachings of Christ.[78] The Old Testament is replete with examples of legitimate warfare undertaken by the Jewish people and sanctioned by God. The Lord rescued the people of Israel by drowning Pharaoh's crack troops as they chased the Israelites through the parted Red Sea. Witnessing the destruction of their enemy, the Israelites shouted in joy, "The Lord is a warrior; the Lord is his name."[79] Additionally, the Israelites were commanded by God to fight the tribes inhabiting the Promised Land in order to remain pure in their worship to God and not succumb to pagan practices. Once in the Promised Land, warfare did not cease as the Israelites throughout their history were ordered by God to fight their enemies.[80]

The justification for warfare in the New Testament is more nuanced than in the Old Testament, for the teachings of Christ demand more deliberation concerning the use of violence. On one hand Jesus seems to discourage the use of violence, as when he rebuked Simon Peter for cutting off the ear of Malchus in the Garden of Gethsemane;[81] on the other hand, Jesus acknowledged division in the world and the possibility of violence when he said, "Do not think that I have come to bring peace on earth; I have not come to bring peace, but a sword" (Matt. 10:34). Elsewhere in the New Testament the military profession is shown in a positive light. Centurions (Roman officers) are presented as examples of great faith in several episodes, including at the Cross.[82] The conversion of the centurion Cornelius is a defining moment in the Acts of the Apostles and justifies the missionary outreach efforts to the Gentiles.[83] John the Baptist also influenced Christian understanding of the warrior when he instructed soldiers to "rob no one by violence or by false accusation, and be content with your wages" (Luke 3:14). Since his admonition did not repudiate the military profession, the Church acknowledged the legitimacy of soldiering.

However, the question of whether Christians could serve in the imperial Roman army was greatly debated in the early Church. This is understandable given the historical situation of a Church under persecution by the state, whose instrument of persecution was the army. Some early Christian writers believed members of the Faith could serve in the army while others disagreed.

Although the nascent Church wrestled with this question, soldiers embraced the Faith and even gave the ultimate witness of their faith through martyrdom.[84]

Once the Emperor Constantine legalized the existence of the Church in 313, it grew in membership and began to see itself as part of rather than separate from the empire. As such, the Church used elements of Greco-Roman thought in explaining its understanding of violence and when it can be used, drawing mostly from Aristotle (384–322 B.C.), Livy (59 B.C.–A.D. 17), and Cicero (106–43 B.C.).

Aristotle provided the basic Greco-Roman understanding of violence in his work, *Politics*, where he focused on the ends of warfare. War, for Aristotle, should be waged for the sake of peace and not for its own sake. In other words, there should be a just end for engaging in combat, such as self-defense, to obtain an empire to benefit the state's citizens, or to enslave non-Greeks.[85]

The Roman writer Livy added to Aristotle's "just ends" by also focusing on the need for a "just cause" to enter into combat, which could include the breaking of an agreement or retribution for an injury. Such reasons illustrate that an understanding of what constitutes "just cause" can be influenced by the historical situation and by those responsible for making the determination. Modern sensibilities recoil at any mention of a "just cause" in a holy war, but those who participated in the Crusades did not share that sentiment.

The Roman thinker Cicero further enhanced Greco-Roman thought on warfare by placing it in a legal context, requiring a formal declaration of war by the state, an expressed purpose to the conflict, and by allowing for the recovery of lost goods or punishment as "just causes" to go to war.[86]

The major influence in Christian thinking on the causes of and purposes for warfare is St. Augustine of Hippo (354–430). In his work, *City of God*, Augustine consolidated the Jewish and Greco-Roman traditions into a Christian understanding of legitimate warfare. The modern world sees violence as inherently evil, but Augustine believed violence could be used for

legitimate reasons including the restoration of order and property. In special circumstances, war could be a holy undertaking.
Using Augustine's writings, the Church identified four criteria
that must be satisfied: a just cause, which can involve past or present aggression; proclamation by legitimate authority; defense or
recovery of rightful possessions; and right intention or pure motives of the participants. Additionally, war should be undertaken
only as a last recourse and the violence unleashed must be pro-
portionate to the threat.[87] In the eleventh century the writings
of Augustine on religious war and the secular concerns for just
war merged to form a holy just war in the Crusades.[88]

This Christian understanding of holy war differs greatly from
the Muslim teaching on *jihad*. *Jihad* is incumbent upon all Muslims and is a foundational teaching of Islam. Christian holy war
is not incumbent on every believer; indeed, participation in the
Crusades was always voluntary, and violence is seen as a necessary evil that can only be entered into for serious and just reasons. Christian teaching even places restrictions on the nature
of warfare and on the intentions of those who participate; *jihad*
harbors no such limitations. The main purpose of *jihad* is offensive through the conquering of territory in order to spread
Islam throughout the world; Christian holy war is defensive and
primarily involves the recovery of territory lost to an aggressor.

War as Pilgrimage

Urban's plan for the recruitment of western warriors to march to
the Holy Land, liberate Jerusalem, and alleviate Muslim pressure
against the Byzantine Empire was placed within the context of
the spiritual journey of pilgrimage. The birth of the Crusades
occurred in a time of intense pilgrimage throughout Europe.
This was a time of faith and its public expression was a staple of
life. Pilgrims throughout Christendom frequented Santiago de
Compostela, St. Martin of Tours, Rome, and Jerusalem. The
landscape of Christendom was full of national, regional, and local shrines to various saints and relics. Jerusalem was a particular

focus for pilgrims, especially those from France. Urban's idea to marshal Western warriors to liberate the Holy City was not only revolutionary but pastoral. Before Clermont, pilgrims were not allowed to carry weapons, which caused deep consternation for those trained from an early age to defend themselves. This prohibition against bearing arms on pilgrimage presented a special challenge for the nobility, some of whom could not bring themselves to lay down arms even for the spiritual benefits of pilgrimage. Hence, "the summons to Crusade was a pastoral move, giving arms bearers the chance of contributing to their own salvation by undertaking a severe penance which did not entail the abandonment of their profession of arms and the humiliating loss of status involved in pilgrimaging abroad as normal penitents, without weapons, equipment, and horses."[89]

In a certain sense, Urban's summons to Jerusalem was a "universal call to holiness" oriented specifically to the laity, who otherwise believed the only sure way to contribute to their salvation was to renounce the world and enter the monastery. A Crusade was not seen as just another pilgrimage but as the greatest pilgrimage.[90]

Answering the Call

Urban knew his exhortation to those assembled at Clermont would not produce enough warriors to ensure the success of the Crusade, so he planned an elaborate and lengthy road trip throughout France in order to recruit as many warriors as he could. His preaching tour encompassed 2,000 miles and required an entire year to complete. He made a huge impact on the people of France, most of who had never seen the pope, and a good number of Crusaders came from the areas he visited.[91] Preachers were sent throughout Christendom, including England, Germany, Iceland, Sweden, and Italy, and the response was immense. Some estimates indicate 100,000 people may have taken the cross, of which 60,000 were warriors; of those, 6,000–7,000 were knights.[92]

In order to appreciate the extent of Urban's preaching and the significant response it engendered, a comparison of populations to respondents in the modern world can be made. The total population of France, Italy, Germany, and England combined in the late eleventh century is estimated at 20 million people; the modern populations of those same countries total 264 million people. If the same ratio of population to respondents were applied, the modern number of Crusaders would be 1.3 million![93]

Although Urban desired and asked for soldiers, the devotion to Jerusalem was so widespread that large numbers of non-combatants, who would hinder the armies on the march, also took the cross. So Urban charged bishops and priests with screening potential *crucesignati*. Those who could not fight were asked to stay in Europe and help the cause through prayer. Urban forbade monks from leaving their monasteries and did not want large numbers of priests to participate. He also stipulated that Spanish soldiers should not take the cross since they were already engaged in the fight against Islam in their home country: the *Reconquista*. Concerned for the well-being of women, Urban forbade married men from going on the Crusade without permission from their spouses.[94] (Later, Pope Innocent III would change this stipulation because too many men were using this rule as an excuse not to go on Crusade!)

The huge response to Urban's call at the council of Clermont is even more amazing when considering the cost to go on Crusade—for a knight, four to five times his annual income.[95] Although some modern critics assert that the Crusades were focused on the accumulation of wealth, the historical record shows that the vast majority of those who took the cross suffered financial hardship as result. They certainly did not profit from it. In order to finance such an expensive undertaking many knights and their extended family sold or mortgaged their land and possessions. Once the Crusading movement had taken root in Christendom, alternative means of finance were developed in order to shift the full burden from the individual Crusader. Kings instituted taxes on all their subjects, for example, and popes taxed bishops and the clergy in order to raise necessary funds.

Why Did They Go?

Despite the enormous financial burden involved, staggering numbers of Catholics answered the call to Crusade, raising the question: why? It is a question with an answer that eludes modern man, but was clear to medieval man. Although there is no simple explanation for the overwhelming response to Urban's Crusade, there is one factor that outweighs all others: faith. Medieval people were steeped in the Catholic Faith; it permeated every aspect of society and their daily life.

This is not to say that every Crusader was a saint or that every warrior who participated in this movement did so for pure and virtuous reasons. Nonetheless the medieval worldview was shaped and heavily influenced by the Faith of the Catholic Church and "for the majority of participants it is undeniable that the crusade proved to be a profoundly (though not obsessively) religious experience."[96] Medieval people saw Urban's call to Crusade as a highly unique, once-in-a-lifetime opportunity to provide for their spiritual health and increase their chance of salvation. This recognition is reflected in the commentary of Robert of Rheims who believed "only the creation of the world and Christ's Crucifixion could match the Crusade."[97] In that vicious and violent age most laymen, especially the nobility, believed it was extremely difficult for those not in a monastery to go to heaven. The Church constantly warned warriors that battling over land holdings against fellow Christians placed their souls in danger, and this alone provided sufficient motivation for many to take the cross. The desire of warriors to perform penances for their sins and the ability to utilize their martial skills in an armed pilgrimage was "one of the chief attractions of the First Crusade . . . now at last the laity had a task to perform, pleasing to God, for which they were especially equipped and which professed religious were not permitted to undertake."[98] Again, this is not to argue that faith was the only motivator for warriors on Crusade, but it was the primary reason why the majority participated.

Faith is certainly a more reasonable explanation than material gain. If material reasons had been paramount, would it not have been far easier and safer for Western warriors to stay home and fight their neighbors rather than travel 2,500 miles to a distant and completely alien land? It used to be fashionable in academic circles to attribute motivation for participating in the Crusades to second- and third-born sons who, due to the traditions of inheritance in medieval Europe, could not inherit property. Faced with a large population of marauding and landless warriors, it was said, the Church marshaled these forces and sent them to the Holy Land where they could acquire land.

This theory has been thoroughly debunked by examining the actual records of those who went on Crusade. It was not the younger but rather the first-born sons of French families who overwhelmingly participated in the First Crusade. In other words, it was the men who stood to *lose everything*. And indeed, participating in the Crusade was a bad investment for medieval warriors, the vast majority of whom returned (if they returned) materially poorer for the experience.

We know, too, that most of those who survived the expedition and made it to the Holy Sepulchre returned home afterward; they did not stay to acquire feudal land holdings. The Crusade was a pilgrimage, and just like modern-day pilgrims who visit a shrine or church for a period of time and then return home, so did the warriors of the Crusades. After the First Crusade, there were some nobles who stayed in the Holy Land and created what are known as the Crusader States, but these areas always suffered from a lack of military manpower because of the very episodic nature of Crusading and the desire of most warrior-pilgrims to return home.

War as Penance

Although his calling of the Crusade was unprecedented, perhaps Urban's most revolutionary act was creating the view that war could be a penitential act in the same vein as prayer and fasting. Participants in a Crusade believed that its religious value derived not just from its achievement of an objective like the capture or recovery of Jerusalem, but also from the way the combatants behaved while fighting to bring this about."[99] Crusaders were expected to act as penitents during the expedition by dressing simply, and were forbidden from activities usually associated with armies: swearing, gambling, and prostitution. Violating these rules could result in death, mutilation, or public humiliation.[100]

Crusaders spiritually prepared themselves to go on Crusade by seeking forgiveness for their sins from the neighbors, by asking those remaining at home to pray for them while on Crusade, and through various personal spiritual devotions and exercises.[101] Before departing, many warriors visited local or regional shrines, fasted, prayed, and gave alms.

Medieval writers understood the Crusades were penitential wars and exhorted their readers/listeners to participate in the expedition because of the spiritual benefits provided to the penitent. Eudes of Châteauroux clearly identified the holy war of the Crusade with penance when he wrote, "[T]hose who take the cross deny, that is to say renounce, themselves by exposing themselves to mortal danger, leaving behind their loved ones, using their goods, carrying their cross, so that afterwards, they may be carried to heaven by the cross."[102] The fact that the Crusade was considered inherently dangerous and risky proved its penitential foundation, as James of Vitry recorded:

> What greater almsgiving can there be than offering oneself and one's belongings to God and risking one's life for Christ, leaving behind one's wife, children, relations and birthplace for the service of Christ, exposing oneself to dangers on land, dangers at sea, dangers from thieves, dangers from plunderers, the danger of battle for the love of the Crucified?[103]

War as an Act of Love

Faith and love of God, neighbor, and self were the main reasons why medieval people participated in the Crusades. This is clear from the written evidence contained in the charters of the time, which were documents recording property transactions.

For example, the knightly brothers Geoffrey and Guy indicated they were going to Jerusalem for "both the grace of the pilgrimage under the protection of God, to exterminate wickedness and unrestrained rage of the pagans by which innumerable Christians have already been oppressed, made captive and killed."[104]

Odo of Burgundy clearly articulated his understanding of the penitential nature of the Crusade and concern for his salvation as the primary motivation for participation when he explained that he undertook "the journey to Jerusalem as a penance for my sins . . . Since divine mercy inspired me that owing to the enormity of my sins I should go to the Sepulchre of Our Savior, in order that this offering of my devotion might be more acceptable in the sight of God."[105]

Odo's sentiment was shared by the knight Ingelbald, who decided to go on Crusade because of his recognition of the great gift of redemption: "Considering that God has spared me, steeped in many and great sins, and has given me time for penance, and fearing that the weight of my sins will deprive me of a share in the heavenly kingdom, I, Ingelbald, wish to seek that sepulchre from which our redemption, having overcome death, wished to rise."[106]

Popes, preachers, and saints throughout the Crusading movement focused their exhortations on the recognition that service in God's army arose from love of God, love of neighbor, and concern for one's salvation. At Clermont, Urban urged knights to sacrifice themselves for Christ as the Lord had done for them: "It ought to be a beautiful ideal for you to die for Christ in that city where Christ died for you."[107] In the thirteenth century, Eudes of Châteauroux identified participation in the Crusade with an expressed and devoted love of God: "It is a sign that man loves God, when he casts aside the world. It is a sure sign that he burns with love for God and with zeal when for God's sake he leaves his fatherland, possessions, houses, sons and wife to go across the sea in the service of Jesus Christ."[108] The chronicler Guibert of Nogent aptly summarized the purpose of the Crusade and why warriors took the cross when he wrote, "[T]he

Crusader set himself the task of winning back the earthly Jerusalem in order to enjoy the celestial Jerusalem."[109]

The testimony found in these written records is compelling, but it is nonetheless wise to recognize that human motivations are not always pure and virtuous, and they are usually complex. Some who went on Crusade probably hoped they *would* benefit materially. Crusade expeditions comprised large groups of warriors centered on their own vassal lord, and although they may have been primarily motivated by holy reasons that does not mean they were all saints. "They were men of the sword: pious and idealistic, but also crude, arrogant, and at times savage."[110] Crusade armies were "a curious mix of rich and poor, saints and sinners, motivated by every kind of pious and selfish desire."[111] Crusaders indeed went to war not only for reasons that men have gone to war for centuries—glory, adventure, love of country—but also because they recognized the Crusade as a unique opportunity to participate in their salvation and give a witness of their love for God.

Wars of Conversion?

A final brief clarification is in order. Despite the belief of modern-day critics, the Crusades were not wars of conversion comparable to those that had helped Islam spread by the sword. Indeed, engaging in warfare simply for the conversion of others was never a criterion for just war, nor does the historical record indicate that this is what motivated the Crusaders. For the individual Muslim, conversion to Christianity was (and still is) rare and dangerous; any such conversions were only a subsidiary benefit to the Crusaders, who saw their expeditions primarily as defensive, just, holy wars designed to reclaim Christian territory from the hands of aggressive and harassing Muslims. "The Crusaders weren't fighting in the East to save the souls of unbelievers or to extend the bounds of the Christian religion. They fought to win salvation for themselves and to recover or defend sites that were sacred to their faith."[112]

★★★

Urban's speech at the council of Clermont in November 1095 gave birth to the Crusading movement that would span several centuries in the life of the Church. The Crusades began in the Church, were fostered by the Church, and were fought by baptized warriors who loved the Church. Urban pleaded with the knights of medieval Europe to embark on an armed pilgrimage to liberate the Holy City of Jerusalem. The story of those who responded is one of great drama, adventure, miracles, and divine protection.

3

Jerusalem

When the days for his being taken up were fulfilled,
he resolutely determined to journey to Jerusalem.

Luke 9:51[113]

The forty-one year old Germanic warrior had endured much
over the prior three years. He had sold much of his land holdings to finance his journey to Jerusalem. He had survived a bear
attack, extreme heat and cold, starvation, political struggles with
the Byzantine emperor, and numerous battles and skirmishes
with the forces of Mohammed. He and his brother, Eustace III,
were among the first over the walls at Jerusalem and had fought
bravely to liberate the city of the Lord. With his armed pilgrimage now at an end, it can be surmised that Godfrey de Bouillon
looked forward to journeying home to his beloved Lorraine.

His plans, however, were not God's plans. Although he had
never contemplated it, the Lord's warrior was asked, "because
of his noble excellence, the proven worth of his military service,
his patient temperance, and also the elegance of his manners," to
become the first Western king of Jerusalem.[114]

Tradition holds that Godfrey rejected the title of king out
of deference to the King of Kings. He reputedly remarked, "I
will not wear a crown of gold in the city where the Savior wore
a crown of thorns." Instead he took the title "Defender of the
Holy Sepulchre" and renewed his pledge to serve God in his
army. This noble Catholic warrior was not given much time
to consolidate and fortify the land holdings of the Crusaders
after the First Crusade, as he died only a year after the fulfillment of his Crusader vow. The Kingdom of Jerusalem would

flourish and then founder under future rulers (who exhibited no qualms about taking the title "king"—including Godfrey's brother, Baldwin); none of them would compare to the First Crusader, Godfrey, who risked and suffered much for the glory of God and his Church.

Organization of the Crusader Armies

The politics of Christendom in the Middle Ages were regional rather than national, and the organization of medieval armies followed suit. Unlike modern armies with a unified command structure and highly organized bureaucracy of support, medieval armies were organized by personal relationships. Recruitment, combat operations, and command structure centered on the relationship between individual warriors and individual rulers.

As a result, there was not one army that went on Crusade but multiple armies, and they were even more distinct than normal medieval armies. "The diversity, the random appeal of the Crusade and the different kinds of contingents raised, the lack of any central command—all of this meant that Crusader armies were even more ad hoc than most medieval armies."[115] Crusade armies, as a result, were "in effect, a loosely organized mob of soldiers, clergy, servants and followers heading in roughly the same direction for roughly the same purposes."[116]

The loose structure and organization of Crusade armies might seem to foster disunity and lead to disaster, but the unifying force was the Catholic Faith. These Catholic warriors banded together to fight for the Cross in "God's army" motivated by their concern for their personal salvation, the relief of their fellow Christians in the Holy Land, and the desire to serve Christ and his Church.

Since the Crusades were called and approved by popes, their personal representative (a legate) accompanied the armies. Most papal legates did not command troops in the field and had very little practical authority. Some were excellent leaders and held the Crusade together through their diplomacy and tact in dealing with internal squabbles of the various leaders; others were abject failures that inappropriately inserted themselves, to the ultimate failure of the Crusade. Later popes would try to control Crusades through these legates but found that medieval armies mirrored the structure of medieval society, which was not highly organized or easily controllable.

The "People's Crusade"

Pope Bl. Urban II set an official departure date of August 15, 1096 and while major noble leaders throughout Christendom prepared their armies to leave on or near that date, others endeavored to leave before.[117] Preachers throughout Christendom exhorted people to take the cross. One extremely skilled and persuasive preacher was Peter the Hermit, a holy man with a "swarthy and a long face, horribly like the donkey he always rode and which was revered almost as much as himself. He went barefoot; and his clothes were filthy. He ate neither bread nor meat, but fish, and he drank wine."[118] Peter attracted large groups whenever he preached and miracles followed in his wake.[119]

Peter preached the Crusade in April 1096 in Cologne and his persuasiveness motivated tens of thousands to undertake the journey to Jerusalem. Although this following is usually known as the "People's Crusade," this is a misnomer. The name implies that Peter's following consisted only of poor non-combatants; in reality, Peter's group consisted of 700 knights and 28,000 infantry plus non-combatants.[120]

One knight who led the "advance guard for Peter the Hermit's army" was Walter, lord of Boissy-sans-Avoir from the Ile de France.[121] Walter is usually known as Walter Sansavoir or Walter the Penniless. He left with a group of eight knights and an infantry force after Easter in April 1096. Walter's group followed the traditional land pilgrim route and reached Constantinople on July 20, 1096. A few weeks after the advance guard left on the march to Jerusalem, Peter's group followed, reaching Constantinople on August 1, 1096.[122] The Byzantines were unprepared for the early arrival of these Crusaders and did not have the necessary provisions. As a result, rioting broke out in the Crusader camp. Desirous to rid themselves of the rioting and thieving horde, the Byzantines transported the army to Anatolia on August 6.

Once in Muslim territory, Peter's army foundered due to lack of leadership and planning. (It seems Peter the Hermit was a great preacher but he was not a military strategist.) The Crusade divided into German, Italian, and French contingents and each decided to follow its own objectives, to the detriment of all. The French group raided the city of Nicaea and returned with a good haul of loot. Envious of the French success, the German contingent decided to launch its own raid on Nicaea and set out with 200 knights and 7,000 infantry.[123] The Turks, after encountering the French, were prepared and easily captured the German raiding party. The prisoners were offered the choice of conversion to Islam or death; some chose Islam, the rest were executed.[124]

The Turks sent a letter, supposedly from the Germans, to the remaining Crusaders telling of huge amounts of treasure in the city. Duped by the Turkish letter, the remaining Crusaders marched to Nicaea.[125] This large army was ambushed and slaughtered by the Turks. Walter Sansavoir was pierced through his coat of mail by seven arrows and killed.[126] The few survivors, including Peter the Hermit, made their way back to Constantinople and eventually joined the main armies of the "Prince's Crusade."

The so-called People's Crusade failed miserably primarily because of a lack of unifying leadership. The presence of Peter the Hermit's army in Muslim territory in the fall of 1096 was nothing more than a minor irritant to the Seljuk Turks of Rum.

Persecution of the Jews

Jewish communities existed throughout Christendom at the beginning of the Crusading movement. Christian attitudes towards the Jews differed from region to region, but papal policy centered on toleration and protection—indeed, the Jews were the only non-Christian community officially protected in medieval society. Regardless, some of those who took the cross used the Crusades as an excuse to harass Jews for their wealth; this was especially evident in the Rhineland. One individual unworthy to be called or even considered a Crusader was Count Emich of Flonheim. A Jewish chronicler named Solomon ben Simson described Emich and the havoc he wreaked on the Jewish population of the Rhineland:

> Count Emich was the enemy of all the Jews—may his bones be crushed to pieces in millstones of iron. He was known as a man who had no mercy on the old, or on young women, who took no pity on babies or sucklings or the sick, who pulverized God's people like the dust in threshing, who slew their young men with the sword.[127]

Emich and his followers marched down the Rhine plundering and massacring Jews in the cities of Speyer, Worms, Mainz, Trier, and Cologne. He attacked the Jews of Speyer on May 3, 1096, killing twelve. The death toll would have been much higher had John, the bishop of Speyer, not intervened and given shelter to the Jews, earning him praise from a contemporary Jewish chronicler as a "pious one among the nations."[128] Bishop John not only saved the Jews in his community, he also sought out and prosecuted those who had participated in the pogrom. Those caught were tried and when found guilty they were punished by losing a hand.[129]

Emich and his murderous horde continued their march and arrived at Worms. The Jewish community divided into two groups; some stayed in their homes, hoping and praying for deliverance, others sought protection from the local bishop. Emich marched into the town and began perhaps the most deadly of all his pogroms. Hundreds of Jews were slaughtered. Some committed suicide rather than face death at the hands of the Christians, and some converted in order to survive.

Not sated with the blood of the Jews in Worms, Emich proceeded to Mainz, which was a major center of Jewish learning, culture, and business. The Jewish community tried to forestall the pogrom with the payment of seven pounds of gold.[130] The bribe did not work. Many Jews accepted the invitation of Bishop Rothard, who opened his palace to them. The ecclesial sanctuary of the bishop's personal residence meant nothing to Emich, who stormed the palace and massacred the sheltering Jews; perhaps as many as 700 were killed.[131]

Due to the ecclesial interference he experienced in several cities, Emich changed tactics during the course of his persecution and took his army to towns without a resident bishop. Eventually Emich's band made their way to the city of Cologne, where they burned the synagogue and Torah scrolls. After leaving a trail of death and destruction in the Rhineland, Emich tried to march through Hungary on his way to Jerusalem. He was denied entry and soon thereafter his army dissolved. Emich went back to Flonheim and never traveled to the Holy Land.

These marauding murderers in the Rhineland in the late eleventh century can hardly be called authentic Crusaders. Although these warriors may have taken the cross and endeavored to follow Urban's call by journeying to Jerusalem, they never completed their pilgrimage. Contrary to a modern myth, the persecution of the Jews, which occurred at the beginning of the Crusading movement, was not "the first holocaust" or the beginning of a long period of Christian anti-Semitism. Rather, these horrible pogroms were motivated not by love of Christ and concern for personal salvation, but by mammon.

The First Crusade

The 60,000 warriors who embarked on the First Crusade knew they were involved in something exceptional and unique; they were members of "God's army" and "possessed a special sense of identity"; they were warriors of the cross fighting for God.[132] Despite the fact that the First Crusade "lacked unified leadership, a coherent political strategy or an agreed military plan," the warriors were confident in their martial abilities, buoyed by the promise of spiritual benefits, and fixated on liberating Jerusalem from the hold of Islam.[133]

The First Crusade is occasionally known as the "Prince's Crusade" because the major leaders were dukes and counts, rather than monarchs. Most of the major kings at the time of Urban's call were engaged in political or personal feuds with the Church and so either would not or could not participate.[134] A result of this is that the armies of the First Crusade became a multinational force, representing all of Christendom.[135] It was France, however, from which came the majority of warriors.[136]

The French First Crusaders were divided into two main groups, the northern and the southern. Hugh of Vermandois (1053–1101)—the younger brother of Philip I the Fat, King of France—commanded the northern group. The forty year old Hugh was an ineffectual military commander, but nonetheless so carefully planned his route that his was the first army group to arrive in Constantinople in November 1096. Commanding the southern group was Count Raymond of Toulouse, a fifty-five year old veteran of conflicts against Muslims in Spain, where he lost an eye in combat. He was one of the first warriors to take the cross at Clermont and was extremely wealthy. Unlike most Crusaders, Raymond traveled with his wife and planned to stay in the Holy Land. Joining his army was the papal legate Bishop Adhemar of Le Puy. Raymond's force left in October 1096, after the official departure date, and was the last of the major army groups to arrive in Constantinople on April 21, 1097.

Another group of French crusaders left in late September and early October and traveled to Italy. There, in late October, they met with Urban II at Lucca. This was an eclectic group that included Robert Duke of Normandy, Stephen, Count of Blois, and Robert II, Count of Flanders.

Robert of Normandy, who was nicknamed "Curthose" ("short stockings"), was the eldest son of William the Conqueror, the Norman prince who had successfully invaded and conquered Anglo-Saxon England. Robert conducted himself well on the First Crusade and played a pivotal role at the battle of Dorylaeum and

the sieges of Antioch, Jerusalem, and Ascalon. He survived the
Crusade and upon his return home he "found himself the hero of
instant legend, his alleged deeds enshrined in stained glass at the
royal abbey of St. Denis within a decade of his death."[137]

Count Stephen of Blois was the son-in-law of William the
Conqueror and is believed to have been a somewhat reluctant
Crusader. He was strongly urged to go on the journey to Jerusalem by his overbearing wife, Adela, daughter of the Conqueror.
Stephen was extremely wealthy and had much to lose by going
on Crusade. He later abandoned his fellow Crusaders at the siege
of Antioch and returned to France in disgrace. His sullied reputation and the constant nagging of Adela forced him to return
to the Holy Land to fulfill his Crusader vow, and in the 1101
Crusade he died of wounds sustained in battle.

The family of Robert II was well aware of the risks involved
in a pilgrimage to Jerusalem. A decade before the First Crusade,
his father had made the journey and had even sent 500 knights
in service to Emperor Alexius in 1090.[138]

The armies of Robert Curthose, Count Stephen, and Robert
of Flanders arrived in Constantinople in the spring of 1097.

For Godfrey de Bouillon (1058–1100), the First Crusade was
the culmination of years of training. Raised to be a great military commander, Godfrey began his martial training at an early
age and was a combat-ready warrior by the age of sixteen.[139] He
was the prototypical medieval military commander: personally
leading his troops into harm's way and exhorting and encour-
aging them from within the ranks rather than from the safety
of the rear. His brothers, Eustace III and Baldwin, also took
the Crusader vow and made the journey to Jerusalem. Crusade
preaching was very effective in Godfrey's lands, enabling him
to assemble a vast army containing several thousand knights and
soldiers along with two future kings of Jerusalem.[140] He departed
on the official departure date, August 15, and eventually reached
Constantinople on December 23, 1096.

The infamous Norman warrior, Bohemond, commanded
the last major army group. Bohemond was the son of Robert

Guiscard, who was the leader of the Normans in southern Italy. "Bohemond" was a nickname given by his father and referred to a legendary giant. His baptismal name was Mark.[141] Bohemond was perhaps the most fascinating Crusader, since he personally knew Urban II, was fluent in Greek (a rarity among the Western Crusaders), and was a brilliant military strategist and field commander. He was "swashbuckling, overbearing, uproarious, at his best making a last stand, at his worst when involved in political intrigue, simple and sincere in his Christian faith, yet a great sinner."[142] Bohemond assembled his army and formed the core from close relatives whose loyalty he trusted, including his nephew, Tancred of Lecce. His army began the march to Constantinople two months after the official departure date and took six months to arrive in Constantinople.[143]

At Byzantium

The Crusaders were excited to reach the great city of Constantinople, which was larger and more majestic than any city in Christendom. The Byzantines, on the other hand, were shocked at the number of Crusaders and were not prepared for the arrival of such large groups of warriors from Western Europe.

The Crusaders were unaware that they had marched into a politically dangerous situation, and the actions of Emperor Alexius (r. 1081–1118) perplexed them. Alexius was a cunning ruler whose primary aim was safeguarding his own position and power. He was not a great soldier and had no intention of placing his military reserves at the disposal of the Crusaders since the "spirit of the Crusade was deeply alien" to him.[144] The consummate politician, Alexius was wary of openly supporting the Crusaders in case they failed, which would make relations with the Seljuk Turks on his borders difficult. His strategy focused on playing the odds: He "would support the Franks as long as they succeeded."[145]

Large foreign armies near his capital city made Alexius nervous. In order to safeguard his throne, the Byzantine emperor decided to isolate the Crusade leaders and demand their personal loyalty. The Crusaders unwittingly assisted this plan by arriving separately in Constantinople over the course of the fall and winter. Alexius's desire to receive personal pledges of loyalty from the major Crusade leaders took the form of personal oaths, which were an essential element of feudal society. Although some demurred initially, all the leaders eventually took the required oaths in order for the transportation of their armies across the Bosporus. The Crusaders, as vassals of the emperor, now expected Alexius to protect them and preserve their interests while on the march to Jerusalem. It quickly became apparent to the Crusaders that their understanding of Alexius's role and his vision were quite at odds. The manipulative politician would seek his own interests over the Crusaders throughout the campaign.

Nicaea

The Crusaders decided to liberate the ancient Christian city of Nicaea—site of two ecumenical councils, in 325 and 787—as the first step on their long journey to Jerusalem. Godfrey's army was in the vanguard and arrived at Nicaea on May 6, 1097. His 3,000-man army cleared and cut back the overgrowth on the old Roman road leading to the city and placed crosses along the path as guideposts for the rest of the army.[146] Providentially, the Crusaders arrived and were allowed time to set up their siege positions due to the absence of the main Seljuk army under Kilij Arslan, who was off fighting the Danishmend Turks elsewhere in Anatolia. However, news soon reached Kilij Arslan that the city was surrounded and he rushed to its rescue, arriving on May 16. He attacked the Crusader force, and although there were heavy losses on both sides, the Crusaders emerged victorious, which was a "a remarkable achievement for such a novice and fragmented army."[147] The destruction of Kilij Arslan's relief army opened the way for the Crusaders to besiege the city of Nicaea.

The siege of Nicaea lasted six weeks and was witness to actions both heroic and atrocious. The Crusaders built siege engines, which they used to destroy the city's walls. Inevitably,

Crusaders were killed near the walls, which provided opportunities for the Turks to demoralize the living Crusaders as recorded by Fulcher of Chartres: "Truly, you would have grieved
and sighed with compassion, to see them [the Turks] let down
iron hooks, which they lowered and raised by ropes, and seize
the body of any of our men that they had slaughtered in some
way near the wall. Having robbed the corpse, they threw the
carcass outside."[148] The Crusaders responded to the mutilation of
their dead comrades by cutting off the heads of Turkish soldiers
and flinging them into the city.[149]

The presence of Byzantine naval vessels on the Ascanian Lake
led the Seljuk garrison to open negotiations with imperial repre-
sentatives for surrender terms. These negotiations were kept secret
from the Crusaders, who continued to prepare for a general assault.
The emperor promised the Seljuks safety of persons and property
and ensured the Crusaders would not be allowed in the city.

On June 19, 1097, the Crusaders awoke stupefied to see imperial banners flying from the city walls, and although Alexius
gave them expensive gifts, they felt cheated of the opportunity to
plunder the city, which was standard practice in medieval warfare.

The Crusaders knew they would not have been able to keep
possession of Nicaea even if they had entered it, since it was a
former imperial city and in accordance with their oath to Alexius it would revert to imperial hands. Regardless, Alexius's actions at Nicaea set the stage for future conflict when another
former imperial city capitulated to the Crusaders.

The Anatolian Death March

Buoyed by their victory at Nicaea, the Crusaders began their
march to Antioch at the end of June 1097. The journey would
take them through Anatolia, and the summer heat of 1097 was
a brutish and nightmarish event for all involved. Sustenance was
scarce as the Turks destroyed sources of food along the route and
the lack of water caused many Crusader deaths. When water
sources were found, some even died of excessive drinking![150]

Many starving warriors sold their military equipment in order to buy overpriced food, and others abandoned their gear because it was too heavy to carry without a beast of burden.[151] The toll on horses and other animals was also great, and most knights arrived at Antioch without any horses at all.[152]

On this Anatolian Death March, Crusaders suffered not only starvation but also sickness; Count Raymond of Toulouse became so ill that he received the Sacrament of Extreme Unction (Anointing of the Sick).[153] Godfrey also suffered, though the circumstances that caused it were unique: He rescued an unarmed pilgrim from an attacking bear and, although he killed the bear, was seriously wounded in the encounter.[154]

Yet, in the midst of the terrible march, the Crusaders' mettle was tested in a major battle that proved their fighting capability and united their resolve.

The Battle of Dorylaeum

Kilij Arslan, who you will recall had recently warred against the Danishmends, now allied himself with them in order to destroy the Crusaders in revenge for the loss of his capital city at Nicaea. Forty-five miles southeast of Nicaea, near the town of Dorylaeum, the forces of Kilij Arslan set upon the Crusader vanguard commanded by Bohemond.

Muslim troops were mostly fast-moving cavalry who relied on the bow to pepper the Crusaders with arrows. These mounted archers loosed deadly volleys, then feigned withdrawal in order to entice their enemy to break ranks and advance in pursuit; once the enemy took the bait, the archers moved to attack the enemy flanks and rear with the goal of a complete encirclement and subsequent annihilation.

Kilij Arslan believed the vanguard was the main Crusader body and ordered the attack. Bohemond quickly assessed the situation and ordered his infantry, clerics, and non-combatants to make a defensive camp at a marsh, which also protected their back and right flank. The knights were ordered to line up and advance.

The volleys of the Turks left the knights with so many arrows stuck in their armor that they resembled porcupines. Eventually, the knights were driven back to the defensive camp with the infantry and civilians. Bohemond's warriors fought alone in this defensive posture for five to six hours before the main body came to the rescue and beat back the Muslim assault.

The Battle of Dorylaeum taught the Crusaders an invaluable lesson: They learned how to fight and defeat the mounted Turkish warrior in open combat by maintaining discipline rather than breaking ranks and pursuing the enemy. News of the Crusader victory spread rapidly throughout Anatolia and caused panic in the Turkish world. Christian populations in towns with a Turkish garrison revolted against their Muslim overlords and welcomed the advancing Crusaders. The Turks now viewed the Crusaders as invincible and did not harass them further on their march to Antioch.

Antioch – home to St. Peter·

The main army groups continued their march through Seljuk territory and arrived at the outskirts of the great city of Antioch on October 20, 1097, ending their grueling four-month march through the Anatolian plain.

Antioch was an ancient city originally founded in 300 B.C. by Seleucus Nicator, a general in Alexander the Great's army. It grew into a large and important city in the Roman Empire with an estimated population of 300,000.[155] After the Catholic Faith arrived in Antioch it was home to St. Peter for a time. In the early second century, the great St. Ignatius, bishop of Antioch, was arrested by order of the Emperor Trajan and hauled to Rome so that his execution could serve as an example of imperial policy toward Christians. The city of Peter and Ignatius was conquered by the forces of Mohammed in 637 and held for over 300 years until the Byzantines reclaimed it in 969. The Seljuk Turks returned the city to the sphere of Islam in 1085.

The Crusaders recognized the great challenge ahead of them when they observed the impressively fortified city. Antioch rested partly on a mountainside with a defensive citadel perched a thousand feet above the main city. The steep slopes of the city were surrounded by seven miles of walls, doubled at the northern end and studded with 360 towers. The size of Antioch was its greatest strength for the defenders and the bane of any attacker, as even a large army was forced to disperse troops around its walls, thereby diminishing its attacking power.[156] The siege of Antioch would test the Crusaders in every way, and although they would eventually succeed in liberating the city, it would come at a heavy cost.

First Contact

In the first engagement with the Muslim forces at Antioch, the Crusaders fought the Battle of the Iron Bridge to secure the northern approach to the city. The Iron Bridge was an old fortified bridge, northwest of Antioch, built in the sixth century with two towers, one at either end, across the Orontes River. Holding the Iron Bridge was crucial to any successful siege of Antioch because "possession of this crossing made it impossible for any large enemy force to surprise the crusaders encamped around Antioch and it provided a bridgehead for raids out into Syria."[157]

Knowing the northern approach to the city was secure, the Crusaders marched to the walls, formed defensive positions around it, and settled in for the siege. Unfortunately, the Crusaders were ill-prepared for a siege and soon found themselves engaged in a long, drawn-out stalemate of raiding, sallies, and counter-sallies by Turkish forces.

Albert of Aachen recorded the state of affairs and constant attacks by the Turks: "Morning, noon and night every day there were sudden attacks, sallies, scenes of carnage, and endlessly you could hear in the Christian camp always new lamentations over further losses."[158] As the stalemate progressed through the winter, the Crusaders' sufferings intensified. By Christmas most of the available food near the city was consumed, and knights were forced to kill their horses so that "those who used to carry them

. . . they now carried in their stomachs."[159] The rank and file suffered horribly and time was spent not in combat but in searching
for food. The lack of food resulted in many deaths in the Crusader camps, and those alive were forced to find and eat small
amounts of food even in the most disgusting of places:

> At that time, the famished ate the shoots of beanseeds grow-
> ing in the fields and many kinds of herbs unseasoned with
> salt, also thistles, which, being not well cooked because of the
> deficiency of firewood, pricked the tongues of those eating
> them; also horses, asses, and camels, and dogs and rats. The
> poorer ones ate even the skins of the beasts and seeds of grain
> found in manure.[160]

Eventually, the situation became so intolerable that the Crusaders were forced to mount foraging parties to secure food.
Harassment from the Turks hampered their ability to find food,
which tied up critical manpower as the Crusaders were forced to
forage in well-armed groups.

The Crusaders were in the worst possible position: trapped in
between the walls of the city and the impending arrival of a Muslim relief army. To many, the situation looked hopeless. Desertions,
even by well-known personages, became rampant. Even Peter the
Hermit, who had joined this group of Crusaders when they arrived
in Constantinople, deserted the cause at Antioch, although he was
later arrested and forced to return to the camp. In order to stem
the desertions and improve morale a series of temporal and spiritual regulations were promulgated and enforced. Bishop Adhemar
instituted penitential fasting, processions, almsgiving, intercessory
prayer, and celebration of special Masses throughout the Crusader
camps in order to beseech God to end their suffering.[161]

Liberation!

The rapidly deteriorating situation, the desire to end the months-
long siege, and news of a relief army under Kerbogha, the

commander of Mosul, on its way to Antioch, prompted Bohemond to craft a plan to liberate Antioch.

An Armenian convert to Islam named Firuz al Zarrad, who was a captain of one of the tower guards near the St. Paul gate, began negotiations with Bohemond—whose ability to speak Greek facilitated the exchanges—to allow his troops into the city. Before Bohemond allowed the operation to commence, he approached the other Crusade leaders and asked their permission to keep and rule the city should they liberate it. The only leader who balked at Bohemond's bargain was Raymond of Toulouse, who reminded the leaders that Antioch was imperial territory and their oaths demanded return of the city to Emperor Alexius. The discussion was heated but eventually Raymond agreed to allow Bohemond to rule the city until the emperor came in person to claim it.

Secure in his position, Bohemond worked with Firuz on the operational details of entering Antioch. The plan entailed a commando-type raid involving sixty knights climbing a ladder to Firuz's tower just before dawn. But only a few knights successfully made the climb before the ladder broke. Adapting to the situation, the knights in the tower discovered a small, undefended gate, which they opened to allow the main body of troops into the city. Once inside, the Crusaders fanned out while the remaining Turkish troops retreated to the citadel. Yaghisiyan, the ruler of Antioch, managed to escape the city in the chaos and confusion (he was later discovered by a group of local Armenian Christians and beheaded).[162]

The liberation of Antioch, brought about through the skilled negotiations of Bohemond, was a miracle. Achieving their objective of returning the ancient Christian city of Antioch to the Faith was a momentous and happy occasion for the Crusaders. But their joy was soon forgotten when the forces of Kerbogha arrived.

From Besiegers to Besieged

Kerbogha had assembled a large allied force to relieve Antioch and crush the Crusaders. On the march to Antioch, he diverted his force to Edessa in the hopes of taking that city from Baldwin of Boulogne. Baldwin's defense of Edessa during the three-week siege bought time for the Crusaders at Antioch. Kerbogha's expedition to Edessa proved a costly mistake, as he failed to capture the city and only arrived at Antioch on June 4, 1098—one day after the Crusaders had entered the city.

The Crusaders who had been the besiegers now became the besieged. They were caught between the Muslim forces inside the citadel, which still held out and proved a nuisance for the Christians, and the forces of Kerbogha outside the walls of the city. Once again the situation looked hopeless.

The Crusaders were dealt another blow when Count Stephen of Blois deserted. Stephen and a detachment of Crusaders were north of Antioch when the city was liberated, and when they marched back to the city they saw Kerbogha's forces outside the walls and the citadel still in enemy hands. This situation led Stephen to believe that the Crusaders would soon be crushed, so he decided to leave the Holy Land. On the march home he stopped at Philomelium, where Emperor Alexius was encamped. He described for the emperor the dire situation at Antioch and expressed his belief that all was lost. Alexius agreed and took his army back to Constantinople. Upon returning to France, Stephen was berated and shamed by his wife. The guilt of leaving the Crusade and failing to fulfill his vow (certainly exacerbated by Pope Paschal II's (r. 1099–1118) excommunication of those who had deserted during the siege of Antioch[163]) weighed heavily on him. He later returned to the Holy Land in the minor Crusade of 1101, and was killed.

News of Alexius's return to his capital was received in Antioch with anger. The Crusaders now firmly believed that Alexius had betrayed them and their oaths were null and void.[164]

The Visions

Trapped between the forces in the citadel and the forces of Kerbogha, the Crusaders began to despair. The Lord, as he had done throughout the expedition, came to the rescue.

Peter Bartholomew, a layman, told the Crusaders that St. Andrew had recently appeared to him and revealed the location of the Holy Lance of St. Longinus, the Roman legionary who pierced the side of Christ on the Cross. Debate raged among them over the veracity of Peter's vision. Bishop Adhemar was highly skeptical, primarily because he had seen the purported Holy Lance in Constantinople. Others, including Raymond of Toulouse, believed.

A search was conducted in the church of St. Peter to find the Lance. The Crusaders dug for hours throughout the morning but did not find anything, and as the day wore on everyone began to lose hope. Just when the search was about to end, a worn lance head was found. The Crusade leaders, in a letter to Pope Urban II in September 1098, wrote, "We were so comforted and strengthened by finding it, and by many other divine revelations that we, who before had been afflicted and timid, were then most boldly and eagerly urging one another to battle."[165] The finding of the Holy Lance greatly improved Crusader morale and "transformed the army's mood from terrified inertia to awed encouragement."[166]

Victory at Antioch

The time was at hand to deal with Kerbogha's relief army. To spiritually prepare for battle, the Crusaders proclaimed a three-day fast. They conducted processions to the churches within Antioch and received the sacraments of confession and the Eucharist.

Once more the Crusaders turned to the military genius of Bohemond, who organized the disparate troops into four divisions of two squadrons of infantry and knights in two lines each. Bohemond's plan was for each division to advance out of the city gate in a column but then in the open field perform the complex maneuver of changing formation from column to line. This tactic was brilliant, for it allowed each division to face the enemy ready to attack and covered the deployment of each subsequent division. Bohemond also took advantage of geography, using the Orontes River on the right and high ground on the left to cover the Crusader flanks. This arrangement avoided the trap of encirclement and mitigated the Turks' main battle tactic.

Another key to the Crusader victory over the numerically superior Muslim forces outside the walls of Antioch was Kerbogha's crucial mistake of allowing the Crusaders to march out of the city unopposed. This gave the Crusaders time to organize into their battle formation. Apparently, Kerbogha had been informed of the Crusader advance but could not be troubled to interrupt his chess game.[167]

The Crusaders then engaged the Turks and slaughtered them. Those Muslim troops not killed by the Crusaders fled the field in a panic. Witnessing the destruction of their only hope, the defenders in the citadel surrendered and finally, after almost eight months of siege and constant combat, the Crusaders were victorious.

Part of the reason for the overwhelming success of the Crusaders against Kerbogha was their faith in Christ and the deep conviction that they were fighting and suffering for love of him. The Crusaders were "sustained by faith and determination, by that driving religious enthusiasm which was the motor of the crusade, they fought for the chance to live."[168]

Another reason was the miraculous appearance of a heavenly army of angels, saints, and the ghosts of dead Crusaders, as recorded in the *Gesta*:

> There came out of the mountains, also, countless armies with white horses, whose standards were all white. And so, when our leaders saw this army, they were entirely ignorant as to what it was, and who they were, until they recognized the aid of Christ, whose leaders were St. George, Mercurius, and Demetrius. This is to be believed, for many of our men saw it.[169]

The victory at Antioch solidified the First Crusade and drove it to ultimate victory later at Jerusalem. Although thousands of miles from home, the Crusaders had persevered through intense suffering and proved to be one of the finest fighting forces in history. The liberation of Antioch has since been well remem-

bered in Christendom as "a terrible struggle, a military epic indeed, the success of which was more than adequate demonstration that their journey was the work of God."[170]

Departure for Jerusalem

After the defeat of Kerbogha's army, the Crusaders rested and
replenished their supplies while they planned for the eventual
assault of Jerusalem. During the rest, internal politics among the
leaders once more returned to dominate the Crusade. Unfortunately, Bishop Adhemar, the papal legate and the chief mediator
among the personality conflicts of the nobles, died of typhoid
fever on August 1, 1098. The loss of Adhemar was a huge blow
to the Crusade that "further fractured the expedition's cohesion
and direction by removing the one accepted figure of moral
authority and religious stature who transcended factional and
regional divisions."[171]

As any field commander recognizes, it is extremely difficult
to keep an army on the march or in the field for an extended
period of time without a mission or objective to accomplish. By
the fall of 1098 the rank-and-file soldiers were restless and eager
to march on Jerusalem.

Cannibalism – brought about by external hunger

While the Crusaders waited to march on Jerusalem, they decided to try and consolidate their hold on Antioch by liberating
territory near the city. In late November 1098, the forces of
Godfrey and Bohemond besieged the city of Marra, which "was
neither a large nor an important place and its defenses were not
strong."[172] The siege of Marra provided one of the most infamous events in Crusading history: cannibalism by Crusaders.
Fulcher of Chartres records what happened:

> Here, when the siege had lasted twenty days, our people suf-
> fered excessive hunger. I shudder to tell that many of our people,

harassed by the madness of excessive hunger, cut pieces from the buttocks of the Saracens already dead there, which they cooked, but when it was not yet roasted enough by the fire, they devoured it with savage mouths.[173]

Most accounts indicate that only a small minority of Crusaders, perhaps a group of landless knights known as the Tafurs, engaged in cannibalism, and only due to their state of near starvation. The awful event illustrates the extreme situations Crusaders encountered throughout their journey—situations that the vast majority of Crusaders endured without resorting to desperate acts.

The Siege Begins

In January 1099, the order was given at last, and the Crusaders departed for the Holy City. Raymond of Toulouse began the 450-mile journey barefoot and dressed as a humble pilgrim.

From an original force of 6,000 to 7,000 knights and 60,000 fighting men, the total that left Antioch was only 1,200 knights and 12,000 infantry; the events of the Crusade had certainly taken their toll.[174] In May they entered Fatimid territory north of Beirut and marched by the cities of Sidon, Tyre, Acre, and Haifa, each of which gave the Crusaders provisions in exchange for safety.

In early June the lead elements of the Crusade army reached the inland road to Jerusalem, their objective within reach, a full two years after the liberation of Nicaea. A great sense of relief combined with the expectation of much suffering ahead must have pervaded the armies. By the time they arrived at the walls of the Holy City on June 7 they were certainly aware that the liberation of Jerusalem was not an easy proposition. The city had double walls, along with moats. The defenders were not as numerous as the attacking Crusaders, but they were well supplied.

Iftikhar al-Dawla, the Fatimid governor, took extra steps to make conditions for a long-term siege intolerable to the Crusaders. He ordered all animal herds driven from the environs of the city in order to deny the Crusaders easy access to food. He also poisoned the wells near the city, forcing the Crusaders to haul water from the Jordan River and other sources that were miles away.

Almost a week after their arrival on June 13, the Crusaders, despite the lack of proper siege equipment, decided to attack the city. Utilizing only one scaling ladder, they managed to breach the outer wall of defense. They were unable to surmount the inner rampart, however, and after heavy losses were forced to retreat.

While the Crusaders pondered how they could possibly gain entry without proper siege equipment, the Lord once again provided a solution. On June 17 six Genoese and English ships sailed into the port city of Jaffa. The ships carried not only provisions and wood for siege equipment but personnel who could construct proper siege engines and towers.

Arrival of the ships and construction of the siege equipment came at the perfect time, for in early July the Crusaders discovered that a Fatimid relief army was on the march from Egypt and would arrive at Jerusalem within a month. The Crusaders, as they had been at Antioch, were now engaged in a race against time.

Imitating Joshua

The death of Bishop Adhemar almost a year earlier at Antioch was still keenly felt, but the papal legate returned once more to exhort the Crusaders to complete their pilgrimage. The priest, Peter Desiderius, announced that the spirit of Adhemar had appeared to him and rebuked the Crusade leaders for their personal quarrels:

"Speak to the princes and all the people, and say to them: 'You who have come from distant lands to worship God and the Lord of hosts, purge yourselves of your uncleanliness, and let each one turn from his evil ways. Then with bare feet march around Jerusalem invoking God, and you must also fast. If you do this and then make a great attack on the city on the ninth day, it will be captured. If you do not, all the evils that you have suffered will be multiplied by the Lord.'"[175]

The Crusaders heeded the advice of Adhemar in Peter's vision. They fasted for three days, and on July 8 they processed around the city, barefoot and unarmed, singing prayers and bearing relics, including the Holy Lance from Antioch. The Muslim defenders mocked the Crusaders' imitation of Joshua and the Israelites at Jericho by hitting and abusing crosses that they hanged over the city walls.[176] Miraculously, the defenders never sallied forth from the city to engage the Crusader host while it was the most defenseless. The great procession ended at the Mount of Olives where Raymond d'Aguilers, Arnulf of Choques, and Peter the Hermit encouraged the warriors of Christ with their preaching.

The Final Assault

The Crusaders attacked Jerusalem on July 13, using siege towers and battering rams at two locations. Godfrey had positioned his tower at a northern area of the city near Herod's Gate and the church of St. Mary Magdalene; this crucial placement ended up catching the defenders by surprise. As the city's occupiers struggled to repair the wall, they desperately fired catapults at the attacking Crusaders.[177] Raymond's army in the south met with less success; they had placed themselves near Zion Gate, a location that could be defended by nine of the city's fourteen catapults. Raymond's warriors suffered heavy causalities.

Although the two army groups were separated, they maintained cohesion of attack by communicating with signalers who used reflectors that had been placed on the Mount of Olives.[178] At three o'clock in the afternoon, the hour of Crucifixion, on Friday, July 15, the Feast of the Dispersal of the Apostles, the Crusaders achieved their final objective and entered the Holy

City. 460 years from its initial capture by the forces of Mohammed, Jerusalem was once again in Christian hands.

The "Massacre"

As was common in medieval warfare, in Christendom as well
as in the Islamic world, a city that refused surrender found itself
at the mercy of the attacking army once it forced its way in,
which is the reason why many leaders came to terms with an attacker rather than risk a siege.[179] Most attacking armies preferred
the city's surrender since it spared the army from causalities and
prevented destruction of the city. Once inside Jerusalem, the
Crusaders went on a rampage and killed many Muslim troops
as well as non-combatants. This event has been described as the
"Massacre of Jerusalem" and is used as a weapon for attacking
the Crusades and the Church. Detractors, without attempting to
understand the historical context of warfare at the time, reference this "massacre" to cast doubts on the morals and motivations of the Crusaders. Many even point to this event as a reason
for the recent attacks by Islamic terrorists on the West. Former
President Bill Clinton did so in a speech at Georgetown University on November 7, 2001:

> Those of us who come from various European lineages are
> not blameless. Indeed, in the First Crusade, when the Chris-
> tian soldiers took Jerusalem, they first burned a synagogue
> with 300 Jews in it, and proceeded to kill every woman and
> child who was Muslim on the Temple Mount. The contem-
> poraneous descriptions of the event describe soldiers walking
> on the Temple Mount, a holy place to Christians, with blood
> running up to their knees. I can tell you that that story is still
> being told today in the Middle East, and we are still paying
> for it.[180]

While there is no doubt many were killed, we must not exag-
gerate what happened. Many inhabitants of the city (including

Jews) were not killed but captured and ransomed; others were expelled from the city.[181] The idea that this event, which occurred over 900 years ago, is the reason for Muslim hatred of the West is absurd and illustrates a complete misunderstanding of the Crusading movement and its impact on the Islamic world.

The event is well known because both Islamic and Christian chroniclers recorded it, although there are discrepancies among the various accounts: some claim the massacre went on for several days, others that it occurred on the first day only. The Christian sources do not agree on how many were killed; Fulcher records that 10,000 were massacred, while others indicate only several hundred. Some Islamic sources provide widely inflated numbers, claiming upwards of 75,000 killed (the city's entire population was between 20,000 and 30,000). It is probable that anywhere from several hundred to 3,000 were slain by the Crusaders.

One interesting thing is the similar language used in the Christian sources to describe the bloodshed. The *Gesta* records that "the slaughter was so great that our men waded in blood up to the ankles."[182] Fulcher of Chartres recorded that "within this Temple about ten thousand were beheaded. If you had been there, your feet would have been stained up to the ankles with the blood of the slain."[183] In a letter sent to Pope Paschal II, the Crusade leaders informed the pope about the killings, writing "and if you desire to know what was done with the enemy who were found there, know that in Solomon's Porch and in his temple our men rode in the blood of the Saracens up to the knees of their horses."[184] Finally, Raymond d'Aguilers recalled this event and wrote, "[I]t is sufficient to relate that in the Temple of Solomon and the portico crusaders rode in blood to the knees and bridles of their horses."[185] Most Christian accounts of the initial events in Jerusalem after the Crusader liberation utilize similar language in describing the amount of blood spilled by those killed, the same expression used by President Clinton: The blood of the slain was either ankle-deep, calf-deep, or up to the knees of horses.

What most modern people, including the former president, fail to understand is that this language was not meant to be taken literally or to leave a factual record of the numbers of those killed. Rather it was intended to recall passages of Scripture that medieval people would instantly recognize—such as Revelation 4:20, which says, "and the wine press was trodden outside the city, and blood flowed from the wine press, as high as a horse's bridle for 1,600 stadia."[186] In the Old Testament this image of "treading a wine press" was "without exception a metaphor of judgment."[187] (See, for example, Isaiah 63:3.)

The city in that passage from Revelation is a reference to Jerusalem as the true city of the saints, and the imagery of blood and divine wrath refers to the judgment of unbelievers.[188] At first glance the precise figure of 1,600 stadia seems superfluous, but the figure would have been known in the Holy Land since it is the approximate length of Palestine as measured from Tyre to the border of Egypt.[189] Blood flowing up to a horse's bridle, meanwhile, "is figurate battle language and functions hyperbolically to emphasize the severe and unqualified nature of the judgment."[190] In using well-known language and imagery from Scripture, First Crusade commentators made the point that victory over Muslim forces throughout the Crusade and specifically at Jerusalem was ordained by God as a judgment against unbelievers.[191]

Although the killing of innocent civilians in Jerusalem cannot be justified, it can be explained as the actions of an army with "heightened emotions . . . which had been through terrible trials."[192] Some Christian sources suggest the killings were undertaken to cleanse the holy places from Muslim profanation and others see the massacre as retribution for Crusader sufferings throughout the campaign.[193] Additionally, the military position of the Crusaders also influenced their actions, for "they had engaged in a race against time and the gamble had succeeded. But now they anticipated the coming of an Egyptian army and it was fear of leaving an enemy in the nest that brought about this atrocious killing."[194]

War is a nasty affair and massacres were by no means the sole province of Christian warriors. The Muslim warlord Zengi massacred 6,000 Christian men, women, and children on Christmas Eve 1144 when he conquered the city of Edessa.[195] Likewise Baybars, the thirteenth-century Mamluk general-turned-sultan of Egypt, pursued a policy of aggressive *jihad* in his campaigns against Christian settlements. After conquering Antioch, he ordered the city gates closed and locked with the entire Christian population trapped inside. All were massacred in a bloodbath so repulsive that it shocked even Muslim chroniclers.[196]

Defender of the Holy Sepulchre

After achieving their objective, the Crusaders were faced with the reality of protecting, consolidating and organizing the territory they had liberated during the First Crusade.

The noble leaders of the Crusade gathered on July 17, two days after their momentous and miraculous victory, to choose a leader for the city. The nobles called for Raymond of Toulouse to be named king, but he refused (possibly out of a religious sense of unworthiness but also possibly because he really wanted the crown but did not want to *appear* to desire it). The nobles then looked to Godfrey, a warrior who had performed heroically throughout the Crusade, and offered him the crown on July 22. He accepted, but refused to be called king, taking instead the title, "Defender of the Holy Sepulchre."[197]

Going Home

Their vow fulfilled and Jerusalem secure, the vast majority of Crusaders still alive after their grueling three year journey turned west toward home.

Those who made it back to see loved ones again were a blessed few; eighty percent of those who participated in the First Crusade never returned, most dying from disease and starvation rather than from battle wounds.[198] A few Crusaders remained in the

Latin East but they were never numerous and, as a result, the Crusader States always suffered from a lack of internal manpower to defend and expand their meager outposts. After the final battle at Ascalon, Godfrey was left with only 300 knights and 2,000 infantry to defend Jerusalem and other Crusader territory.[199]

It is estimated that only 11 percent of the surviving Crusaders remained in the Holy Land after the First Crusade, and by the year 1100 there were a maximum of only 4,000 Western Europeans total.[200] This confirms that most participants did not view the Crusades as a source of wealth or an opportunity to increase land holdings. The Crusade was primarily a pilgrimage. When it was over, the pilgrims returned whence they had come.

4

Warrior-Monks, Preachers, and the Second Crusade

Edessa is taken, as you know, and the Christians are sorely
afflicted because of it; the churches are burnt and abandoned.
God is no longer sacrificed there. Knights, make your decisions,
you who are esteemed for your skill in arms; make a gift of
your bodies to him who was placed on the cross for you.

Chevalier, *Mult Estes Guariz*[201]

We believe that it has come about through the providence of divine
counsel that so great a multitude of the faithful from diverse
regions is preparing to fight the infidel, and that almost the whole
of Christendom is being summoned for so praiseworthy a task.

Pope Bl. Eugenius III[202]

The fifty-six year old Cistercian was exhausted. His normal spiritual practices placed great strain on his body and forty years of such practices had taken their toll. Pope Eugenius III had entrusted the holy monk with the task of generating support for the journey to the Holy Land. Despite his ill health, Bernard of Clairvaux had persevered in his mission and now, in 1146, his preaching journey was almost complete.

He had traveled several hundred miles throughout Flanders and the German Empire in mid-winter over the prior seven months and given dozens of sermons to the warriors of Christendom. He had even personally motivated the two greatest monarchs of the time to attend to the "business of God."[203] Such success had followed Bernard throughout his life, especially in his monastic work, and his preaching tour had accomplished his papal tasking. Bernard had done his part. Christendom was mobilized; warriors were making preparations once again to fight the forces of Islam and aid their Latin brethren in the East.

The Latin East

Although nearly all of the surviving First Crusaders journeyed home to Europe, a few settled in the Holy Land. Over the next fifty years, they consolidated, expanded, and solidified control of what became known as Outrémer,[204] stretching 600 miles from north to south.

The activity of the First Crusade produced three Crusader States: the County of Edessa, the Principality of Antioch, and the Kingdom of Jerusalem. The County of Tripoli, another Crusader State, was established during the reign of King Baldwin I. The Kingdom of Jerusalem was "the emotional, political and strategic heart of Outrémer."[205] Important religiously and politically but not economically, the kingdom suffered greatly from succession problems throughout its history; only twice in its eighty-eight year history did son succeed father as king, and the two times it happened, one son was a minor and the other a sickly leper.

After the death of Godfrey de Bouillon, who had refused out of humility and faith to accept the title of king, his brother Baldwin hurried to Jerusalem to take the throne. He was "fittingly sad at his brother's death but even happier with the expected inheritance."[206] Baldwin had no qualms about taking the title "king of Jerusalem" and was crowned in the Church of the Nativity in Bethlehem on Christmas Day, 1100.

Life in the Latin East

The Latin settlers were never numerous during the twelfth and thirteenth centuries and were minority rulers of large Muslim populations.[207] The "Franks," as their Muslim neighbors called them, soon found that accommodation with the local populace was the path to growth and success. Relations between the Franks and Muslims were shaped by mutual benefit and general indifference. "Spontaneous uprisings against the Franks were rare; active collaboration with them was limited."[208]

There was very little cultural exchange and there were very few conversions. One reason for the lack of conversion was the allowance by the Latin settlers for Jews and Muslims to openly practice their faith. The Crusades were not wars of conversion. Although Muslims were not allowed to reside in Jerusalem itself and the Dome of the Rock was turned into a church, Muslims were permitted to visit the area and pray.[209]

The policy of general accommodation by the Latin settlers with the Muslim populace became a point of contention with Crusaders traveling from Europe, who were horrified at the Franks' willingness to negotiate and even enter into treaties with Muslims. It was a difficult balancing act for those who lived in the Crusader States. They were no longer soldiers on the march; they recognized the need to live prudently with their Muslim neighbors. Yet they needed assistance from Christendom to maintain and sustain their settlements. Arrivals from Europe failed to understand the position of the Latin settlers and "as time passed, a gulf opened between the new crusaders, who arrived from the West to fight Muslims and the local residents, who would have to live with the Muslims after the pilgrims returned home."[210]

Defense of the Latin East

The security of the Crusader States was always precarious. The one constant in the Holy Land was a lack of sufficient manpower to police, govern, and defend the 600-mile region.

In order to compensate for this lack of manpower, an intensive castle-building campaign was undertaken from 1115–1150. Castles were sited in strategic locations in order to control the surrounding territory and were used as forward operating bases

for incursions into Muslim territory. The shortage of manpower "demanded fortifications so strong they could be garrisoned
with comparatively small bodies of men."[211]

The celebrated castle Krak des Chevaliers is a great example.
It was built in Syria (near the modern-day border with Leba-
non) in the County of Tripoli and had an inner wall a hundred
feet thick as well as an outer wall fixed with round towers. It
enclosed a 390-foot-long Great Hall, quarters for soldiers, sta-
bles for horses, several wells and cisterns, and had windmills to
process corn and sugar cane. Krak des Chevaliers was virtually
impregnable and withstood multiple attacks including one by
Saladin in 1188. The Mamluk general Baybars captured it finally
in 1271 after more than a yearlong siege.

As beneficial as castles were to the Crusaders, they were costly to maintain. Even if built efficiently, they required manpower
to defend and utilize. To garrison these castles and defend the
Latin East, the rulers of Outrémer turned to an innovation in
the spiritual life of the Church.   Monks

The Warrior-Monks

Crusading was originally a temporary action undertaken for a
specified goal. With the establishment of the military religious
orders in the twelfth century, that "temporary act of devotion
became warfare as a devotional way of life."[212]

The development of these religious orders, whose members
took a vow to live the evangelical counsels of poverty, chastity,
and obedience with the added vow of military service for Christ
and the Church, can be traced to those warriors who came to
the Holy Land after the First Crusade. The founding of their
orders, like the founding of most religious orders throughout
Church history, was not a planned event; rather it "was the completely spontaneous response of some Christians to the problems
facing them in the Holy Land. The pilgrims had to be protected
and the sick and needy among them cared for, and above all else,
the safety of the captured holy places had to be assured."[213]

Over time, four main groups of warrior-monks developed: the Hospitallers, the Templars, the Teutonic Knights, and the Knights of the Holy Sepulchre. Believing that "fighting was a charitable activity," members of these orders "said the office and then rode out to kill their enemies."[214] Some questioned whether these orders were in keeping with the dictates of the gospel of Christ, but the reality of life in the twelfth century was such that "if the mendicant brothers preached the gospel, the military brethren defended it."[215]

The Hospitallers

The Hospitallers began as an independent religious order founded in 1113 by Bl. Gerard Tenque, whose initial role was caring for sick pilgrims in a hospital. Recognized by Pope Paschal II, these monks followed the Rule of St. Augustine, wore a black cloak with a white cross, and were especially devoted to St. John the Baptist. Their official name, the Order of the Hospital of St. John of Jerusalem, reflected this devotion. The Hospitallers served the poor, considering themselves "serfs of the poor of Christ."[216] The Grand Master of the order was called "the guardian of the poor" and the brothers were allowed to wear only humble clothing because "our lords the poor . . . go about naked and meanly dressed. And it would be wrong and improper for the serfs to be proud and the lord humble."[217]

The Hospitallers cared for the sick in the most luxurious manner possible in their Jerusalem hospital, which was a world-class facility that admitted patients regardless of illness (except leprosy), nationality, or sex. Not only did they admit Jews and Muslims but they accommodated their dietary laws.

The hospital in Jerusalem was a massive facility with a maximum capacity of 2,000 separate beds, and in overflow situations the brothers' dormitory was used by the sick while the brothers slept on the floor. Patients were provided excellent food and care including meat portions three times a week and white bread—quantity and quality foreign to all but the noblest members of medieval society. Four surgeons and physicians attended at the hospital and practiced Western medicine based on the techniques taught at the medical school in Salerno. When the kingdom's army mobilized, the doctors attended in the field.

The Templars

King Baldwin II supported a group of knights organized by the Frenchman Hugh of Payns and gave them part of his royal palace in the Temple enclosure as their quarters. Accordingly, the religious order originally known as the Poor Knights of Christ became known as the Knights of the Temple, or the Templars.

Hugh and eight companions including Andrew of Montbard (the uncle of St. Bernard of Clairvaux) founded the Templars. They lived by the Cistercian rule and took vows to live the evangelical counsels, adding a special vow to protect Christian pilgrims traveling from the port of Jaffa to Jerusalem.

The order received recognition in 1128 from Pope Honorius II (1124–1130), and over time grew in prestige and influence through the granting of large amounts of land from the nobility of Christendom. The Templars were known for their discipline in battle and strict obedience; a Templar was not allowed even to adjust his stirrup without permission from his superior![218]

Templars lived by the five major rules of the order: 1) to fight to the death for the holy places of Christendom; 2) to refuse to be ransomed if captured; 3) to accept every combat regardless of the odds; 4) to refuse quarter or ransom to Muslim prisoners; and 5) to give their lives to defend any Christian attacked by a Muslim.[219] Despite the strictness and difficulty of Templar life, many were drawn to it. St. Bernard helped recruitment through his general support and the writing of a treatise, *On the Praise of the New Knighthood,* in which he highlighted the meritorious aspect of fighting for Christ with the potential for martyrdom: "Life indeed is fruitful and victory glorious, but according to holy law death is better than either of these things. For if those are blessed who die in the Lord, how much more blessed are those who die for the Lord?[220]

The order grew in membership, prominence, and influence in the Holy Land and Europe. By 1150, the Templars could muster 600 knights, which combined with the Hospitallers amounted to half the total available knights in the Latin East.[221] Their power in Christendom was rooted in the 9,000 feudal lordships and manors they owned, providing a large base of resources and financial influence.[222] Templar houses became known as important financial centers in Europe and served as places of deposit for Crusaders traveling to the Holy Land. This, in turn, inaugurated the first primitive system of ATMs, since those who deposited funds in a Templar house in Europe could withdraw that amount minus a fee at Templar houses in the Latin East.

As the number of transactions grew so did the Templar coffers. Their financial holdings and power became the envy of royalty and nobility throughout Europe, but especially in France. This situation would incite the jealousy of the despotic Philip IV "the Fair" of France in the fourteenth century, who arrested the master of the order and other knights on false charges. The king convinced Pope Clement V to order the suppression of the Templars, which occurred at the Council of Vienne in 1311. Despite their inauspicious ending, during their existence the Templars faithfully served Christendom, especially through the witness of the 20,000 brothers who gave their lives for their fellow Christians.[223]

Knights of the Holy Sepulchre

Godfrey de Bouillon, the hero of the First Crusade, founded the Knights of the Holy Sepulchre in 1099 as the military guard for the Church of the Holy Sepulchre. In 1138 Pope Innocent II (r. 1130–1143) approved their religious charism as canons of the Church embracing the evangelical counsels. The order also contained knights living a secular life who vowed to defend the tomb of Christ.[224] Operating so closely with the kings of Jerusalem initially made the order a powerful institution, but it steadily became a ceremonial and service organization. In 1847, the order was reconstituted, reorganized, and modernized by Pope Bl. Pius IX, who took on the role of grand master. The Knights of the Holy Sepulchre continue to serve the Church through their spiritual devotion to the Holy City and their assistance to Christians in the Holy Land.

The Teutonic Knights

The Teutonic Knights of St. Mary's Hospital of Jerusalem originated through the actions of German merchants at the siege of Acre in 1190, during the Third Crusade. They began by simply establishing a hospital in the Crusader camp to care for the sick, wounded, and dying combatants, but within a decade their focus shifted to military matters. Like the other military religious orders, they bound themselves in service to Christ and the Church. They embraced a personal identification with the Savior, evidenced by the adoption of the motto, "Who fights us, fights Jesus Christ."[225]

Although never influential in the Holy Land, the Teutonic Knights became a powerful political and military force in Eastern Europe. In spite of this, they were decisively defeated by Polish forces at the Battle of Tannenberg on July 15, 1410. The devastation wrought by this defeat severely limited their influence and effectiveness. Although their numbers dwindled through the centuries, they continued to exist as a small order of nobility centered in Austria. Already limited in activity, they suffered even greater loss when twelve knights were hanged in 1944 by the Nazi German government for their role in the assassination plot against Adolf Hitler.[226]

Military Orders and the Church

The modern Catholic may wonder why the Church recognized and supported the creation of religious orders whose members lived the evangelical counsels but also fought in combat. The same question was also raised by some Catholics during the twelfth century, but the Church rightly emphasized the difference between killing an innocent person and an enemy soldier. St. Bernard used the term "malecide"—the killing of evil; it was "the extermination of injustice rather than of the unjust, and therefore desirable."[227]

The military religious orders were a unique spiritual innovation in the life of the Church. While the Crusades gave the medieval warriors of Christendom a temporary outlet for spiritual benefits through the use of their martial skill, the military orders provided a permanent place for the knight in monastic life: "The warrior, a strong man, taking pride in his strength, was asked to use this strength and his sword in the service of the weak, to step out of his own world and become a monk, yet keep his sword by his side and his lance in his hand."[228]

The Rise of Zengi

The Islamic world in the east was fractured in the late eleventh century with competing caliphs in Baghdad and Cairo. The call to *jihad* after the First Crusade to force the Christians out of Outrémer was centered in Damascus through the preaching of Ali as-Sulami (1039–1106). A year before his death, as-Sulami gave a series of public lectures in the Great Mosque in Damascus, which were published as a book entitled *Kitab al-jihad* or *The Book on Holy War*. As-Sulami argued that the solution to disunity among Muslims was the expulsion of the Outrémer Christians through *jihad*. His contemporaries paid little heed to as-Sulami's exhortations, but fifty years later Nur al-Din would lay the groundwork for the famous general Saladin to implement the plan of as-Sulami to destroy the Latin East.

Imad al-Din Zengi was the ruler of Mosul and Aleppo and struck a fearful figure; he was "a sadistic monster, at the sight of whom one man was supposed to have dropped dead from fright, [and] who crucified his own troops found marching out of line and trampling crops."[229] Zengi desired to unify the Muslim cities and create an empire for himself. He also desired to expand his holdings by pushing the Franks out of the Holy Land through *jihad.* Edessa

A great opportunity came to Zengi when King Fulk of Jerusalem died unexpectedly in 1143 from a horrific head injury sustained while hunting. His oldest son, Baldwin, was too young to assume the throne outright but was proclaimed king under the regency of his mother Queen Melisende. Seizing on the political weakness in the Kingdom of Jerusalem, Zengi marshaled his army for an attack on the Crusader State of Edessa.

Once his army arrived at Edessa, Zengi's engineers began the task of undermining the walls by digging tunnels. Four weeks after their arrival, on Christmas Eve, they brought down a portion of the walls and poured into the city.

The defenders and populace of Edessa made a mad dash for the citadel in the hopes of survival; Archbishop Hugh was accidentally crushed to death by the fleeing masses.[230] Zengi's army rampaged through the fallen city, pillaging, plundering, raping, and massacring 6,000 Christian men, women, and children.[231]

Edessa was the first of the Crusader States and, after only forty years, the first to fall back into Muslim hands. The fall of Edessa was a serious blow to the Christian strategic situation in Outrémer since it guarded the approach to Antioch.

Zengi's success at Edessa emboldened him. He set his sights on Jerusalem, but before he could act he was killed in 1146 by his favorite Frankish slave who murdered him after Zengi engaged in a night of heavy drinking. Zengi's empire was divided between his sons, Sayf al-Din, who received Mosul, and Nur al-Din, who received Aleppo. The dream of a united Muslim kingdom waging *jihad* would have to wait a little longer. Although he did not accomplish his major goal, Zengi did significantly alter the political and military landscape in Outrémer. His success at Edessa "had a profound effect on Christians and Muslims alike. The Christian aura of invincibility was shattered. A new generation of Muslims who had thought of the Crusader States as permanent entities now began to think again."[232]

The loss of Edessa demanded a Christian response. No new Crusade had been called in a generation, but now the warriors of Christendom were asked once more to risk their lives to recover what had been lost.

Calling the Second Crusade

News of the fall of Edessa sent shockwaves throughout Christendom. An entire generation had been raised since the First Crusade and most in Europe to take for granted the continued existence of the Crusader States. Now, just as Bl. Urban II had sprung to action fifty years before, the successor of St. Peter once more rose to the occasion to motivate Catholic warriors to embrace the cross at the service of the Church.

Bernardo Paganelli was the first Cistercian monk to be elected pope, taking the name Eugenius III (r. 1145–1153). Bl. Eugenius III knew the events at Edessa required papal exhortation of another major expedition to the East, and so he issued the bull *Quantum Praedecessores* on December 1, 1145. Addressed to King Louis VII of France, Eugenius III's short document set the stage for the Second Crusade as well as provided an official listing of the privileges granted to Crusaders. Eugenius exhorted the warriors of France, and later those throughout Christendom, to take the cross in order to return Edessa to the patrimony of Christ. As at Clermont fifty years before, Eugenius III used his papal authority to grant the spiritual incentive of the indulgence for those who undertook the journey:

> By the authority of omnipotent God and that of Blessed Peter the prince of the apostles conceded to us by God, we grant remission of and absolution from sins . . . in such a way that whosoever devoutly begins and completes so holy a journey or dies on it will obtain absolution from all his sins of which he has made confession with a contrite and humble heart.[233]

Half a century before, Urban had utilized the French people's intense devotion to Jerusalem in motivating warriors to go on the

First Crusade. Now, because Jerusalem was in Christian hands, Pope Eugenius III had to find a new method of motivation. His exhortation for the warriors of France to take the cross centered on recalling the brave and noble deeds of the ancestors of his audience as well as an appeal to their sense of honor as Christian knights. The deeds of the First Crusaders were well known throughout Christendom and remembered in art, architecture, song, and stories. Eugenius utilized this memory to evoke a sense of family honor in the listeners of his day and to encourage knights to defend what their ancestors had liberated half a century before:

> It will be seen as a great token of nobility and uprightness if those things acquired by the efforts of your fathers are vigorously defended by you, their good sons. But if, God forbid, it comes to pass differently, then the bravery of the fathers will have proved to be diminished in the sons.[234]

Eugenius's bull had a lasting impact on the Crusading movement and was possibly the most widely circulated papal document in medieval Europe.[235] Nonetheless, *Quantum Praedecessores* could not, on its own, motivate warriors to risk certain death thousands of miles from home. Following Urban II's strategy, Eugenius also commissioned preachers to travel throughout Christendom in order to make the contents of *Quantum Praedecessores* known so that the Second Crusade could become a reality.

Preaching the Second Crusade

St. Bernard of Clairvaux was the third son of seven children born to a noble family near Dijon in the Burgundy region of France. He was "passionate, full of inner fire" and totally devoted to the Catholic Faith. He had a special reverence for the Blessed Mother that had been inculcated by his own mother.[236]

Bernard was endowed with the gift of preaching which, at the insistence of Pope Eugenius, he used to maximum effect for the Second Crusade. Theophilus Reynauld's sixteenth-century book

The Gallic Bee referred to Bernard as the "mellifluous" or "honey-sweet" Doctor of the Church, a name that has stuck through the centuries.[237] Pope Pius XII used this moniker as the title for his encyclical on St. Bernard in 1953 on the 800th anniversary of his death. Bernard's preaching was like "the fragrant aroma of an incense burning in a heart on fire with the Holy Spirit," which flowed from his in-depth study of the Faith, through which, like "a diligent bee, he has extracted the sweet essence from Scripture and the Fathers and refined it in loving meditation."[238]

St. Bernard undertook his papal-directed preaching tour seriously and, despite his ill health, ventured across Christendom for nine months through the spring and winter of 1146 and into 1147, preaching numerous sermons and traveling several hundred miles. He recognized that the "business of God" was necessary and he endeavored to raise the warriors required to restore Christian lands in the East.[239]

Bernard preached the Crusade in France, Flanders, and throughout the German Empire. To those regions he could not visit he sent letters urging the faithful to take the cross to fight in a worthy cause: "[N]ow, O mighty soldiers, O men of war, you have a cause for which you can fight without danger to your souls: a cause in which to conquer is glorious and for which to die is gain."[240]

As with the First Crusade, it was the spiritual benefit of the indulgence that motivated participants, and it was this aspect that Bernard emphasized:

> I call blessed the generation that can seize the opportunity of such rich indulgence as this, blessed to be alive in this year of jubilee, this year of God's choice. Take up the sign of the Cross and you will find indulgence for all the sins which you humbly confess. The cost is small, the reward is great.[241]

Radulf and the Jews

Bernard was certainly the most well-known preacher of the Second Crusade, but he was not the only one. Other preachers, some approved and others not, traveled throughout Christendom to dispense exhortations, some of which deviated from the official message and instead promoted persecution and harassment of the Jews. Bernard heard of such preaching and made it known that the Jews were not to be harmed: "We have heard with joy that zeal for God burns in you, but wisdom must not be lacking from this zeal. The Jews are not to be persecuted, nor killed, nor even forced to flee."[242]

A fellow French Cistercian monk named Radulf failed to heed the words of Bernard. Traveling to the Rhineland, Radulf incited anti-Semitic fervor in the same cities of Count Emich's pogroms during the time of the First Crusade.[243] Radulf's message against the Jews was the same as the one used by Emich a generation previously: why risk life to travel far from home when enemies of Christ were near at hand? Although Radulf's preaching led to outbreaks of violence against certain German Jewish communities, such pogroms were "isolated incidents . . . not systematic slaughter."[244]

Bernard was greatly upset when news of his fellow Cistercian's preaching reached him. He expressed his holy anger at Radulf when he wrote, "I find three things most reprehensible in him: unauthorized preaching, contempt for episcopal authority, and incitation to murder."[245] Bernard was so disgusted that he traveled to Mainz in November 1146, confronted and rebuked Radulf, and ordered him to return to his monastery.

Conrad III and the Germans

Bernard's preaching tour and written exhortations were a resounding success as warriors took the cross in great numbers, equaling and perhaps rivaling the total forces of the First Crusade. In some ways, Bernard's preaching mission was made easy due to the vivid memory of the First Crusade present in twelfth-century Christendom. Knights and nobles spent their evenings regaled with tales of heroics from the First Crusade in the *chansons* of the troubadours. The warriors of Christendom who heard St. Bernard were honor-bound men who recognized the Second Crusade as an opportunity to measure themselves against the "honor, valor, [and] nobility" of their ancestors who participated in the First Crusade.[246]

The most powerful ruler in Christendom, however, was not interested in going on Crusade. There was a plethora of political issues to deal with in imperial territory and, even if there hadn't been, an exhausting, risky journey to the east was not looked upon favorably by the fifty-four year old monarch.

Conrad III was not opposed to the Crusade or the Crusading movement; he had previously taken the cross in 1124 and made the pilgrimage to the Holy Land before his coronation as king of the Germans. Indeed, he was the only major monarch of Christendom to go to Jerusalem twice. The problem was that political unrest in his lands, motivated by those angry at his accession to the throne, weighed heavily on his heart and he sincerely believed it was not prudent for him to go to Jerusalem again.

St. Bernard had already preached the Crusade to King Louis VII of France, who responded and was busy making preparations to depart. Now it was time for Conrad to follow suit. The "Honey-Sweet" Doctor arrived at the king's Christmas Court in Speyer in December 1146 and met privately with Conrad. History does not record what was said between the powerful king and the humble preacher, but it does record the actions of both men the next day.

After celebrating Mass in the cathedral, St. Bernard turned toward Conrad and personally and publicly called him to take the cross. Conrad responded, "Now I recognize clearly that this is a gift of divine grace, nor now shall I be found to be ungrateful . . . I am ready to serve him!"[247] Bernard went to the altar, retrieved a prepared cloth cross, and pinned it on the king.

The interaction made for great theater, which medieval people highly enjoyed, but more than likely the king had agreed to take the cross the day before during his private meeting with Bernard. Conrad's embrace of the cross motivated other leading nobles and clergy to do the same, including his half-brothers

Duke Henry of Bavaria and Otto of Freising, and his nephew, Duke Frederick of Swabia—the future holy Roman emperor known as Frederick Barbarossa. Now that the king and his leading nobles had taken the cross, preparations were undertaken to ready the massive German army for its march to the east.

The Road to Constantinople

Since French preparations were already well underway, it was decided a meeting of the allies should be held to discuss the logistics involved in transporting the two hosts to the Holy Land. King Louis VII, St. Bernard, and several French nobles met on February 2, 1147 with German ambassadors. They agreed that the armies would follow in the footsteps of their ancestors from the First Crusade and take the land route to Constantinople and onward to northern Syria.

The Germans made efficient preparations. Within six months (the French took fifteen months) Conrad was ready, and in May 1147 he departed Nuremburg with an army of 30,000 to 35,000 soldiers plus noncombatants.

They had a fairly uneventful trek through Eastern Europe until they reached Byzantine territory,[248] where they suffered harassment by imperial troops. Regardless, the Germans eventually reached Constantinople in September.

The Byzantines viewed the Germans as "greedy and fickle barbarians and heretical."[249] Like Alexius I before him, Emperor Manuel was fearful, suspicious, and anxious about them and believed their true objective was to conquer Constantinople. In order to mitigate the risk of such an operation, Manuel entered into an alliance with the Turks and may have even supplied them with information on the numbers and route of the Western armies. He also encouraged the Turks to attack the French Crusade forces on their way to Antioch.[250]

The task of journeying to the Holy Land and liberating Edessa was already a difficult one; it was made far more so by the treachery of the Byzantines. "At most, Manuel helped only when and how it suited him; at worst, he ensured, if only passively, that the odds were stacked against the Westerners."[251]

Retracing the Steps of the First Crusade

The Byzantine navy transported the German army across the Bosporus, and it made its way to Nicaea. Conrad's force left Nicaea on October 15, but only ten days out it became clear the army was consuming too much food and marching too slowly, partly due to constant Turkish harassment. In late October, the army was badly mauled by the Turks near Dorylaeum, the site of victory for the First Crusaders fifty years before. The army had been encamped near Dorylaeum when Conrad allowed the cavalry to leave the main body to search for water. This proved a tactical blunder with severe consequences. The rapid mounted Turkish archers set upon the undefended infantry and slaughtered many. Although the cavalry returned and beat back the Muslim force, the damage had already been inflicted. The killing was so great that veterans, years after the battle, were said to weep at the memory of that day.

Despite the heavy losses at Dorylaeum, Conrad's army continued the march. After three days it became apparent that they should not continue. The leading nobles demanded a council with Conrad to discuss the future of the army. Morale was low and casualties continued to mount.

Things went from bad to worse when Conrad was struck by two Muslim arrows—one was to the head, causing a gruesome injury. The nobles begged Conrad to retreat. He agreed. The mighty German army, once full of promise and hope of victory, was demolished as an effective fighting force. The weeks-long march had brought nothing but a 20-percent casualty rate, a demoralized army, and a severely wounded king.

They returned to Nicaea in early November. Louis VII's French army soon joined them and was shocked to hear of the German defeat. The two armies marched together to Ephesus to celebrate Christmas, and it was then that Louis decided to move

out and continue his journey through Anatolia. Conrad, still suffering from his arrow wound, decided to go to Constantinople
to convalesce. After spending the rest of winter and early spring
there, he informed Emperor Manuel that he was leaving to re-
join the Crusade. Conrad's group celebrated Easter at Acre and
then marched to Jerusalem, were he visited the holy sites. In May
1148 he entered into an agreement with King Baldwin III and the
Templars to lead his remaining forces to Damascus.

Louis VII and the French

The twenty-six year old Louis VII (1120–1180) was a pious and
devoted Catholic steeped in the Crusading history of his ancestors. The heroic tales of the First Crusade were read aloud at his
coronation ceremony in 1137.[252] His pious and austere lifestyle
contrasted greatly with that of his wife, Eleanor of Aquitaine,
the most famous woman of the medieval period.

Pope Eugenius knew of Louis's interest in the Crusade, which
is why he addressed the bull *Quantum Praedecessores* to the French
king and his subjects. Louis eagerly took the cross because the
martial ethos of the medieval French demanded it, and a desire
to emulate the actions of the First Crusaders pushed him. Of
course, it was no easy decision, since "to raise the money necessary for the Crusade, to be away from one's lands for two or
three years and to stand a fair chance of losing one's life constituted a serious set of calculations for any individual, let alone
one with the God-given responsibilities of a crowned head."[253]

St. Bernard traveled to Vézaly at Easter in 1146 to attend an
assembly called by Louis. Here the Second Crusade would be announced and French warriors would be urged to participate. The
choice of Vézaly was deliberate. It was well known as the starting
point for the pilgrimage, or *Camino*, to Santiago de Compostela.
There could be no better place to call forth soldiers to engage in
the penitential and armed pilgrimage of the Crusade.

Bernard preached eloquently and the nobility and clergy of
France responded. The great French fervor manifested itself in an

unexpected multitude of individuals taking the cross; so many, in fact, that the cloth crosses ran out and Bernard improvised by tearing his own habit to make more![254] Louis VII's family and relatives joined him in taking the cross, including his wife (one of several women who joined the Crusade), his brother Robert of Dreux, and his uncle Amadeus of Savoy. Crusading veterans and sons of First Crusaders also signed up.

Over the next fifteen months, Louis assembled the men and materiel needed to conduct combat operations in the east. Besides the military and political preparations Louis focused on spiritual preparation. In a show of immense humility and penance, the king visited a leper house outside of Paris to minister to the poor souls by washing their feet.[255]

By the summer of 1147, Louis VII must have felt confident and hopeful for the journey ahead. He had spent over a year getting ready for the grand adventure. Political and military preparations were complete. His spiritual preparations helped center the true nature of the expedition in his heart. All was ready for the king of France and his mighty soldiers to march to war.

The French Head East

The French, as the Germans had before them, enjoyed an uneventful march through Eastern Europe but troublesome setbacks once they entered Byzantine territory. Emissaries from Emperor Manuel demanded the French agree to return any liberated former imperial territory, just as Alexius had demanded of the First Crusaders. The French had believed Greek towns along the way would be open to them in order to buy food, but most refused to allow them entry and instead lowered (insufficient) food in buckets by ropes over the city walls. Advance units of Louis's army were even attacked by Byzantine forces outside the walls of Constantinople.

Despite Byzantine harassment the main French army arrived at Constantinople in early October 1147. After being transported to Anatolia they proceeded to Nicaea, where they watched in horror as the battered army of Conrad III returned from its disastrous march.

Louis and his army moved inland and were ambushed and constantly harassed by the Turks. The king countered the mobile tactics of the Muslims by organizing his army so that the knights were in the front and sides, protecting the infantry and baggage train within a shell of heavily armored soldiers. Although the march was difficult due to constant Muslim attacks, the army was holding and Louis was confident of their safe arrival in the Holy Land.

Disaster at Mount Cadmus

As the French army approached Mount Cadmus in southern Anatolia, Louis gave strict orders that the line of march should not be broken for fear the Turks would exploit the gap. Unfortunately, his orders were not followed. The vanguard made good time through the mountain pass but allowed a gap to form between its units and the long, slower-moving baggage train. The rearguard had not even moved out of camp yet. Seeing the baggage train exposed, the Turks attacked.

The news reached Louis in the rearguard and he immediately sprang into action, leading his elite personal bodyguard into the fray. After heavy fighting and narrowly escaping capture, the king made his way back to the shattered remnant of his army and surveyed the scene. Many of his nobles were now dead, along with a number of infantry. On top of that, the marauding Muslims had plundered his baggage train. The once-promising Crusade was in crisis.

The Antioch Affair

Louis and his nobles finally arrived in Antioch on March 19, 1148. Their time in that city produced the most salacious story of the entire Crusade. It was a tale of political intrigue and marital difficulties that became one of the most remembered episodes of the Crusading movement.

Prince Raymond of Antioch welcomed King Louis but saw in his arrival an opportunity to increase his control over the surrounding countryside. Raymond hoped the consolidation of territory using French muscle would secure his independence from the Byzantines, who had attacked the city a decade previously and still maintained that the city was imperial territory. Raymond also wanted to take advantage of the local Muslim political situation and believed the time was right for an attack on Aleppo, ruled by Zengi's son Nur al-Din.

Louis recognized that an attack on Aleppo would not be advantageous and decided the best course of action was to march south to Jerusalem and link up with Conrad's remaining forces. This decision infuriated Prince Raymond and set into motion the "Antioch Affair."

Louis's wife Eleanor of Aquitaine had been pleased with the decision to travel to Antioch. Prince Raymond was her uncle, although he was only eight years older, and they had known each other for years. Raymond spent a great deal of time with Eleanor during her stay in Antioch and after Louis's rebuff of his plans, his time with the Queen increased. Eleanor welcomed the attention. She "was indeed flirtatious, flighty, and already tired of her husband."[256] Sources differ and historians argue over what did or did not occur between Prince Raymond and Eleanor, but the historian of the Latin East, William of Tyre, believed the queen was "a foolish woman" who, "contrary to her royal dignity," was unfaithful to Louis.[257]

Throughout this time in which she was possibly having an adulterous—and incestuous—affair, Eleanor tried to convince Louis to support Raymond's plan to march to Aleppo. She was furious at Louis's decision to travel to Jerusalem instead and threatened to seek an annulment on the grounds of consanguinity (they were third cousins once removed) if Louis refused to go to Aleppo. The queen's threat did not move Louis to reconsider and he marched to the Holy City.

After they returned from the Crusade, Eleanor did follow through on her threat and sought an annulment, which was

granted in 1152. Two months later she married Henry Plan-
tagenet, the future king of England. That marriage produced
eight total children; three of the sons became kings of England—including Richard I the Lion-Hearted and his infamous
rival, John.

Damascus

By the summer of 1148 the Second Crusade was in near shambles. The major armies had suffered horrific casualties during
their marches through Anatolia and the remnants arrived in Jerusalem disheveled and disheartened.

Louis, Conrad, King Baldwin III, and the local Christian nobility met to determine the course of the Crusade. They faced
three choices of targets: Aleppo, Damascus, or Ascalon. Aleppo
was least viable, as Nur al-Din was well entrenched and too
far north. A good tactical and strategic argument could have
been made to attack the Fatimid city of Ascalon, the gateway to
Egypt; its capture would provide a base of operations to launch
raids into Egypt and solidify the Kingdom of Jerusalem's southern border. However, the local nobility preferred an attack on
Damascus. Damascus and Jerusalem had been allies until Nur
al-Din, the ruler of Aleppo, married the daughter of the ruler
of Damascus. The local Latin nobility were afraid that the marriage would lead to Nur al-Din's total control of Damascus in
the future, which would threaten the survival of Christian Jerusalem. So, they convinced Louis and Conrad to join forces and
march with local troops to Damascus.

The combined army arrived near Damascus on July 24, 1148.
Damascus was protected not only by its defensive walls but also
by orchards, which surrounded most of the city "like the halo
around the moon."[258] The orchards comprised plots surrounded by dry mud walls which served as a natural defensive barrier.
Some plot owners had constructed towers as well. The army that
controlled the orchards had Damascus by the throat—the Crusaders recognized this and therefore focused their initial attack here.

The German army led the way through the orchards and pushed the Muslim defenders back. Conrad was seen engaging in personal combat as he severed the head, neck, and shoulder of one Muslim defender. This display of strength caused other Muslim troops to retreat.[259]

By the end of the first day of fighting the Crusaders were in an excellent tactical position. They were in control of most of the orchards and had pushed the outer defenses of the city back to the walls. They had plenty of food and water, and set their camp on a plain on the other side of the orchards in front of the city. Curiously, the army had not brought along any siege equipment, nor did it construct any, indicating that the leaders expected a rapid assault or quick surrender to bring them victory.

On the second day of fighting the defenders counterattacked and made small gains, but the Crusaders were still in a dominant position. By the third day, at the suggestion of the local Christian nobles, the Crusaders broke camp and shifted their point of attack to what they believed to be a weaker section of the walls on the eastern side of the city. Their belief was not accurate, as the eastern walls were heavily defended. Meanwhile, Damascene troops reoccupied the orchards, preventing the Crusaders from returning to their original attack position. Separated from their previously abundant food and water supply and aware of advancing Muslim relief armies, Louis and Conrad made the heart-wrenching decision to end the siege and withdraw to Jerusalem. The Crusade was over; it had accomplished nothing and was an abject disaster.

The Blame Game

Why did the Christian armies fail? William of Tyre tried to answer that question a quarter century later by interviewing surviving veterans in France. Unfortunately, his research did not provide a definitive answer, but it did point to the belief that treachery was involved. Conrad III believed blame should be placed squarely on the shoulders of the local Christian nobility:

With general consensus we reached Damascus and set up our camp in front of the city gate. Although our men faced considerable danger, there can be no doubt at all that the city was close to being captured, and surrendering. But then, those whom we had no reason to distrust behaved in this way: they claimed that the side of the city we were on was impregnable and intentionally led us to another district where there was neither water for the army, nor was it possible to gain entry. Everyone was angered by this and turned around and retreated in grief with the siege a failure.[260]

The story circulated in the West that Jerusalem's nobility had been bribed to betray the siege; this belief would sour European relations with the Latin East for the next thirty years.

Muslim sources, though, provide more awareness of what happened that fateful July in 1148. Although the generally accepted Western narrative was that the Crusaders were in a very favorable position of attack after the first day of fighting, the reality was more nuanced. The first day did result in Crusader success, including the killing of two well-known and important Muslim religious figures. However, the notion that the city was on the brink of surrender was not accurate. The inhabitants of Damascus had no intention of surrendering and were motivated by deep religious piety to fight and defend their city. Damascus held a special place of importance for Islam, as it was reportedly the site where the messiah would come before the day of judgment at the end of the world; the slopes of Mount Kaisoun allegedly were the birthplace of Abraham; and it was the city where God gave asylum to Jesus and Mary.[261] The city known as "God's Paradise on Earth" would not have fallen without tremendous effort, and with Muslim reinforcements rapidly approaching, the Crusader belief in a "quick win" did not fit the reality of the situation.

The bottom line was that King Louis VII and Conrad III found themselves in a dire predicament before the gates of Damascus. It was "a choice between a brave and dangerous assault . . . and an ordered withdrawal, [so] retreat may have appeared the sensible path. Only it was not the path of heroes; the miracle of Antioch in 1098 was not to be repeated."[262] Had Damascus fallen into Crusader hands it would have meant the recovery of Edessa, the strengthening of the northern frontier, and the destruction of the possibility of Muslim unity in the Holy Land. The failure at Damascus was a lost opportunity that ultimately lost Outrémer.

The End of the Crusade

Conrad III left the Holy Land in September of 1148 after a very difficult year that left him with a severe wound and the loss of his army and a good portion of his wealth. He was the "leader of the largest army to set out in 1147, [and] Conrad lost most and gained least."[263]

One member of Conrad's army did not forget his experience during the Second Crusade. The lessons learned in that expedition helped Frederick of Swabia, Conrad's nephew and the future holy Roman emperor known as Frederick Barbarossa, plan and execute his journey during the Third Crusade.

King Louis VII stayed in the Kingdom of Jerusalem until Easter of 1149. He departed on contracted Sicilian ships, which were set upon by the Byzantine navy. The ship carrying Queen Eleanor was seized and detained for a time. The royal couple eventually made their way to Sicily where they traveled to the Italian mainland. They met with Pope Eugenius, who tried to mend their rapidly unraveling marriage but to no effect. Louis and his estranged queen finally arrived home in France in November.

Results of the Crusade

The Second Crusade not only failed to liberate Edessa (which had been the primary objective) and Damascus, but it produced several other negative effects. It was such a disaster that "it is no exaggeration to say that the crusader states would have fared better had the Crusade never been launched."[264] The failure of the Byzantines to lend adequate support to the French and German armies and Manuel's policy of benign neglect furthered the Western understanding that the Eastern Christians "were part of the problem rather than the solution" to the issues affecting Outrémer.[265] The military blunders by both the French and German armies on their marches through Anatolia and the bad decisions at Damascus weakened the aura of invincibility surrounding Crusade armies in the Holy Land. The Muslims were no longer afraid of Christian armies.

Perhaps the most deleterious effect of the failure of the Second Crusade was the lowering of morale and a general questioning of the Crusading movement. The First Crusade had been a miraculous success, so Second Crusade contemporaries expected the same. When failure was the result, questions were raised and answers posited in a negative way that affected Christendom's view of its leaders and the Crusading movement as a whole. Eugenius III believed the failure of the Second Crusade was "the most severe injury of the Christian name that God's Church has suffered in our time."[266]

Those who preached the Crusade and assisted with its prosecution were not immune to criticism. St. Bernard suffered such intense denunciation that he referred to that time in his life as the "season of disgrace."[267] Responding to the personal reproaches, Bernard offered his own explanation as to why the Crusade failed—it was the benevolent and mysterious will of God:

> How can human beings be so rash as to dare to pass judgment on something that they are not in the least able to understand? It might perhaps be a comfort for us to bear in mind the heavenly judgments that were made of old . . . For . . . it is true that the hearts of mortal men are made in this way: we forget when we need it what we know when we do not need it . . . The promises of God never prejudice the justice of God.[268]

Other commentators leveled their ire at the Templars, accusing them of accepting Muslim bribes during the siege of Damascus.[269]

Although it is human nature to imagine overly complicated explanations for life's setbacks, the reality is that the answers are often very simple. The failure of the Second Crusade was neither Bernard's fault nor the Templars'; the Byzantines are not to blame, either (even though they did not assist at the level hoped for by Louis and Conrad). The Second Crusade failed because it was a poorly funded enterprise led by over-optimistic leaders who committed too many military blunders.[270]

The Death of the "Honey-Sweet" Preacher

Pope Eugenius III died in July of 1153 and, a month later, his trustworthy and loyal mentor and friend, Bernard of Clairvaux, followed him into eternal glory. Bernard was canonized twenty-one years after his death and officially declared a Doctor of the Church in 1830 by Pope Pius VIII. Despite the criticism of modern-day writers, St. Bernard's preaching of the Second Crusade was not "sinful" behavior; rather, it was the work of a man totally dedicated to Christ, his Church, and his vicar on earth.[271] The pope had called the Crusade and authorized Bernard to spread its message and motivate warriors to undertake its burden. Bernard understood the need for the Second Crusade and he worked tirelessly to promote it. His mission was far from sinful; it was the work of holiness. "The Church has had great saints since, perhaps even greater, but none ever again whose life and universal impact quite matched that of Bernard of Clairvaux."[272]

5

The Sultan and the Kings

[We want to fight] . . . until you see Jesus fleeing from Jerusalem.

Ibn Munir of Tripoli[273]

We have heard things that make us tremble at the severity of the judgment that the divine hand has executed over the land of Jerusalem.

Pope Gregory VIII[274]

The count of Poitou heard the devastating news and knew immediately what he had to do. The pope had once more called to arms the warriors of Christendom. The Holy City of Jerusalem had fallen into enemy hands; the Christians of the Latin East were in desperate need.

The count had plenty to keep him occupied at home, including incessant political intrigue. None of it mattered now. Christ's patrimony was in peril, and the pope's call moved this warrior to forget the cares of home to embrace the cross. The count made his way to Tours, and there in the city of St. Martin, in November of 1187, he took the vow to go on Crusade. He was determined to utilize all the means at his disposal to muster a formidable army motivated by one mission: the recovery of the Holy City.

Spiritually prepared and armed with the resources of the kingdom of England and his extensive holdings in Aquitaine, the thirty-two-year-old count was confident that his mission would be accomplished. In the summer of 1190, medieval Europe's greatest military commander departed his home, not to see it again for the next four years. The time was at hand: Richard the Lion-Hearted was going to war.

Their Worst Fear—the Rise of Saladin

Less than thirty years after the failure of the Second Crusade, the Christians of the Latin East found themselves surrounded by a unified Islam whose ruler pursed a campaign of *jihad* to push them out of the Holy Land forever. William of Tyre, the historian of the Latin East, described the military and political situation of Outrémer with the ascendancy of the infamous Saladin:

> [A]ll the kingdoms round about us obey one ruler, they do the will of one man, and at this command alone, however reluctantly, they are ready, as a unit, to take up arms for our injury. This Saladin . . . a man of humble antecedents and lowly station, now holds under his control all these kingdoms, for fortune has smiled too graciously upon him.[275]

Saladin was a Kurd born in the town of Tikrit in modern-day Iraq—the same birthplace as Saddam Hussein. The man who would wreak havoc among the Christians in Outrémer was known as Yusuf Ibn Ayyub during his lifetime, but he became known in western literature and history as Saladin, from the Arabic title *Salah al-Din* ("Restorer of Religion)."[276] He was a pious and observant Muslim who fasted, slept on a rough mat, and gave generous alms to the poor. His spiritual practices were rooted in a desire to do the will of Allah and imitate the example of Mohammed and even exceed it, for "while he emulated the temperance he surpassed the chastity of his Arabian prophet."[277]

Saladin believed that God had chosen him to recapture the Holy City of Jerusalem. This conviction fueled a fierce commitment to *jihad*, as his biographer, Baha al-Din Ibn Shaddad commented:

> The Holy War and the suffering involved in it weighed heavily on his heart and his whole being in every limb; he spoke of nothing else, thought only about equipment for the fight, was interested only in those who had taken up arms, had little sympathy with anyone who spoke of anything else or encouraged any other activity.[278]

Collapse of the Fatimid Caliphate

Saladin began his rise to power and influence as an assistant to his uncle, Shirkuh, who was sent to Egypt by Nur al-Din in 1163. Shirkuh's reign as Egyptian vizier was short—he died suddenly on March 23, 1169, after eating an "exceptionally rich meal."[279] Saladin was appointed vizier in his place, but as the fifth vizier in six years his position seemed very tenuous. "His political position appeared hopelessly anomalous: an orthodox Sunni Kurd, nominally subject to a foreign overlord, sustained by a dwindling Turkish army from Syria, attempting to rule a large, unsubdued and populous country in the name of a Shi'ite caliph."[280] Despite his weakened political position, Saladin engaged in a series of administrative reorganizations of Egyptian society and the army in order to undermine the existing institutions and eventually replace them with elements loyal to himself.[281]

In June of 1171, Nur al-Din ordered Saladin to forbid mention of the Fatimid caliph's name during Friday prayers in mosques; it was replaced with the name of the Abbasid caliph in Baghdad. Although this exchange of names seems a simple matter, it was a significant move that had far-reaching implications. In effect, this was the opening salvo in a fight to restore Sunni leadership to Egypt (a country where the majority of the population was Sunni) and replace the Shi'ite dominant Fatimid family.

On September 11, 1171, Saladin conducted a large military parade in Cairo in which 14,000 troops marched through the town in a demonstration of power and intimidation.[282] When the Fatimid family was subsequently placed under arrest, Saladin was firmly in control of Egypt but his ambition was far from sated. He sought nothing less than the complete unification of the Muslim world under his suzerainty. This goal required the conquest of the Muslim lands controlled by Nur al-Din and the territory occupied by the Crusader States.

Saladin began his unification of Muslim territory upon the death of Nur al-Din on May 15, 1174. Saladin marched to Nur al-Din's capital at Damascus, conquered his city, and married his widow in a move designed to present himself as the successor to the great ruler.

Two years later, the Abbasid caliph proclaimed Saladin the ruler of Egypt, Yemen, and Syria and ordered him to expel the Latin Christians from the Holy Land and recover Jerusalem.

Saladin is often portrayed in the West as a great general and military thinker. The reality is far different. He was "a cautious, at times nervous field commander, better at political intrigue, diplomacy, and military administration than the tactics of battle or the strategy of a campaign."[283] His troops fought in the standard Turkish behavior of harassment with mounted archers charging enemy formations, feigning retreat and counter-charging in the hopes of separating the foot soldiers from the cavalry. In so doing, they lured the cavalry into a fight on open ground without the protection of their infantry where they could be picked off one by one by the archers. Saladin's archers, much to the chagrin of Latin knights, specifically targeted enemy horses. This irritated western knights because "in the Western tradition of knightly warfare it was considered bad form, as well as financially stupid, to kill or injure an enemy's horse."[284] Saladin's forces conducted harassment operations and raids against the Latin settlers eight total times in the 1170s and 1180s.

The Leper King

King of Jerusalem Baldwin IV (r. 1174–1185) was a leper, diagnosed by his tutor, William of Tyre, when he was still a child. By the early 1180s, the disease was consuming his body even as political intrigue in the kingdom was consuming his mind and energy. But "whenever he tried to relinquish the increasingly intolerable burden" of responsibility, the heroic and faithful king met only incompetence.[285] Despite the disease that left him partially paralyzed, nearly blind, and suffering immense agony at the physical disintegration of his body, Baldwin was an able military commander who defeated and almost captured Saladin at Montgisard in November 1177.[286] Baldwin's fate was not to suffer in quiet agony the perils of his debilitating disease; instead, he spent his time dealing with the political intrigue of the factions within his court.

One faction was led by Count Raymond III of Tripoli, the great-grandson of Raymond of Toulouse, one of the leaders of the First Crusade. He became count at the age of twelve when assassins murdered his father. Later in life he was captured by the Muslims and held in Aleppo for eight years, during which time he took advantage of the situation to learn Arabic.

The other faction that sought to control Baldwin IV was led by his mother, Agnes of Courtenay, and included the infamous Reynald of Châtillon as well as Joscelin III, the titular count of Edessa and Baldwin IV's uncle. This group controlled access to the king and sought to ensure that their vision for the kingdom was in place when the sickly king died.

The key actor in the kingdom's succession was Baldwin's sister, Sybilla, who married William of Montferrat in 1176. The marriage ended at the untimely death of William in 1177, but the union produced a son, the later Baldwin V. Sybilla was too young, beautiful, and politically connected to remain a widow for the rest of her life, and three years after the death of her husband a handsome minor nobleman from the West came into her life and changed the history of Outrémer forever.

Guy de Lusignan

Guy de Lusignan was that handsome nobleman. He had a "daring and swashbuckling demeanor," and left Aquitaine in search of fame and fortune in the Latin East.[287] He found the vehicle by which he could accomplish his goals in a marriage with Sybilla. With the help of Baldwin's mother, Sybilla persuaded the Leper King to appoint Guy as regent in 1181.

The choice was a bad decision: Guy was an ineffective ruler and an incompetent military commander. His ineptitude was on full display in the fall of 1183, when Saladin crossed the Jordan River to besiege the fortress of Kerak east of the Dead Sea. Guy marshaled a 15,000-man army, but failed to engage Saladin, thus allowing the invader to slip back over the frontier and out of harm's way.

Baldwin IV was greatly upset at this debacle and he accused Guy of cowardice and treason in the face of battle. The king then removed Guy as regent and even tried to force Sybilla to divorce him. Baldwin appointed his five-year-old nephew, Baldwin V, the son of Sybilla and William of Montferrat, as heir, with Count Raymond III of Tripoli as regent.

A disaster was on the horizon, and Baldwin IV could see it. He knew Saladin was consolidating his power and that it was only a matter of time before he launched a full-scale invasion of the kingdom. He knew the dynastic disputes and court factions drained the kingdom of the unity it desperately needed in such a time. The Leper King did what he could, but the disease that would eventually take his life hampered his abilities. Yet his dedication and devotion to the kingdom were without compare. His sacrifice was heroic, but not even the actions of a truly saintly leper could forestall the end, which was near at hand.

The Beginning of the End

Baldwin IV died on May 16, 1185, at only twenty-four. In eleven years as king, Baldwin had tried to buttress the kingdom from the coming Islamic tide, but his actions came to naught when his successor, the boy Baldwin V, only eight years old, died in September 1186. Baldwin V had agreed to the proposal of the regent Raymond III of Tripoli that if Baldwin V should die before the age of majority, a committee of the major rulers of Christendom would gather to choose the new monarch. Vying for the throne were the daughters, from two separate marriages, of King Amalric: Sybilla and Isabella. Sybilla was married to the former regent Guy de Lusignan and Isabella was married to Humphrey III of Toron; neither man was a great choice for king.

In an action of political intrigue worthy of a Hollywood film, the party favorable to Sybilla, including the masters of the Templars and Hospitallers, asked Patriarch Heraclius of Jerusalem to crown Sybilla queen while Raymond III was away in Tiberias.

Before Sybilla was crowned she had to promise to divorce Guy, who was intensely disliked by the local barons.

Sybilla agreed to the divorce[288] with three conditions. First, their children (all daughters) were to be declared legitimate heirs to the throne. Secondly, Guy would continue to remain Count of Ascalon and Jaffa. Finally, she must be free to choose another husband.[289]

The conditions were granted. Sybilla, immediately after her coronation, announced her choice of husband: Guy de Lusignan! She then crowned Guy as king.

Upon hearing the news of the outrageous events in Jerusalem, Raymond III marshaled his troops from Tripoli and deployed them to Tiberias with plans to attack Jerusalem. Civil war was in the offing. Raymond's bitterness so overwhelmed his judgment that he rashly entered into a treaty with Saladin against King Guy and Queen Sybilla.

Saladin was upset with the frequent raids by Reynald of Châtillon and issued a summons for volunteers to join the *jihad* in order to increase the size of his army.[290] Once assembled, he invaded the Kingdom of Jerusalem on June 27, 1187, bent on the eradication of Outrémer.

The Horns of Hattin

News of Saladin's invasion reached King Guy, who issued the summons for all able-bodied free men in the kingdom to muster for defense of the realm. Count Raymond III of Tripoli broke his alliance with Saladin and rushed to the banner of the king. The summons produced a grand army of 20,000 men, 1,200 of who were knights (600 Templars and Hospitallers, and 600 local nobles).[291] It was the largest army ever assembled in the kingdom, and its muster depleted the garrisons throughout Outrémer to mere skeleton crews. Estimates vary on the size of Saladin's army, but by all accounts, it was larger than the Christian force.[292]

King Guy hoped to follow the traditional Christian strategy when confronted by a Saladin raid: refrain from a decisive engagement by deploying the army defensively and waiting for

Saladin's advance to lose steam and retreat. Conversely, Saladin's goal was to force the Christians to fight in order to compel a decisive battle. In the 1187 invasion, Saladin divided his army, with one element advancing against Tiberias in a move designed to draw out the kingdom's forces.

The Christian army was instructed to muster at Sephoria, where the kingdom's high command would meet to discuss the best course of action. "On their decision hung the future of nine decades of western European settlement in the Near East."[293]

News arrived that Saladin's army was besieging the city of Tiberias, which had fallen except for the citadel. The debate raged among the barons over whether to march the kingdom's army to break the siege or to hold back, trusting that Saladin would retreat.

Count Raymond III argued against a march. He knew that the topography of the region would not favor the Christians: it was a vast, barren, waterless wasteland. Any march through it in the summer heat would spell certain death. Raymond suggested that the army abandon Tiberias and instead march to Acre to await Saladin behind its well-fortified walls.

Although there were those in the group who doubted Raymond's authenticity because of his recent alliance with Saladin, his opinion made tactical and strategic sense. King Guy agreed. However, later that night, Gerard of Ridefort, the Master of the Temple and a personal enemy of Raymond, met the king and convinced him to change his mind. On July 3, 1187, the army broke camp and then began the twenty-mile march to Tiberias.

The day was hot and the march was across hilly terrain. The Christian force hoped to reach the water source at Hattin twelve miles away before the day ended. Saladin heard that Guy was on the move, so he broke off the siege of Tiberias and organized his army to meet the Christians. After an exhausting march the warriors of Outrémer reached the "horns" of Hattin, a hill with two peaks, toward the end of July 3.

On the morning of July 4, 1187, King Guy's army awoke to the realization that they were surrounded by Saladin's troops.

The Muslims knew the tired and thirsty state of the Christians, and taunted them by pouring out cups of water onto the ground.[294] Muslim forces added to the Christian discomfort by lighting fires from gathered brushwood filled with dry thistles in order to fill their camp with smoke.[295]

Despite the intolerable conditions, the Christians defended their position. Count Raymond and some knights broke through the Muslim line but soon found themselves at the bottom of a hill. Cut off from the battlefield and knowing an uphill charge would result in heavy casualties, they retreated.

The rearguard under Balian of Ibelin and the Templars broke under the heavy onslaught. The situation was hopeless, and annihilation seemed imminent, but Balian and a few other knights were able to escape. King Guy tried to turn the tide with two brave and bold cavalry charges toward Saladin's position and, although they came close to the sultan, they were beaten back.

Horse casualties and the lack of cover forced the knights to dismount. They continued the fight on foot, but the Muslim pressure was too much for the exhausted and thirsty Christians. Their line broke, and Saladin's forces swept through the Christian army.

The cause was lost. Muslim soldiers found King Guy and his drained knights slumped on the ground physically unable to continue the fight. Roughly 3,000 warriors had fled the battle, including Count Raymond and Balian of Ibelin, but the vast majority were either killed or apprehended.[296] Among the captured were King Guy, his brother Aimery, Humphrey of Toron, William III of Montferrat, Reynald of Châtillon, and Gerard of Ridefort, the Master of the Temple. They were all sent to prison, except for Reynald, whom Saladin personally beheaded. Two days after the battle, all captured Templars and Hospitallers were also executed on the direct orders of Saladin, "because they were the fiercest of all Frankish warriors."[297] Not content with the deaths of those captured at Hattin, Saladin ordered further executions of all Templars and Hospitallers in captivity in Damascus. Given the choice of death or conversion to Islam, most remained true to the Lord Jesus: 230 were martyred for the Faith.[298]

The defeat at Hattin also saw the capture of a relic of the True Cross. The Bishop of Acre held the relic throughout the battle but was struck down, and the relic was confiscated by Saladin's forces. It was taken to Damascus and paraded through the city upside down in a gesture of ultimate insult. The loss of the True Cross, "even more than the defeat itself, resonated throughout Christendom, raising the military disaster into a spiritual catastrophe."[299]

Ultimately, the disaster at Hattin happened because Guy committed the most basic mistake of military strategy: He allowed his enemy to fight him "where he wanted, when he wanted and how he wanted."[300]

The loss was devastating for Outrémer. The massacre of so many knights "removed the kingdom's main defense, and the slaughter of the infantry must have annihilated most of the rest of the male population."[301] The kingdom was left virtually unguarded.

The Fall of Jerusalem

Having barely escaped the disaster at Hattin with his life, Balian of Ibelin made his way to the coastal city of Tyre. However, he was worried about the safety of his wife, Maria Comnena, and their children, who were in Jerusalem—Saladin's next target. Balian sent a message to the sultan asking for safe conduct to move his family out of harm's way. Saladin agreed as long as Balian traveled unarmed and spent only one night in the Holy City.

When the citizens of Jerusalem found out Balian was there, they begged him to lead the defense. Jerusalem, like the other cities of Outrémer, had sent the vast majority of its fighting men to annihilation at Hattin. Balian did not want to break his promise to Saladin, but the insistence of the Jerusalemites and the pitiable condition of their defense changed his mind. A chivalrous man, Balian sent a letter to Saladin explaining why he had to renege on their agreement. His family was safely transported to Tyre, escorted by Saladin's troops at his order.[302]

The defense forces of Jerusalem when Balian took charge consisted of two knights and the city militia. Balian made the bold decision to knight all noble boys over sixteen as well as thirty handpicked men in the city. These knights provided him with a corps of troops who could help him organize the defense and motivate the militia during the siege.

Saladin's army arrived on September 20, 1187. Balian, recognizing the situation was hopeless, proposed terms of surrender to Saladin. The sultan rejected them outright, demanding the unconditional surrender of the city. This was an unconventional response, for most besieged towns were given the opportunity to surrender with terms by the besieging army.

Saladin's army began the attack. Balian's meager militia withstood five days of near-constant bombardment by siege engines. Impatient with the stubborn resistance of the Christian defenders at the western wall, Saladin broke camp and shifted his point of attack to the eastern wall, establishing his headquarters on the Mount of Olives. This location was the site of the successful sieges of the Roman army under Titus in A.D. 70 and the First Crusaders in 1099. On September 29, only nine days into the siege, Muslim sappers opened a breach in the northeastern section of the wall.

Balian asked for an audience with Saladin in the hopes of convincing him to provide terms of surrender. Once again, the stubborn sultan denied the Christians' terms, which infuriated Balian who replied to the rejection:

> O sultan, be aware that this city holds a mass of people so great that God alone knows their number. They now hesitate to continue the fight, because they hope that you will spare their lives . . . because they love life and hate death. But if we see that death is inevitable, then, by God, we will kill our own women and children and burn all that we possess. We will not leave you a single dinar of booty . . . not a single man or woman to lead into captivity. Then we shall destroy the sacred rock, al-Aqsa mosque, and many other sites: we will kill the 5,000 Muslim prisoners we now hold. In the end, we

will come outside the city, and we will fight against you as one fights for one's life. Not one of us will die without having killed several of you![303]

Balian's threat worked. Saladin presented terms that allowed Christians to purchase their freedom. There was concern about the vast amount of poor people in the city who did not have the necessary funds to buy their freedom, including a good number of recent widows who had lost their husbands at Hattin. Saladin agreed to a lump sum payment for the poor.[304] Unfortunately, not enough money was raised to redeem all the poor in the city, so a large number were captured and sold into slavery.[305]

Saladin entered the city on October 2, the same day (according to Islamic tradition) that Mohammed's night journey to heaven from Jerusalem occurred. Once in the city, Saladin ordered the removal of every external Christian image and cross. Most of the churches in the city were turned into mosques, except the Church of the Holy Sepulchre,[306] or were taken from Latin clergy and given over to the Orthodox.[307] From the moment Godfrey de Bouillon scaled the parapet to the moment of Balian's departure, the Holy City had remained in the hands of Christians for only eighty-eight years.

The Calling of the Third Crusade

The defeat at Hattin, the loss of the True Cross, and the capture of the Holy City by Saladin shocked and horrified the inhabitants of Christendom. Pope Urban III (r. 1185–1187) died in grief upon hearing the disastrous news from Outrémer. His successor, Gregory VIII (r. 1187) issued a summons for the Crusade nine days later in the document *Audita Tremendi*, promulgated on October 29, 1187. Gregory called all Christendom to an examination of conscience and a commitment to penance for the sins that had contributed to the victory of the enemy and the capture of Jerusalem.[308]

"After forty years of complacency, indifference, and lip-service, Christendom's response to Gregory's call was overwhelming."[309]

The loss of Jerusalem awakened the warriors of Christendom in a way not seen for close to a hundred years. Even those not able to go on Crusade responded to Gregory's call as monks took the cross; they went "from the cloister to camp, threw off their cowls, donned mail shirts, and became knights of Christ in a new sense, replacing alms with arms."[310]

The desire to liberate the city of Christ, as it was in the First Crusade, was the primary driver for the success of the preaching campaign. Jerusalem was also a popular pilgrimage destination in the late eleventh century and had become more so by the end of the twelfth century. Warriors from all over Christendom took the cross in imitation of those who went before them in the First and Second Crusades. Their motivations were varied, but one reason for the large response was the role of the three major monarchs in Christendom, who made the Crusade a priority.[311]

Frederick Barbarossa and the Germans

As a young man in his twenties, Frederick fought in the Second Crusade in the army of his uncle, Conrad III. The failure of that campaign remained with him, and he vowed not to make the same mistakes. Frederick was the leading monarch of Christendom; appointed king of the Germans in 1152 and anointed holy Roman emperor by Pope Alexander III in 1181, he controlled all of modern-day Germany and northern Italy. He was a man of intelligence, vitality, willpower, and a full red beard, hence the moniker *Barbarossa*.

On Laetare Sunday, March 27, 1188, the old warrior answered the summons to Jerusalem issued by Pope Gregory VIII. Frederick was the last of the major monarchs of Christendom to answer the call, but he was the first to leave. Frederick's Crusade was very much a re-enactment of the First Crusade and a re-fighting of the Second. The German king recognized the one aspect that could either sink the Crusade or help it succeed was an alliance with the Byzantines. He well remembered the Byzantine betrayal of the Second Crusade, and he knew the stories of their selfish priorities during the First. He decided to send envoys to the Byzantines and to all the rulers along the route he intended to take.

Despite Frederick's diplomatic outreach, the Byzantines rejected his pleas and imprisoned his envoys. Frederick was so upset at the Byzantine response that he asked the pope's approval to change the focus of his Crusade from Jerusalem to Constantinople.[312] The request was rightly denied.

Emperor Isaac II (r. 1185–1195) actively sought to undermine Frederick's Crusade because he embraced the traditional Byzantine paranoia of a Western conquest of Constantinople. Isaac entered into a secret treaty with Saladin, pledging to hamper, as much as possible, the progress of Frederick's army.[313]

Despite these hostile actions, the imperial army left Mainz on May 23, 1189, taking the land route used during the First Crusade. By all accounts it was a huge army, perhaps the largest ever assembled in Christendom during the Crusading movement. One estimate puts the host at 100,000 men with 20,000 cavalry; so large that it took three days for the army to pass a single point on the march.[314]

Frederick decided on an overland journey because it was more convenient for the bulk of his force. The emperor demanded discipline and pious behavior on the march, and his army behaved accordingly as it marched through Christian territory on the way to the frontier with Byzantium, which it reached on July 2, 1189. Once they were inside the Byzantine border, imperial forces harassed the Germans and the promised provisions did not materialize. Isaac II clearly did not like Frederick, his treaty with the Normans, his use of the title "Roman emperor," or his large army. Negotiations between the two men over the army's march and provisioning broke down, resulting in Frederick's capture of Adrianople.

On February 14, 1190 an agreement was reached wherein Isaac promised to transport the German army to Anatolia in exchange for the return of the captured city. Free passage through Byzantine territory was also granted the Germans along with access to markets at reasonable rates. Frederick agreed to avoid the capital city and indiscriminate foraging in imperial territory. The following month the German host was transported to Anatolia, and reached enemy territory there in April of 1190. The march through Anatolia was difficult; as the supply system collapsed both man and beast suffered from exhaustion and sustained Turkish attacks. The army was kept together mainly through Frederick's sheer will and excellent leadership, which instilled hope in the hearts of the soldiers. The emperor's leadership was on full display at the city of Iconium, where he urged his troops to capture the city by crying, "Why do we tarry, of what are we afraid? Christ reigns! Christ conquers! Christ commands!"[315] The Germans won a pitched battle outside the city and were able to claim the necessary supplies for the continued march.

By May, the German army reached the relative safety of Christian Armenia, and already had "achieved what the Crusaders of 1101 and the Second Crusade could not. In two months since crossing to Asia, he had brought his vast army, depleted but intact, in the face of sustained Turkish hostility, difficult terrain, heavy casualties, and shortages of supplies, to a welcoming Christian territory."[316] Unfortunately, the success of Frederick's army would prove fleeting when a month later on June 10, 1190, the aged emperor died while fording the Saleh River. It was a catastrophe from which the Crusade would not recover.

There are various accounts as to what actually happened to Frederick. Some believe he slipped on rocks while in the water and drowned; others think he had a heart attack. An anonymous German chronicler believed the current was too strong for the old monarch.[317]

Saladin's camp welcomed news of Frederick's demise. The sultan was recorded to have said, "God thus liberated us from the evil of such a man."[318]

The emperor's death was a huge blow to the German host. Despite suffering near sixty percent casualties on the march through Anatolia, the German army was still a disciplined and effective fighting force; it was, however, without a commanding leader.[319] The loss of the emperor, who had kept the army together through his charisma, willpower, willingness to lead from the front, and concern for his troops, was too much for the other nobles to overcome, and most of the demoralized troops began the march home. Some warriors remained in Outrémer and those divided into two groups. One group, under the command of Duke Frederick of Swabia, the emperor's son, traveled by sea to Antioch and later Tripoli. This group would later participate in the Christian siege of Acre. The other group decided to try its chances by continuing on the original overland route to Syria. It was effectively wiped out.

Although Frederick's death was a huge setback for the Third Crusade, there were other monarchs in Christendom assembling large armies in defense of Outrémer. The time of Frederick Barbarossa had come to an end. The time of Richard the Lion-Hearted and Philip Augustus was beginning.

Richard the Lion-Hearted, King of England

The count of Poitou was the first nobleman to take the cross upon the promulgation of *Audita Tremendi* in 1187 and was eager to journey to Jerusalem. Richard (r. 1189–1199) was thirty-two years old when he assumed the throne of England upon the death of his father, Henry II. His martial qualities were unrivaled and he endeared himself to his troops by being the first in every attack and the last to withdraw. Richard's reputation was such that Muslims in the Holy Land considered him their worst enemy; after the Crusades, Muslim mothers threatened misbehaving children by telling them "King Richard" was coming for them.[320]

Richard's reign in England lasted a decade but he only lived on the island for six months, as he preferred his extensive land holdings in France. Although English actors have portrayed him in Hollywood movies, Richard spoke only French throughout his life.

Richard's preparations for the Crusade were extensive, and with the large amounts of money raised from the "Saladin tithe"— a tenth of income and property value for those who did not take the cross—and from selling his own lands, he raised a fleet of a hundred ships, with 9,000 sailors and soldiers to transport his army to the Holy Land.[321] Richard received the pilgrim staff, and allegedly carried King Arthur's famed sword Excalibur with him on the Crusade.[322] His army was ready, and the time was at hand to depart England to link up with the French.

Philip II Augustus, King of France

This twenty-five year old king was born of great Crusading stock, the son of the Second Crusader, Louis VII. Philip's reign was marked by political struggles with the kings of England, who were also his vassals as lords of Aquitaine. In many ways he was the polar opposite of Richard the Lion-Hearted. He was not a great warrior or military strategist like Richard, and rarely took great risks. Instead, he was "a calculating, cautious, and resourceful opportunist who tended to wait on favorable events rather than risk grand gestures."[323]

He was not impressive to look at—he had already lost the sight of one eye—and ten years of government of France had made him cautious and distrustful, cynical and nervous. He was not clever or well educated, but he was sharp, with a practical intelligence, and he had a capacity for hard work and taking pains, combined with self-control, a disposition towards prudence and equity. Ruthless he might be but he was usually ruthlessly fair.[324]

Despite his lack of military acumen and political focus, Philip took the cross and made preparations to travel to Outrémer.

On July 2, 1190 the kings of England and France met at Vézelay, the famed site of the great St. Bernard's preaching of the Second Crusade. They agreed that all conquered land would be split between them, and that the armies would travel by sea.

The 219 ships carrying the Anglo-French Crusaders sailed through the Mediterranean on their way to Crete. Unfortunately, several ships were scattered from the main fleet due to a severe storm and were wrecked on the island of Cyprus. The shipwrecked Crusaders were not greeted warmly by the Byzantine rebel in control of the island, Isaac Comnenus, and were imprisoned. News of the shipwreck and imprisonment reached Richard, who demanded that Isaac release his men. Isaac, foolishly, refused to do so. That decision prompted Richard to invade the island to rescue his men. But "what may have begun as a rescue soon became a conquest."[325]

The Conquest of Cyprus

In May 1191, Richard's Crusade host embarked on a fourteen-day campaign that changed the history of the Crusading movement. Richard's invasion seemed a foolhardy adventure: His force was greatly outnumbered by a foe behind defensive fortifications on its own territory. Yet this was exactly the type of fight Richard specialized in. The chronicler Ambroise recorded a story that illustrates Richard's risky behavior and the jovial manner in which he engaged in it.

> A cleric, Hugh de la Mare, came to the king attired for war, and with advice the monarch cumbered: "Sire, we are fearfully outnumbered; Let us retreat at once!" whereto the king replied, "Sir Clerk, for you a pulpit were a fitter post than here amid an armored host: For God's sake and his mother's, then, leave the affairs of war to men!"[326]

Richard launched an amphibious attack on the city of Limassol and forced Isaac to flee inland. (Before pursuing the Greek upstart, though, Richard took the time to get married to Berengaria of Navarre.) Embarking his troops on their transport ships, Richard sailed around Cyprus to Famagusta, where another amphibious landing caused Isaac to retreat again. Richard's army pursued the rebel into the interior, where they defeated his army in a series of skirmishes. Toward the end of May Isaac realized that he could not defeat Richard, so he agreed to surrender on the condition that Richard not clap him in irons. Richard agreed, and when Isaac surrendered, Richard ordered him clapped in silver shackles instead![327]

Although the conquest of Cyprus was not on the Crusade agenda, its capture proved providential. It was an excellent base of supply for the Third Crusade and future Crusades and became "the most lasting Crusader achievement in the eastern Mediterranean," remaining in Christian hands for the next 400 years.[328]

Breaking the Siege of Acre

The campaign season of 1190 was a frustrating time for the Christians besieging the city of Acre, who had arrived under the banner of the released King Guy in the summer of 1189. Their action consisted of continually assaulting the walls to no effect, and defending their fortified position from assaults by Saladin's relief army. The stalemate was grating on the nerves of the soldiers, and one estimate indicated disease and starvation killed 100 to 200 warriors each day.[329] Conditions in the Christian camp were disgusting, as the corpses of men and animals attracted large number of flies. Food was so scarce that knights succumbed to eating their mounts and the bones of dogs.[330]

Thankfully, King Philip's army arrived on April 20, 1191. The army built siege engines, including a massive catapult nicknamed the "Evil Neighbor" and a large siege tower to help with the assault on the walls.[331] After his delay at Cyprus, Richard reached the siege on June 8. His arrival tilted the siege in favor of the Christians; on July 12 the Muslim garrison finally realized its valiant two year defense was at an end and asked for terms of surrender. The Christians allowed the garrison to leave unmolested in exchange for the return of the True Cross captured at Hattin, payment of 200,000 dinars (gold coins), the release of all Christian prisoners, and Saladin's fleet of seventy galleys.[332]

The Massacre of Muslim Prisoners

Despite the generous terms, Saladin did not fulfill most of the conditions. He refused to hand over the True Cross, did not deliver the first payment of money on the due date and failed to release the promised Christian prisoners on time despite given thirty days to comply. Ten days after the due date, on August 20, 1191, in retaliation for Saladin's non-compliance, Richard ordered the execution of 2,700 Muslim prisoners. Richard explained in a later letter why he gave the order:

> On Saladin's behalf it had been agreed that the Holy Cross and 1,500 living persons would be handed over to us, and he fixed a day for us when all this was to be done. But the time limit expired, and, as the pact which he had agreed was entirely made void, we quite properly had the Saracens we had in custody—about 2,600 of them—put to death. A few of the more notable were spared, and we hope to recover the Holy Cross and certain Christian captives in exchange for them.[333]

Modern-day critics of the Crusades frequently cite the massacre of Muslim prisoners at Acre as a prime example of sinful and shameful behavior of Christian warriors in the name of God. But, like the massacre at Jerusalem in 1099, this action must be viewed in its historical context and with full presentation of the facts. Frequently, the mention of Richard's massacre by Crusade critics omits the relevant context of Saladin's reneging on the terms of surrender, and the fact that Saladin performed equal and greater acts of barbarism on Christian prisoners. Indeed, more than likely Saladin was not surprised at Richard's reaction. "The sultan probably recognized the massacre for what it was: a deliberate act of policy for which his own actions were in part responsible. Over the following weeks he treated captured Christian soldiers with summary execution, occasionally allowing their corpses to be mutilated out of revenge."[334]

Although the execution of these prisoners cannot be condoned, it can be explained. Richard was leaving Acre soon, and did not want a large body of hostile Muslims behind him. Medieval warfare allowed such butchery when terms of surrender were not obeyed. Richard also understood the action would send a clear signal to Saladin that future negotiations and agreements should be honored. Although horrific to the sensibilities of modern readers, "Richard I's butchery of his Muslim captives was an atrocity not uncommon in war. It was not an act of random sadism, less so, for example, than Saladin's own execution of the Templars and Hospitallers after Hattin."[335]

The Departure of Philip

Less than a month after the Muslims surrendered Acre, the Christian camp was abuzz: King Philip had announced that he was leaving the Crusade. The bulk of the French army would remain under the command of the Duke of Burgundy and fight under Richard's command for the remainder of the Crusade.

Philip was ill and upset that Richard received most of the glory and recognition for ending the siege at Acre. He also desired to gain control of Richard's land holdings in France, although before he left he had sworn that he would not do so upon his return.[336] Philip was heavily criticized in France for leaving the Crusade, just as previous deserters had been. Although he stressed the illness he contracted at Acre as a main reason for his departure, this was not considered a legitimate excuse to leave the Crusade—to retreat from battle, yes, but not from a Crusade. The Crusade vow was a sacred oath that medieval people believed could not be easily ignored or left unfulfilled. Regardless of the reason for his departure, "Philip's actions left a sour taste for generations."[337]

The March of the Lion-Hearted

Less than a week after the massacre of Muslim prisoners, Richard ordered his army to leave Acre and march eighty miles to the port city of Jaffa. Controlling Jaffa was necessary for logistical supply before any assault on Jerusalem. Saladin's army shadowed the Crusaders and repeatedly tried to harass them into an open battle. Richard countered by forming his army into a hollow formation in which the cavalry was placed inside a protective box of infantry on one side and the coast on the other.[338]

This formation required strict discipline and coordination between cavalry and infantry. The Crusaders marched in three divisions with the Hospitallers in the rear and Templars in the vanguard, and the Mediterranean protecting their western flank. When the eastern flank of infantry grew weary from the harassing Muslims' constant arrow barrage, a complicated maneuver of replacement occurred with forces marching along the coast.

Richard's fleet followed the progress of the army offshore, providing relief and supplies when needed. Although the Crusaders exhibited great endurance and discipline, the march was very slow, and there were many wounded from the Muslim attacks, including Richard. The situation could not continue without decisive action. Saladin needed to force a confrontation before Richard arrived at Jaffa. He decided to order a general attack outside the town of Arsuf.

The Battle of Arsuf

The Crusaders broke camp and began the march to Arsuf on the morning of September 7, 1191. It was an extremely hot day and Saladin hoped to utilize a familiar tactic of attacking at the end of the day when soldiers were "tired, thirsty, and eager to claim a good spot for their tent."[339] His light cavalry would harass the Crusader line in the hopes of provoking a disorganized countercharge, which would allow Saladin's archers to finish off Richard's army. Richard's plan was to withstand the archers' volleys while maintaining ranks and, when the Muslims engaged for close combat on tired horses, he would order a mass cavalry charge and win the day. Saladin ordered the attack and the Muslims rode to battle with a deafening roar designed to strike fear in the hearts of the Crusaders.[340]

The battle grew in intensity and the situation became desperate in the section commanded by Garnier de Naples, the grand master of the Hospitallers, who sent messengers to Richard requesting permission to order a charge to alleviate the Muslim pressure. Richard refused because he wanted to wait for the right moment and order a general charge across the line. The Muslim attacks began to take their toll, forcing Garnier to ride to Richard personally and request, once again, permission to charge. A second time Richard refused.

Shortly thereafter, the Muslim infantry supporting the harassing cavalry broke contact, which allowed the Muslim cavalry to charge the Crusader ranks. Garnier was concerned they would break the Crusader line, so he ordered a counter-charge.

The Hospitallers' offensive attack was so sudden that the infantry on the left wing failed to move out of the way in the melee. Seeing the charge, Richard seized the opportunity and finally ordered the general cavalry charge.

It was at the exact moment when Saladin's forces were unprepared for it. Across the battlefield, many Muslim cavalry troops had dismounted to shoot arrows at the Crusaders. The general Crusader charge caught them unawares and unprepared to withstand such an onslaught. Muslim infantry and cavalry elements were smashed in the charge and fled in a disorganized retreat. Some Crusader units chased after the fleeing Muslims, but Richard ordered a halt in order to disengage and fall back in good order to Arsuf.

Richard noted the great victory was achieved on the vigil of the Nativity of the Blessed Mother and gave thanks to God and to her intercession.[341] Saladin never again risked open battle with a Crusader force under the command of Richard the Lion-Hearted.

Richard's Three Options

After the Battle of Arsuf, Richard's army continued their march and arrived at the port city of Jaffa to rest and resupply. At this point in the campaign, Richard realized he had three options.

He could continue the march to Jerusalem, which was the main objective of the Crusade, but success depended on the defense of a long supply chain and a risky siege. The Crusaders could march to Ascalon instead of Jerusalem. Richard knew Saladin had destroyed the defensive works of the city and withdrawn his forces to defend Jerusalem, leaving Ascalon easily conquerable. Controlling the gateway to Egypt would divide Saladin's empire in half, open a two-front war and put the Muslims squarely on the defensive. However, Richard knew the rank and file wanted to go to Jerusalem and were not interested in what they would see as a diversion to another city. His third option was to pursue some semblance of a diplomatic solution with Saladin, in the hope that he could negotiate the return of the Holy City. All of the options involved risk and reward, and none was clearly more favorable than another. So, Richard "pursued a game of two-handed chess . . . military action shadowing detailed negotiations."[342]

By January of 1192, Richard controlled the coastal plain between Jaffa and the Judean hills. Richard's advance was now at a crossroads, and the Crusade leaders needed to determine their next move. The Hospitallers and Templars argued against an attack on Jerusalem because the supply line would be stretched too thin, and the Crusader force would suffer attacks from the besieged city and from Muslim forces trying to relieve pressure on it. The weather was terrible and conditions were not favorable for a siege. Richard recognized that even if his force liberated Jerusalem, his troops would eventually leave, and the native lords did not possess the manpower to withstand the inevitable Saladin counter-attack. The nobles agreed that the only wise military course of action was to withdraw and march to Ascalon. So, "rash in battle, cautious in politics, but expert in military science, on 13 January Richard gave the order to withdraw."[343]

Although it was not the popular decision, Richard made his choice in order to keep his options open. In his mind, he was not abandoning Jerusalem, but biding time for a more advantageous opportunity to besiege the city. However, the rank and file did not view the withdrawal through the same lens. For them, the decision not to besiege Jerusalem was devastating.

In early September 1192, Richard entered into a three-year truce with Saladin. The Treaty of Jaffa maintained Muslim control of Jerusalem, but allowed Christians free access to the city. Most of the Crusaders used the truce to fulfill their vows by going to the Church of the Holy Sepulchre in Jerusalem before departing for home. Richard was not among them. He had sworn to restore Jerusalem to Christ, and would not visit it until he had done so. His decision may have illustrated his belief that the Crusade was not complete, but only suspended until he could return and finish it.[344]

The Departure of Richard

Richard departed for home from Acre on October 9. Despite the favorable treaty with Saladin, the objectives of the Crusade were not achieved, and his earlier promise to remain in the Holy Land until Easter 1193 had been broken. He decided to travel overland since winter weather in the Mediterranean made sea travel difficult. While traveling near Vienna in late December, he was captured by the forces of Duke Leopold V of Austria, who imprisoned him to avenge an insult at the siege of Acre in 1191. Leopold was also a close ally of the Holy Roman Emperor Henry VI, who was not friendly with Richard. Leopold had every incentive to hold the king of England, and when given the opportunity, did so willingly.

Eventually Leopold turned Richard over to Henry VI, who moved him to Worms where he was held for fourteen months until February 1194. Pope Celestine III (r. 1191–1198) excommunicated Henry VI for his incarceration of Richard, since the Church afforded Crusaders the protection and safety of their person and property. Richard was released after a ransom of 150,000 marks was paid (the equivalent of 65,000 pounds of pure silver, three times the annual income of the whole of England). The English people raised the ransom via taxes for the rest of Richard's reign.[345]

Richard had promised to remain in the Holy Land until Easter 1193, but left in the fall of 1192. Since Saladin died on March 4, 1193—three weeks before Easter—one of history's most tempting "what if" questions can be asked of the Third Crusade. The idea of the Lion-Hearted commanding a potent Crusader military force against a Muslim world in disarray following the death of the great sultan leaves the historian imagining what might have been had the king of England kept his promise. Had Richard only stayed until Easter, it is likely that the Third Crusade would have been the most successful of all Crusades, and the entire history of the Crusading movement would have changed.

Saladin's Legacy

The great sultan who united the Muslim world in Outrémer and whose conviction for *jihad* won great victories for Islam died as a result of a life filled with rigorous fasting and the hardships of years spent in the saddle. Saladin's death left unfulfilled his life's greatest desire: to carry the war to Europe and conquer Rome and Constantinople. Ibn Shaddad records Saladin saying in 1189 that once the "Franks" were kicked out of Outrémer he wanted "to set sail to their islands to pursue them there until there no longer remain on the face of the earth any who deny God."[346]

By any assessment, Saladin's life was a success and his legacy reached far beyond the years after his death. He was "born the son of a displaced Kurdish mercenary in the service of Zengi of Mosul, he died the creator and ruler of an empire that embraced Iraq, Syria, Arabia, and Egypt, the effective overlord of the Fertile Crescent, a successful dynast whose arriviste family became the political masters of the Near East for over half a century."[347]

It is one of history's great ironies, then, that Saladin became better known in the collective memory of Europe and Christendom than in the Islamic world. From the Third Crusade to the modern world, the name of Saladin in the West engendered a vision of the perfect knight, perhaps even a secret Christian who was a noble heathen, tolerant and the champion of freedom. This vision is far from the actual man and his exploits, but legend, once enshrined, is hard to remove.

It was the Enlightenment that cemented the modern-day vision of Saladin among Westerners, with eighteenth-century writers building a false image of Saladin that persists to this day. Voltaire helped craft the image of the tolerant and noble heathen in a 1756 essay in which he contrasted the generosity of Saladin with the miserliness of Christian leaders.[348] The myth of the tolerant and benevolent ruler, however, gives way to the reality that Egyptian Jews and Christians were treated better under the Fatimid caliphs, whom Saladin overthrew.

Yet this myth of Saladin persists in the west and continues to shape the memory of the Crusades:

[T]he reality and myth of Saladin epitomize the Western consciousness of Islam and the Middle East as a whole, shaped by centuries of received information, misinformation, and fantasy. . . . here was a Kurd who rose to power in a world dominated by Turks, a Sunni who used a Shi'ite caliphate to launch his rise to fame, a unifier of a world fragmented by religion, ethnicity, and even by the very landscape, a counter-crusader whose largest fan base has always resided in Christendom.[349]

The Death of the Lion-Hearted

Richard returned home from the Crusade after four years of illness, stress, victories, defeats, and a long imprisonment at the hands of the holy Roman emperor. His life and reign continued for another three years until he died on March 26, 1199. While besieging the castle of a rebel, Richard met his end in one of the most perplexing examples of literally lowering one's guard.

Inspecting the siege progress at twilight, Richard noticed on the ramparts of the castle a lone figure: a common soldier with a crossbow, whose only protection was a frying pan. Awed by the man's audacity and courage, Richard lowered his shield and clapped in applause. Richard's display of chivalrous acknowledgment did not impress the enemy soldier, who dropped his frying pan and let loose his bolt. The "extraordinarily well-aimed shot" hit Richard in the left shoulder.[350] An unskilled surgeon attempted to remove the arrowhead, but the tissue damage from the surgery was extensive. Gangrene set into the wound.

Knowing his end was near, the great monarch made preparations for his death. He pardoned the crossbowman (the pardon was ignored upon Richard's death, and the soldier was flayed alive and hanged), confessed his sins, received the Sacrament of Extreme Unction, and died two weeks later at the age of forty-two.[351] He left no children, and so the throne of England passed to his brother John, who became perhaps the worst monarch in English history.[352]

The great Crusader who nearly succeeded against all odds in liberating Jerusalem was dead, but the Crusading movement was not. Several more major Crusades would launch in the future, and Christendom would see the rise of another ruler vigorously committed to the Crusade, who was more than a lion-hearted man: He was a saint.

6

Fiasco of the Fourth Crusade

> *Our Lord commands and tells us all to go forth and liberate the Sepulchre and the cross. Let him who wishes to be in his fellowship die for his sake, if he would remain alive in paradise, and let him do all in his power to cross the sea.*
>
> Raimbaut of Vaqueiras[353]

You are now engaged on the greatest and most dangerous enterprise that any people up to this day have ever undertaken; it is therefore important for us to act wisely and prudently.

Doge Dandolo of Venice[354]

The French noble was a man a principle. Like his peers, he had taken the cross in 1199 amidst much fanfare and dreamed of serving Christ in his army. Confident of his mission and desirous of the spiritual benefits promised to the participants, he left his wife and children and marched to Venice to embark the ships bound for the Holy Land. When insufficient men arrived in the city of St. Mark to pay for the contracted transport, the Crusade plans were altered to attack a Christian city once under Venetian control.

Simon de Montfort was livid. He had not left home and family to attack fellow Christians. His objections were rebuffed, though, and the attack commenced. Simon refused to participate in the siege; he stayed away from the Crusader camp and ultimately left the army. Conscious of his vow, however, he traveled to the Holy Land separately and then returned to France while the remaining Crusader army was sidetracked by the promises of a Byzantine political upstart. Simon became a powerful lord with land holdings in France and England and died prosecuting the Albigensian Crusade[355] against heretics in southern France.

Simon's virtue preserved him from partaking in the fourth and most notorious Crusade, which today continues to be a source of scandal and significantly contributes to modernity's negative impression of the entire movement. Voltaire summarized this flawed and naïve position when he wrote, "The only fruit of the Christians on their barbarous Crusades was to exterminate other Christians."[356]

Innocent III and Crusading

Lothar of Segni was made a cardinal at the relatively young age of twenty-nine and pope at a very young thirty-seven. When he was elected at the beginning of 1198, the cardinals knew he was exactly what the Church needed at that moment in history. Lothar's eighteen-year reign as Pope Innocent III was the most important papacy of the medieval period and one that significantly shaped the Crusading movement. No other pope called as many Crusades as Innocent III or spent as much time focused on the goal of liberating the Holy City. Although he never personally took the cross, Innocent III can rightly be known as the Crusading Pope. A contemporary account of Innocent's life indicates the intense focus he placed on the Crusades: "In the midst of all his work, he quite fervently longed for the relief and recovery of the Holy Land and anxiously mulled over how he could achieve this more effectively."[357] At the very beginning of his pontificate, in a letter to the patriarch of Jerusalem announcing his election, he proclaimed his intention of calling a new Crusade to accomplish the liberation of Jerusalem.[358] The Crusade for Innocent III was the *negotium crucis*, "the business of the cross."[359]

Innocent III's focus on the Crusades is exemplified not only by the number of Crusades he called (seven in total) but also by the innovations he brought to the Crusading movement.[360] In his 1213 bull *Quia Maior*, Innocent made Crusading a moral imperative. He linked Crusading to eternal salvation, writing of those who failed to go: "To those men who refuse to take part, if indeed there be by chance any man so ungrateful to the Lord our God, we firmly state on behalf of the apostle Peter that they . . . will have to answer to us on this matter in the presence of the Dreadful Judge on the Last Day of Severe Judgment."[361]

Innocent envisioned armed pilgrimages managed and administered by the Church, an innovation that was needed but, as events illustrated, impractical to enforce. Money was always an issue during the Crusades, and Innocent tried to address that concern by taxing the Church and its clergy to finance the armed pilgrimages. Previously, married men needed permission from their wives to take the cross; by Innocent's pontificate, men were using that stipulation as an excuse to not go on Crusade. So he abrogated the requirement.

Innocent increased access to the spiritual benefits accorded to Crusaders by granting indulgences not only to those who fought in person, but also for those who paid for proxies to fight in their place, to the proxies themselves, and even to those who provided donations to Crusaders. Furthermore, the Crusading vow had always assumed duration of indeterminate length but Innocent changed that by granting indulgences to men who vowed forty days a year of combat service.[362]

The Calling of the Fourth Crusade

Innocent III called for a new Crusade on August 15, 1198. It was six years after the end of the Third Crusade and 102 years to the day after the departure of the First. This Fourth Crusade would go down in history as "an episode colored by brutality and determination, depravity and avarice, political intrigue and religious zeal."[363]

The notoriety of the Fourth Crusade comes from its (originally) unintended conquest of Constantinople. It was the Crusade in which Christians fought Christians, to the horror of Innocent III and the scandal of modern-day Catholics. The sack of the Queen of Cities was a momentous event, the memory of which reverberates through the centuries to the modern day. Pope John Paul II recalled it when Ecumenical Patriarch Bartholomew I visited Rome in the summer of 2004. The story of how the Fourth Crusade came to Constantinople and how a Flemish knight became the Roman emperor is one of the most intriguing and fantastic in the entire history of the Crusades.

Innocent III could not have chosen a worse time to call a Crusade. The political climate of Christendom was marked by conflict and confusion. Two men contested for the crown of the Holy Roman Empire in Germany and each claimed important allies. Philip of Swabia was allied with France and Otto of Brunswick counted the English in his court. The conflict in Germany prevented a strong ruler from that realm embracing Innocent's call to Crusade. The boy-king Frederick with his mother Constance as regent ruled the Kingdom of Sicily. The important Italian maritime powers of Genoa and Pisa were locked in war, as were the kings of England and France. Recognizing the importance of the English monarch and Third Crusade veteran to his Crusading effort, Innocent sent his legate Cardinal Capuano to negotiate a truce to the war between Richard and Philip. The cardinal successfully negotiated a five-year truce between the warring monarchs, which gave Innocent hope that his Crusade would finally materialize; so the muster date for warriors was set for the spring of 1199. However, King Richard the Lion-Hearted's death in April cast doubt once again that the Crusade would ever form, let alone actually travel to the Holy Land.

The Council of Barons

The Fourth Crusade seemed in doubt until Count Thibaut III of Champagne decided to take the cross. A young man in his twenties, he seemed to have it all. His lands were "one of the largest, richest, and most prestigious lordships in western Europe."[364] He was politically well connected as the nephew of both King Richard and Philip. Thibaut came from illustrious stock that viewed participation in the Crusades as a family obligation. His father, Count Henry I, visited the Holy Land twice, the first time as a participant in the Second Crusade. His older brother was Henry II of Champagne who reigned as ruler of Jerusalem after the death of King Guy de Lusignan. Thibaut's grandparents were the famous King Louis VII, leader of the Second Crusade, and Eleanor of Aquitaine. Thibaut vowed to go on Crusade while at a major tournament he hosted at Ecry-sur-Aisne on an Advent Sunday in 1199. Thibaut's decision at such a large public gathering influenced many others, finally providing the spark needed to light the Crusade—fifteen months after Innocent's call.

Joining Thibaut in taking the cross was the aged Geoffrey of Villehardouin, his chief military advisor. Geoffrey was a veteran of the Third Crusade who had been captured at the siege of Acre on November 4, 1190 and spent four years in a Muslim prison. Despite this negative experience and his age (he was in his fifties) the Crusading zeal burned brightly enough for Villehardouin to go once more unto the breach.

Count Thibaut and the other major French Crusaders met to discuss operational plans for the expedition. The Crusaders discussed the timetable and goals for the Crusade and set their initial objective as Alexandria, with the follow on goal of liberating Jerusalem. The decision to go to Egypt first was kept hidden from the rank and file because the goal of any Crusade for the average soldier was always Jerusalem. Recruitment of the necessary infantry and support personnel might suffer if word of Egypt as the objective leaked out. The meeting of barons also produced the decision to travel by sea rather than over land since a sea journey was substantially faster than a land march. The nobles agreed to pursue the sea route but (since none of them had a fleet) their decision required the assistance of allies.

Mission to Venice

The barons chose six men to travel to Italy and negotiate a contract for transport to Egypt. Genoa and Pisa were engaged in war, so the ambassadors decided to go to Venice, where they knew they would receive a warm welcome and an attentive disposition. Venice's ruler (also known as the doge) was the aged, brilliant, and politically astute Enrico Dandolo (r. 1195–1205).

Dandolo was "benevolent, eloquent, and universally respected. He possessed a great and penetrating sense of politics. He was also an ingenious and skilled diplomat and an equally skilled strategist and tactician. He was one of those men whose qualities make others turn naturally to them for leadership."[365] His leadership skills would be put to the test mightily during the events of the Fourth Crusade.

He came from a family that lived well beyond the median life expectancy for the time. It is believed he was eighty-five when elected doge and ninety-four when the Crusader ambassadors arrived in Venice.[366] Despite his advanced age, Dandolo was in excellent health—except for his blindness, which had resulted from an accident involving a blow to the head.

The Crusade ambassadors arrived in Venice in March of 1201 and were granted a meeting with Dandolo. They requested that the Venetians provide transport for 4,500 horses, 4,500 knights, 9,000 squires and 20,000 infantry, or a combined force totaling 33,500 men. Such a large request demanded a large payment; Dandolo proposed a total cost of 94,000 marks of Cologne for the requested transport. The rate, although high, was not exorbitant for the time period.[367] The Crusaders considered the offer and countered with a rate of four marks per horse and two marks per man for a total of 85,000 marks, which was the equivalent of 60,000 pounds sterling or twice the annual income of the kings of England and France.[368]

Such a large request demanded consultation and discussion. Dandolo informed the Crusaders that he needed to seek the acceptance of the Great Council, an oversight group of forty, and the Venetian people. This consultation was needed because "he would be asking his people to embark upon the most ambitious step in their commercial history."[369] A modern comparison of the immense request the Crusaders were seeking of Venice is a "major international airline ceasing flights for a year to prepare its planes for one particular client, and then to serve that client exclusively for a further period afterwards."[370]

The significant payment was enough of a financial incentive for the Great Council's immediate acceptance of the Crusader's offer, and so all that remained for approval of the treaty was the consent of the people. Dandolo called a popular assembly of 10,000 citizens to participate in a Mass of the Holy Spirit for discernment of the Crusaders' request. After the Mass, Crusader ambassadors were given the opportunity to address the crowd. The oration so moved the people that they cried out, "We consent! We consent!"[371]

The Treaty of Venice was a momentous arrangement for both parties. The Crusaders needed to deliver the large number of troops upon which the cost of the expedition was calculated. For the Venetians, it was the largest enterprise in their history and "the largest state project in western Europe since the time of the Romans."[372] The size of the army expected by the Crusaders required 450 transport ships with a crew of 14,000 men. In order to construct the ships within the stipulated timeframe (ready by the feast of Sts. Peter and Paul: June 29, 1202) Dandolo suspended all commerce for eighteen months—a large risk to the economy of Venice.[373]

The Flaw in the Treaty

The Fourth Crusade would ultimately deviate from its objective primarily due to the fundamental flaw in the treaty the Crusader ambassadors signed with Venice, specifically the calculation of payment based on the number of potential troops. "The terms of the treaty acted as a vice from which the Crusaders were unable to escape for the simple reason that the fundamental calculation on which the agreement was based proved spectacularly wrong."[374] The envoys based the treaty on a future unknown number of potential recruits, not on the known number of warriors at the time of negotiations. They seemed to ignore the reality that warriors not under vassalage to the French barons were not obligated to travel from Venice and could make their own travel arrangements to Outrémer. The fundamental miscalculation of the number of expected troops shaped the later decisions of the Crusade leadership—and guaranteed their failure.

The treaty was sent to Rome for confirmation from Pope Innocent III. He approved it in early May of 1201, with the clear caveat that the Crusaders "should not harm Christians unless they wrongfully impeded the passage of the Crusade or another just or necessary cause should occur."[375]

Leadership of the Crusade

The Crusade faced an immediate crisis when Count Thibaut died unexpectedly on May 24, 1201. Thibaut's burial inscription illustrates his great desire to participate in the Crusade: "Intent upon redeeming the Cross and the land of the Crucified, he paved a way with expenses, an army, a fleet. Seeking the terrestrial city, he finds the heavenly one; while pursuing his goal far away, he finds it at home."[376]

Thibaut's death once more placed the Crusade in jeopardy, as the barons struggled to find a replacement. Faced with the prospect of launching a major expedition without a significant nobleman in command, Villehardouin suggested the nobles seek out the support of Boniface of Montferrat in northern Italy. He was an older man in his fifties and one of the best-known military commanders of the day. It was a controversial suggestion, for the French nobles did not know Boniface personally, but only by reputation. Boniface did not speak French, and his lack of personal commitment to the Crusade became an issue during the expedition.

Arrival in Venice

As the Crusaders made their way to Venice in the summer of 1202, it soon became obvious that the numbers were substantially lower than the Crusade ambassadors had estimated. Ultimately, only 13,000, or a third of the expected 33,500 warriors, assembled in Venice.[377]

The reasons for the low turnout were numerous. Some neglected their vows; others could not afford to fulfill them. There was no papal directive ordering warriors to assemble in Venice, so many troops found their own passage to the Holy Land. The papal legate, Peter Capuano, arrived in late July and was appalled at the number of poor, sick, women, and non-combatants. He dispensed their Crusade vow, which was a humane decision, but it further lowered the number of Crusaders in Venice and deeply upset the Venetians, who refused even to recognize Peter as legate of the Crusade.[378]

When Boniface of Montferrat strolled into Venice on the Feast of the Assumption of Mary, August 15, he faced the first major issue of his command. Since the expected number of Crusaders did not materialize in Venice, the Crusade leaders were unable to provide full payment in accordance with the treaty. The situation was tense as "the greatest commercial city in Latin Christendom faced a financial disaster. The evil consequences of the foolish treaty now stood starkly revealed. The Crusaders could not pay; the Venetians could not renounce payment."[379]

A Solution

As summer turned to fall, Dandolo concocted a plan to remedy the situation. He approached the Crusade nobles with a plan to capture the city of Zara, a town on the Dalmatian coast 165 miles southeast of Venice. The debt owed the Venetians would be suspended until paid through the acquisition of booty.

Zara had been previously under Venetian control but had rebelled. It was extremely important, because it was the first port along the Adriatic coast used by Venice for refurbishment and resupply of ships traveling to Outrémer.[380] Venetians also relied on the oak from Dalmatian forests that flowed through Zara to construct their ships.

Dandolo's plan seemed to solve the problems facing the Crusaders but it produced a new and very serious quandary. King Emeric of Hungary (r. 1196–1204), who had taken the cross in 1200, controlled Zara. His lands, therefore, were protected by the Church; attacking a Crusader's land resulted in excommunication.

The Crusaders needed to fulfill their vows but required Venetian ships in order to do so. They did not have the money to pay the Venetians, whose plan to keep the Crusade from crumbling put their very souls at risk. The choice was between abandoning their vows and attacking a fellow Crusader.

Debate raged among the Crusaders, but eventually most decided to accept Dandolo's offer. Many believed keeping the Crusade intact was paramount, and if that involved attacking a Christian city to raise the money required for transport to Outrémer, then so be it. The papal legate opined that keeping the Crusade intact and paying their debt to the Venetians allowed participation in Dandolo's plan, which was viewed as legitimate since Zara had rebelled against Venetian rule. "It was universally accepted in medieval Europe that a ruler had a right to stabilize his domains, quashing rebels and exacting oaths of loyalty, before leading his armies on Crusade."[381] In this view, Dandolo was merely exercising his rights in asking the Crusaders to help him attack Zara.

The decision to support Dandolo's plan was not unanimous, however, and many Crusaders left Venice, refusing to participate. Some even asked the papal legate to commute their vow. Innocent III did not approve of the diversion to Zara, and after Peter Capuano traveled to Rome to discuss the situation, Innocent sent letters to the Crusaders forbidding them from attacking Zara under pain of excommunication. But the leaders hid the pope's letter from the rank and file.

Arrival at Zara

The Venetian fleet of over 200 ships arrived at Zara on the Feast of St. Martin of Tours, November 11, 1202. The day after the fleet's arrival, emissaries from Zara approached the Crusader camp seeking to negotiate with Dandolo. They agreed to surrender the city in exchange for their lives.

Dandolo agreed but said he needed to consult with the Crusade leaders, which was a bizarre response. The siege was a Venetian affair; the Crusaders only participated out of a need to pay their debts and had no leverage in any negotiation with Dandolo. His "decision was a bad one. Had the doge immediately accepted the surrender much of the trouble that followed would have been avoided."[382]

Simon de Montefort was one of many Crusaders who struggled with the decision to attack Zara and he actively sought to prevent the siege. While the Zarans waited for Dandolo to return, Simon visited them and misrepresented himself, claiming that he spoke for all French Crusaders. Simon told the Zarans the French had no intention of fighting fellow Christians and so they should not surrender to the Venetians. While Simon was convincing the Zarans to hold fast, Dandolo received the consent of the Crusade leaders and returned to find the Zarans missing.

In their place were Simon and Abbot Guy of Les Vaux-de-Cernay, who confronted Dandolo and the Crusade nobles. Holding a copy of Innocent's letter, he commanded, "I forbid you, on behalf of the Pope of Rome, to attack this city, for those within are Christians and you are Crusaders!"[383] Dandolo was furious and said to the Crusade nobles, "Lords, I had this city at my mercy, and your people have deprived me of it; you promised to assist me to conquer it, and I summon you to do so."[384]

Furious at Dandolo's obstinacy in the face of a direct papal order to not attack the city, Simon said, "I have not come here to destroy Christians."[385] Simon refused to participate and retreated from the main host, establishing a camp with his followers some distance from the city. Disillusioned with the events at Zara, Simon eventually left the Crusade and traveled to the Holy Land on his own. He remained committed to the Crusading movement and became the main figure in the later Albigensian Crusade in southern France.

The Siege of Zara

As the Crusaders prepared their siege machines, sharpened their swords, and checked their armor in anticipation of the assault on Zara, its citizens draped crosses over the walls as a reminder to the Crusaders that they were attacking a Christian city.[386] The ingenious tactic did not stop the attack.

After a two-week siege, the Zarans sued for peace and surrendered on November 24. Entry into the city resulted in the plundering of churches, destruction of buildings, and general looting. Dandolo was eager to assert his authority over the city and, mindful of past grievances, ordered the execution and exile of various Zarans.[387]

News of the sack of Zara reached Pope Innocent III, who wrote a letter to the Crusaders denouncing their actions and demanding they restore the city to the Hungarian king:

> Behold, your gold has turned into base metal and your silver has almost completely rusted since, departing from the purity of your plan and turning aside from the path onto the impassable road, you have, so to speak, withdrawn your hand from the plough . . . for when . . . you should have hastened to the land flowing with milk and honey, you turned away, going astray in the direction of the desert.[388]

Innocent told the Crusaders their attack on Zara was "an outrage that is already notorious throughout almost the entire world."[389] Since the Crusaders attacked the lands of a fellow Crusader they were automatically excommunicated, and access to the indulgence—the reason that most joined the Crusade in the first place—was denied.

A group of French envoys left the army and traveled to Rome to discuss the situation with Innocent and to request the lifting of the excommunication. Innocent granted their request on condition that the Crusaders restore Zara to the king of Hungary and promise to not attack other Christian lands, unless a just cause forced them to such an action and only after receiving papal approval. Innocent demanded the Crusade leaders send signed and sealed statements to Rome swearing they would obey all papal orders.[390] Although he was furious at the actions of the Crusaders, "Innocent had no desire to destroy the Crusade by refusing to forgive them if they were truly sorry for their sins and willing to do penance, and as a priest he had no right to refuse absolution to the penitent."[391]

Although the French contingent sought out papal absolution, the Venetians refused to admit any wrongdoing. They believed their attack on Zara was justified and, therefore, they remained excommunicated.

The path to Zara was not a calculated pre-meditated decision on the part of the Crusade leadership and, contrary to popular modern opinion, the Venetians did not secretly force the Crusade toward Zara and ultimately Constantinople. Rather, the reasons for the diversion were "pragmatic, ambitious and opportunistic: to secure the expedition's funding and material resources on one hand and, on the other, to attempt to realign the politics of the eastern Mediterranean in favor of Rome, Outrémer, and the Crusade."[392]

A Byzantine Prince

Travel in the Mediterranean Sea usually ceased during the winter months of November through March, so the Crusaders had to remain in Zara. During their stay, the Crusaders received envoys representing Alexius Angelus, a fugitive from the Byzantine Empire and son to the deposed emperor. The envoys asked the Crusaders to place the prince on the throne in Constantinople.

Alexius had fled the court of his uncle, Alexius III, in the fall of 1201. In order to free his father and return his family to power, Alexius Angelus needed an army; the Crusade army at Zara was in need of cash. So, the envoys presented Alexius' offer to help the Crusade leaders once they had installed him as emperor. He promised to unite the Byzantine Church with Rome; join the Crusade at the head of an army of 10,000 troops;

permanently maintain a corps of 500 knights in the Holy Land; and pay 200,000 silver marks, enough to settle the Venetian debt with a surplus to finance the campaign in Outrémer.

Alexius had previously visited Rome and asked Pope Innocent for assistance, but the pope had rebuffed the prince's request and now told Boniface of Montferrat, the Crusade leader, to have nothing to do with the Byzantine refugee. Despite the papal warning, Boniface and the Crusade nobles agreed to help Alexius. When Innocent heard the news in the spring of 1203 he wrote a letter warning the nobles against traveling to Constantinople and adjuring them "not to return to their previous sins [attacking another Christian city] like dogs returning to their own vomit."[393]

Recognizing that the Crusade nobles might be motivated to help Alexius because he promised reunion with Rome or because the current ruler of Byzantium was a usurper, Innocent wrote: "Let no one among you rashly convince himself that he may seize or plunder Greek lands on the pretext that they show little obedience to the Apostolic See, or because the emperor of Constantinople deposed his brother, blinded him, and usurped the empire."[394] He pointedly told the Crusaders to "give up these pointless diversions and feigned commitments: cross over to save the Holy Land."[395]

Unfortunately, the Crusade leaders did not heed the pope's commands and instead agreed to help Alexius. The "business of the cross" seemed subservient to the business of the Crusade nobles.

The Fourth Crusade nobles were placing their hopes on the promises of a refugee prince with no political experience and unproven popularity. Some modern observers read malice into the Crusade from the beginning, believing that the Venetians, or even the Church, specifically launched the Crusade to attack Constantinople. And indeed, among the general populace, the memory of the Fourth Crusade is one of barbaric acts against fellow Christians. Yet the historical record proves that the results of the Fourth Crusade were not planned from the beginning and were definitely not pursued or supported by the Church. Pope Innocent III specifically and repeatedly exhorted and threatened the Crusaders to choose the correct path and make their way to Jerusalem. It is true that "the diversion to Byzantium was no accident, but [it was] rather the result of conscious choices painfully, openly and controversially reached. [But] the motives behind them were immediate, contradictory, self-deluding and muddled rather than treacherous or malign."[396]

Constantinople—Queen of Cities

The Crusaders arrived at Constantinople on the Feast of St. John the Baptist, June 24, 1203. They were awe-struck by the view. Constantinople was a majestic city unlike anything the Crusaders knew in the West. It boasted a population of 500,000 in the city and another 300,000 in the surrounding area.[397] By comparison, Florence and Venice contained 50,000–100,000 people and London only 25,000–50,000.[398] Constantinople was not only the center of imperial political power but also an economic powerhouse. The inhabitants of the "Queen of Cities" adorned their churches not only in gold, silver, and jewels but also in saintly relics.

The walls of the city were a formidable obstacle and the Crusaders were outnumbered by the garrison three to one. Although the city had surrendered to rival claimants as recently as 1081, in its 900 year history Constantinople had never been conquered by a foreign army.

The Crusaders initially believed the installation of Alexius Angelus would be a peaceful coup, based on Alexius's word and his description of the situation in the city. They soon found out his assessment was completely wrong. When news of the Crusaders' approach reached Alexius III, he sent Nicolo Rosso, a native of Lombardy and resident of Constantinople, to ascertain why the Crusaders had arrived and what they wanted. They told Rosso that they did not recognize the authority of Alexius III and demanded he relinquish the throne in favor of his young nephew.

Dandolo and the Crusade leaders believed that the people of Constantinople were unaware that Alexius Angelus was in their company. To remedy this, Dandolo, Alexius, and Boniface of Montferrat boarded a Venetian galley and sailed along the walls of the city, getting as close as ten feet at times. The Crusaders called out to the citizens gathered on the walls to view the strange flotilla, saying, "Here is your natural lord. If you hold back, we will do to you the very worst we can."[399]

The Crusaders expected the citizens to shout for joy at seeing the return of their lost prince. They were shocked to hear only curses instead, as various objects rained down upon them from the walls. It seemed to the Crusaders as if no one in the city even knew who the prince was.[400]

The rejection of Alexius Angelus at the walls dampened the Crusaders' spirits. A peaceful coup was no longer a viable tactic; the Crusaders now knew they would have to fight. However, the besieging of the Queen of Cities with a force well below the number of defenders was a daunting prospect. Villehardouin succinctly described the situation when he commented, "Never have so many been besieged by so few."[401]

The Main Assault

The Crusade leaders met to plan the main assault and disagreements quickly arose over the plan. The Venetians wanted a marine attack across the harbor with a focus on attacking weak parts of the fortifications, whereas the French, not comfortable fighting from ships, preferred a land assault on the walls. The leaders knew they needed to develop a plan and implement it quickly because they only had enough provisions for a two- to three-week siege.

The nobles agreed on a plan that most military planners would immediately fault: to split their forces and concentrate them on two different points of attack. The Venetians decided to embark on an amphibious assault against the walls whereas the French planned an attack against the walls near the Blachernae Palace. Previous attackers of Constantinople had focused on the middle city walls where the defenses were the lightest. The French chose to attack an area with some of the city's strongest defenses. It was a poor choice.

On July 17, the French Crusaders, using a battering ram and carrying scaling ladders, began their assault. The walls were defended by Pisan troops and by the feared Varangian Guards, and the attack quickly became a disaster: only fifteen Crusaders managed to climb up the walls, and all but two were killed.[402]

The Venetian attack fared better primarily due to their unique ships and the leadership of Dandolo. The Venetians had modified their ships with platforms that provided a location for troops to bombard the defenders with missiles and serve as a heightened position from which to climb on top of the walls. The success of the Venetian attack, which began to push through the city, prompted Alexius III to order an element of the Varangian Guards to break contact with the French and assist the defenders fighting against the Venetians.

The arrival of the Varangians caused the Venetians to fall back. As they did so, they set a defensive fire in the city to separate their line of attack from the Greek defenders. The fire raged out of control and ultimately burned 120 acres in the city and left 20,000 inhabitants homeless.[403] It was the first of three devastating fires the Crusaders would set in Constantinople.

The people of Constantinople were upset at the fire's devastation and clamored for Alexius III, who had been quite passive during the Crusader attack, to do something. Heeding the murmuring of the people, Alexius III launched a counter-attack with more than 30,000 troops against the French Crusader host. The French, recognizing that they were massively outnumbered, sent word to the Venetians to send reinforcements as quickly as possible. In the meantime the French took the drastic measure of outfitting the camp non-combatants—including cooks, tailors, and smiths—for battle. They wore pots from the kitchen for helmets and horse quilts for armor, and used knives and other cooking instruments for weapons.

The Flemish were in the vanguard and began the march toward the Byzantine line, but as they moved farther away from the Crusader camp they suddenly halted, as their commanders became afraid that they were getting too far ahead of the main force. To re-form the line they began a small tactical withdrawal, which from the perspective of those in the main body looked like a general retreat. Medieval chivalry demanded resoluteness in the face of an enemy and retreating was a stain on one's honor, so the Crusaders in the main body charged forward, causing significant confusion within the army. It was a perfect opportunity for the Byzantines to attack but shockingly, the opposite occurred: Alexius III ordered a retreat.

Although the retreat of the Byzantines was perplexing, and devastating to morale, it was in line with Alexius III's goal for the sortie. He did not wish to engage the Crusaders in open battle but rather wanted to halt the Venetian advance by forcing them to divert troops and attention to the French sector. This tactical objective was achieved. At the end of the day's battle, the Venetian advance was halted with heavy casualties and the French were forced to abandon their assault and re-group. Despite the tactical success, the Byzantine failure to engage in combat and drive the French from the field was a strategic disaster. Fleeing in the face of an inferior enemy was tantamount to treason, and the decision increased the people's criticism of Alexius III's behavior during the siege. Alexius III took stock of his situation and decided fleeing was the better part of valor.

So, that evening, with "his city in flames, his enemies intact, his reputation disintegrating, the ill-prepared, discomposed and out-maneuvered Alexius III . . . prudently chose to flee the city."[404]

The Reign of Alexius IV

But the people of Constantinople did not want to immediately install his victorious rival Alexius Angelus due to his close association with the Crusader army outside the walls. Instead, they clamored for the restoral of the blind and aged Isaac II. The old emperor, newly re-installed, sent word to the Crusaders asking for his son Alexius Angelus to join him in the city.

The Crusaders were hesitant to release Alexius Angelus without assurances from Isaac that he would honor Alexius' agreements with them. Although he demurred at first, the old emperor finally agreed. The Crusaders were allowed into the city, and most of them spent time visiting the numerous churches and venerating the many relics.

A few weeks after his father's restoration to the throne, Alexius Angelus was crowned co-emperor, taking the name Alexius IV. Now that he was on the throne, it was time for Alexius IV to deliver on his promises to the Crusaders. A joint letter of obedience from Alexius and Patriarch John X Camaterus was sent to Pope Innocent III reuniting the two Churches. Although this official declaration of reunion was sent per his promise, Alexius IV and the patriarch made no effort to impose Roman doctrine on the Byzantine people. The promise was fulfilled, but it was hollow.

On top of that, Alexius paid the Crusaders only half the amount he had pledged to them—he still owed them the enormous sum of 100,000 silver marks. The Crusaders were able to remunerate their debt to the Venetians, but they needed the remaining amount to finance the Crusade to Outrémer. Pressured by the Crusaders to pay his remaining debt, Alexius sought ways to raise the necessary cash. He first turned to the nobility, taxing the wealthy families of Constantinople, but when even that proved unable to meet the remaining amount Alexius showed no shame in despoiling the sacred. He ordered the tombs of past emperors opened in order to strip the corpses of their rich vestments and precious jewels. When even that amount proved wanting, Alexius commanded the confiscation of sacred icons and vessels whose rich ornamentation was handed over in payment to the Crusaders.

The murmuring and complaining from the citizens of Constantinople over the presence and influence of the Crusaders grew through the summer of 1203, reaching a zenith on August 18, when a riot erupted in the city against Western expatriates in the city. Many were attacked and harassed, including the very Pisans who only a month earlier had fought and died to protect the city against the Crusaders.

The riot caused many Westerners to leave the city and join the Crusaders in their camp. In retaliation for it, a group of

Crusaders (Flemings, Pisans, and Venetians) decided the next day to venture into the city to set fire to a mosque built by Isaac II as a sign of friendship with Saladin.[405] The fire consumed the mosque but then searched for more fuel, beginning a rampage that lasted three days and consumed 440 acres of the densely populated central section of the city, stopping just short of the famed Hagia Sophia. The devastation in lives and property was enormous: 150 people were killed and 100,000 left homeless.[406]

The fires had burned not only the city but also any chance of an amicable relationship between the citizens and Crusaders. The situation in Constantinople was now combustible and neither Isaac II nor Alexius IV were capable of suppressing the inevitable fireworks.

The End of Alexius IV

At the beginning of 1204 Alexius IV was caught in a vicious cycle of trying to appease the anti-Crusader mob while not harming his former friends to whom he owed his reign. Alexius's inability to act decisively either way led to the mob taking matters into its own hands.

On January 25, 1204 the Byzantines descended on Hagia Sophia and compelled the senate and clergy to meet and elect a new emperor. It took three days to find someone willing, but eventually Nicholas Kannovos was selected. The patriarch, however, refused to crown him, so the people performed the ceremony.

Kannovos's reign lasted a mere six days before his death in the chaotic and violent early days of 1204. The news of a mob-elected emperor was a major shock to Alexius IV, who turned once again to his former Crusader friends for help. He offered them possession of the Blachernae imperial palace in exchange for their armed protection. He entrusted this proposal to Alexius Ducas, nicknamed Mourtzouphlus because of his large bushy eyebrows that met in the middle of his forehead.[407]

Unknown to Alexius IV was that Mourtzouphlus hated the Crusaders and was the leader of one of the many anti-Latin groups in the city. This duplicitous imperial bureaucrat would bring about the end of Alexius IV and Isaac II, leading to the Crusader sack of the city. History is not kind to Mourtzouphlus—"few men since Pilate have received such uniformly bad press." In his case, the assessment of history is correct.[408]

The Reign of Alexius V

Mourtzouphlus used his access to Alexius IV and Isaac II to stage a coup with the backing of the military, clergy, and civil service on the night and early morning of January 27–28, 1204. Alexius IV was imprisoned and the popularly elected Nicholas Kannovos was arrested and killed. The aged Isaac II died soon after the takeover. Taking the name Alexius V, Mourtzouphlus was crowned emperor on February 5.

Once installed, he initiated a series of actions designed to force the untenable situation with the Crusaders to a head. Believing the Crusaders would leave if their ally Alexius IV were dead, Mourtzouphlus ordered the imprisoned former emperor strangled. The rank-and-file Crusaders were happy when they heard the news, since they believed the nobles would now leave the city and go to the Holy Land. They were wrong. The Crusade leaders were furious to learn of Alexius IV's death. He still owed them money, and they were determined to receive their promised payment from the Byzantines. The nobles knew they needed food, supplies, and money for a successful expedition to the Holy Land. A second siege of the city was in order.

In an effort to persuade the rank and file, the Crusading bishops presented the case that Mourtzouphlus was guilty of regicide, a usurper, and could be justly deposed. Although the Byzantines saw Mourtzouphlus as just one successful usurper in a long line of such politicians, the Crusaders saw him as a disloyal murderer.

The Second Siege

On April 10, 1204 the second siege of Constantinople began. The Crusaders concentrated their forces on five towers at the northeastern wall near the Blachernae Palace, but the attack was repulsed, with heavy Crusader causalities.[409] The Crusaders were not only defeated in this initial assault but they suffered the taunts of the Byzantine defenders, who "began to hoot and to shout right lustily, and they went up on the walls and let down their breeches and showed them their buttocks."[410]

The siege resumed on April 12. The Crusaders changed tactics in order to successfully capture the towers on the walls. By lashing two ships together, the Venetians could bring superior numbers against a single tower. The ships were then firmly lashed to the tower, and from there troops climbed onto the wall, shouting their battle cry of "Holy Sepulchre!"

As the battle raged, a small group of ten knights and sixty infantry (including the chronicler Robert of Clari) found an undefended walled-up postern gate. Using their hands and swords, the Crusaders began to tear down the wall. Their activity drew the attention of the defenders, who rained down arrows, crossbow bolts, and boiling oil to deter their progress. Finally, the Crusaders succeeded in removing a small section of the wall, which allowed them to see inside the city. The number of soldiers within stunned them. Robert of Clari described the scene and the reaction of the Crusaders: "[I]t seemed as if half the world were there, and they [the Crusaders] did not dare risk entering in."[411] One bold Crusader, Aleaume of Clari (Robert's brother), abandoned caution and began wiggling through the hole, even as his fellow Crusaders tried to stop him by grabbing his feet. Aleaume pushed his way through and found himself on the other side of the wall, cut off from his fellow warriors and facing the Byzantine host. He truly was "one man against a multitude."[412]

Stunned by Aleaume's audacity, the Byzantine troops did the unexpected. Instead of attacking Aleaume and sealing the breach, the Greeks "fled like cattle."[413] The Crusaders had been fortunate in that they had broken through a section of the wall that was guarded by regular imperial troops. These Byzantine troops were "poorly trained and martially inept . . . [and] had shown themselves again and again willing to fight only when the danger to themselves was minuscule."[414] Aleaume leaned back through the wall and yelled to his fellow Crusaders, "Sirs, enter boldly! For I see that they are utterly confounded and are fleeing away."[415]

The remaining Crusaders poured through. They threw open one of the major city gates, and the rest of the army rushed into the city in a wild rampage.

By nightfall the Crusader host was in Constantinople but its hold on the city was precarious. They only occupied a very small area and were still massively outnumbered. In order to solidify their position they lit a defensive fire, which soon raged uncontrollably through the city, destroying homes and businesses. In total, the three Crusader fires destroyed one-sixth of the city and prompted Villehardouin to remark, "More houses had been burned in the city than there are houses in any three of the greatest cities in the kingdom of France."[416]

The next day, April 13, Alexius V fled the city. The Crusaders were victorious. They had conquered "the greatest, most powerful, and most strongly fortified city in the world."[417]

The Sack

Once their position was secure, the Crusaders sacked Constantinople. Their actions over those three days in 1204 set in motion centuries of acrimony and recriminations between East and West.

It is easy to play "armchair historian" and fault the Crusaders for the sack of Constantinople. But to do so projects modern sensibilities onto a past governed by different behaviors and laws. In one sense, the Crusaders cannot be blamed for their actions in 1204. They "found themselves in a treasure-trove of unmitigated proportions."[418] Expecting the Crusaders to ignore the wealth of the city after almost two years of arduous campaigning with frequent diversions, distractions, and disappointments seems unrealistic. But the people of Constantinople were left relatively alone, for the Crusaders were more interested in the riches of the city. There was no wholesale massacre or slaughter, although some people were killed and some Byzantine women, including

nuns, were raped. Lamentably, soldiers have done such things
in every age, and even in an army largely motivated by laudable
religious zeal there was not a total absence of such soldiers.

The economic toll of the sack was more significant, as the
Crusaders sought to remove as much wealth as they could carry
and transport. Bronze statues throughout the city were melted
down or shipped to the West, including the famous four bronze
horses that had been placed over the starting gate of the Hip-
podrome. The horses were shipped to Venice where they were
installed over the entryway to St. Mark's Basilica.[419]

The Crusaders plundered and pillaged sacred items as well, including the vast numbers of relics in the city. Altars were stripped
of ornamentation and even destroyed. Icons were smashed to get
the precious jewels embedded in them. Patens used by priests to
hold the host during the celebration of Mass were used as ordi-
nary bread plates and chalices normally reserved for containing
the sacred blood were used as common drinking cups.[420]

The amount of plunder was devastating to the citizens of
Constantinople. Villehardouin as an eyewitness to the sack remarked that "so much booty had never been gained in any city
since the creation of the world."[421] The estimate of spoils, declared and undeclared, was staggering: 800,000 marks.[422] "The
sack of Constantinople ranks as one of the most profitable and
shameful in history."[423]

Pope Innocent III was shocked, saddened, and angered by the
actions of the Crusaders. He had conceived the Crusade six years
earlier as an expedition to liberate Jerusalem. He did not envi-
sion—indeed, he actively worked against—the many diversions
undertaken by the nobles. In a letter to Boniface of Montferrat,
Innocent condemned the Crusaders' actions and chastised them
for their poor choices:

> You rashly violated the purity of your vows; and turning
> your arms not against the Saracens but against Christians,
> you applied yourselves not to the recovery of Jerusalem, but
> to seize Constantinople, preferring earthly to heavenly riches

. . . These "soldiers of Christ" who should have turned their swords against the infidel have steeped them in Christian blood, sparing neither religion, nor age, nor sex . . . They stripped the altars of silver, violated the sanctuaries, robbed icons and crosses and relics . . . The Latins have given example only of perversity and works of darkness. No wonder the Greeks call them dogs![424]

The Memory and Legacy of the Fourth Crusade

Whatever explanation may be provided for the sack of Constantinople, there is no doubt it has tainted East-West relations through the centuries. Historians who describe the sack and the events of 1204 with great exaggeration have not helped this difficult and complex relationship. Sir Steven Runciman believed "there was never a greater crime against humanity than the Fourth Crusade."[425] Amazingly, he wrote that in 1951, only six years after the Second World War and the worldwide discovery of the full Nazi program of the Final Solution to eradicate the Jewish people. Although indeed devastating in terms of the amount of wealth and relics purloined by the Western warriors, to write, in the wake of the Shoah, that the sack of Constantinople was the greatest crime against humanity is the epitome of hyperbole.

In reality the destruction done to the city and the death of its inhabitants was minimal. Far from committing widespread slaughter, the Crusaders killed only half of one percent of the city's citizens. A three-day sack of cities that initially refused to surrender was the convention in the medieval world. Although "the sack of Constantinople was an atrocity . . . in the terms of the day, [it was] not a war crime."[426] It is true that the sack remains one of the enduring memories of the Crusades. Most people remember the event—or at least remember the anti-Catholic narrative about the event—and it continues to be used to further the falsehood that the Crusades were primarily "land-grabs" or motivated by greed and desire for booty. Yet not even the Fourth Crusade was motivated by greed. The Crusaders desired to campaign in Egypt and then the Holy Land with the ultimate goal of liberating Jerusalem. Due to a series of bad decisions, overzealous calculations, and the need to fulfill treaty obligations, the Crusade veered off course and—ignoring admonitions from the pope—pursued a course that led them to the sack of Constantinople. Although the Eastern world continues to fault the West and the Church for the fiasco of the Fourth Crusade, the simple fact remains that the Crusaders only diverted their expedition to Constantinople at the request of an Easterner. Absent Alexius Angelus's pleading for Crusader help to place him on the throne, his actions while emperor and those of his people, who ultimately overthrew and killed him, there would have been no attack on and sack of Constantinople.[427]

Despite Innocent's unambiguous protestations at the time, blame today is still placed inappropriately on the Catholic Church for the events of the Fourth Crusade. When Pope John Paul II visited Athens in 2001, he was greeted along his route with Greek Orthodox monks protesting his visit while holding signs with "1204" printed on them. Indeed, "the Byzantines' deep sense of betrayal and bitter anger toward the Latins became the legacies of 1204 that would not die with the generation that experienced the events. They would animate centuries of tragic history and, for many, still live today."[428]

Modern critics never tire of pointing out that Pope John Paul II apologized for the Fourth Crusade and the sack of Constantinople. Unfortunately for those who use this "fact" to discredit the Crusade, the pope actually never apologized at all. In brief remarks during the visit of Ecumenical Patriarch Bartholomew I to Rome on the Feast of Sts. Peter and Paul on June 29, 2004, 800 years after the Crusade, John Paul II recalled the events of the spring of 1204 and remembered the prohibitions of Pope Innocent III against the Crusade's diversion to Constantinople:

> On this occasion we cannot forget what happened during the month of April 1204. An army that had set out to recover the Holy Land for Christendom marched on Constantinople, took it and sacked it, pouring out the blood of our own brothers and

sisters in the faith. Eight centuries later, how can we fail to share the same indignation and sorrow that Pope Innocent III expressed as soon as he heard the news of what had happened?[429]

The pope-saint also recognized the complexity of historical events and the inherent problems associated with relying on simple pronouncements of past events from a modern worldview, which leads to false narratives when he added, "After so much time has elapsed, we can analyze the events of that time with greater objectivity, yet with an awareness of how difficult it is to investigate the whole truth of history."[430] In calling on East and West to approach the events of 1204 with greater objectivity, the pope quoted St. Paul: "Do not pronounce judgment before the time, before the Lord comes, who will bring to light the things now hidden in darkness and will disclose the purposes of the heart."[431] Urging the reconciliation of the two halves of the Church, John Paul II offered a prayer appropriate not only for East-West relations but also for the restoral of the proper understanding and memory of the Crusades: "Let us pray together, therefore, that the Lord of history will purify our memory of all prejudice and resentment and obtain for us that we may advance in freedom on the path to unity."[432]   JP II recalling events of Constantinople 1204.

7

A Saint and a Sinner

He [St. Francis of Assisi] *fought in the Crusade,*
in which he and he alone emerged the victor"

Arnaldo Fortini[433]

His [Holy Roman Emperor Frederick II]
conversation reveals that he does not believe in the Christian
religion. When he spoke of it, it was to ridicule it.

Ibn al-Djusi[434]

In early thirteenth-century Italy, the political environment among
the various towns and cities was delicate and tense. When this situation turned into open warfare between the cities of Perugia and
Assisi, many young men on both sides rushed to arms. The Battle of
Collestrada ended in disaster for the smaller city of Assisi, with most
of its forces captured by the Perugians. Among the captives was a
twenty-year-old man from a wealthy Assisi family who had joined
the fight with dreams of glory and honor. His name was Giovanni
di Bernardone, called "Francesco" (Francis) by his father.[435]

Francis suffered for a long year in a Perugian prison until he
was finally released when his father paid a significant ransom.
Several years later, Francis was traveling through the countryside near Assisi when he came upon an abandoned, dilapidated
old church dedicated to the great eleventh-century saint Peter
Damien. The young soldier knelt before the large painted crucifix to pray. During his prayer, Francis witnessed a miracle as the
image of Christ came to life and instructed him, "Go, repair my
house, which, as you see, is falling completely to ruin."[436]

Initially Francis believed the imperative from Christ concerned the specific church of Peter Damien, but the Lord's plan
was much greater. Francis spent time in prayer and finally came
to the decision to renounce his family wealth in order to serve
Christ completely by begging alms for his existence. This radical
approach to holiness soon attracted others, and within five short
years of his dramatic encounter in San Damiano, Pope Innocent
III recognized his followers in a religious order known as the
Order of Friars Minor, or the "Franciscans."

St. Francis saw the need to evangelize those arrayed against
Christendom, especially Muslims. Only two years after the
papal approval of his religious order, the holy friar and several
companions decided to risk martyrdom by preaching the gospel
to Muslims in the Holy Land. However, their ship ran into bad
weather, and they were forced to return home. Undaunted by
this setback, Francis once more planned an expedition to North
Africa. This time he walked to Spain in the hopes of seeking
transport, but became ill and once more was forced to cancel his
plans. It would take several more years before the holy friar from
Assisi could fulfill his desire to preach the gospel to the adher-
ents of Islam, and it was the occasion of another major Crusade
that provided the opportunity.

The "Children's Crusade"

The same century that witnessed the arrival of the holy man
of Assisi and his brown-robed companions also gave birth to
another movement motivated by deep piety. What history records as the "Children's Crusade" occurred "at a time when
Crusading fervor gripped every level of European society . . .
[it] sprang to life in an era of extraordinary religious creativ-
ity."[437] Often cited by critics to invalidate the Crusades, the so-
called Children's Crusade evokes images of toddlers and small
children leaving their homes enthralled with the misguided and
almost perverse prospect of participating in the grand adventure
of military campaigns to the Holy Land. In a sense, the episode

of the Children's Crusade serves as an icon of modern reactions toward the entire Crusading movement. Today's understanding of the Children's Crusade and the Crusades in general is guided more by "mythistory" than actual history.

The term itself is a misnomer, for the event involved neither an army of children nor a Crusade. In essence the Children's Crusade was an urban migration of young people who came from among the poor of society. Their poverty was not the reason for their migration;[438] rather, it came about through their adherence to the mainstream and popular acceptance of the Crusading movement. The participants of the Children's Crusade were "shepherds, ploughmen, carters, agricultural workers, rural artisans [who were] without a settled stake in the land or community, rootless and mobile."[439] Although young people were the primary (though not sole) participants, they were not children but rather teenagers and young adults. The movement was neither an armed pilgrimage (the participants carried no weapons) nor sanctioned by the Church, so it was not properly a Crusade. The Church showed little interest either positively or negatively in this youth movement. There were no condemnations, but no public pronouncements of support either.

What is known for certain about the misnamed Children's Crusade is that between Easter and Pentecost of 1212 young people in the Chartrain region of France (part of the Ile-de-France area near Paris), motivated by religious fervor, took the cross. The specific birthplace of the movement can be traced to the town of Chartres, which was an important religious and educational center in the thirteenth century. Chartres was not only a center of religious devotion but was also an area that specially embraced the Crusading movement. The Chartrain was a major recruiting area for the First Crusade and many of its famous citizens participated in that inaugural event, including Count Stephen of Blois and Fulcher, the First Crusade chronicler. Another reason for the launch of the Children's Crusade may have centered on the failure of the nobility to achieve Crusade objectives, leading people to believe that the "failure of the experienced, rich and proud was to be redeemed by the innocent, pure and humble."[440]

The Leader

Motivated by the general Crusading fervor present in their region, young people and some older men of Chartres began their "itinerant processional" in the spring of 1212.[441] The group carried the typical items of religious processions: banners, candles, crosses, and censers, singing songs with Crusading themes, specifically asking the Lord God to "raise up Christendom!" and to "return to us the True Cross!"[442] The movement grew in strength and numbers when a charismatic youth from Cloyes, a town thirty-five miles south of Chartres, became the *de facto* leader of the movement.

Stephen of Cloyes was a shepherd, a profession that medieval spirituality saw as pure and innocent. Stephen believed the Lord Jesus had appeared to him, giving him letters to be delivered to King Philip II Augustus. His divine mission became the specific objective of the youth in the Children's Crusade and attracted more followers, perhaps as many as 30,000.[443] Stephen and his merry band eventually reached Paris, ninety miles away from Chartres. There they made known their desire to see King Philip to deliver the letters allegedly given to Stephen by the Lord.

The king did not meet the enthusiastic group of young people, but on June 24, 1212, he made known through his officials his command for them to return home to their families. With this kingly imperative, the story of Stephen of Cloyes and the Children's Crusade in France comes to an end. Though disappointed by the king's response, many of the French youth complied, but others ignored the command and continued their procession eastward toward the Rhineland.

The remnant of the French youth movement crossed the Rhine and gathered new members from among the German youth of the Rhineland. Unlike the French movement, which mostly contained young adults, the Rhineland expedition included a wide cross-section of society from urban workers to the elderly to mothers and infants and even entire families. What linked both the French and German movements was the complete absence of armed warriors or clergy. The Rhineland movement, just like the French one, began in a city well known as a pilgrimage site: Cologne, the largest and wealthiest German city in the thirteenth century, and one of four major pilgrimage destinations in Christendom.

Nicholas of Cologne

Just as the French element of the "Children's Crusade" grew in numbers due to the charismatic leadership of Stephen of Cloyes, so too did the Rhineland movement from the leadership of Nicholas of Cologne. There is nothing known for certain about Nicholas's background or motivations for leading the Rhineland element of the Children's Crusade, but it is well accepted that he was a pious man who attracted thousands of people, perhaps as many as 7,000, to join him in taking the cross on an expedition to liberate Jerusalem.[444] Nicholas's objective was to march to the sea to find transport to the Holy Land, and so he led the youth of the Rhineland across the Alps and into Italy in late July 1212.

Once in Italy, initial enthusiasm waned with the weariness of travel and the recognition of reality. As a result, many of Nicholas's followers decided to end their participation by settling in Genoa, while others immigrated to Pisa. Still others, perhaps the remaining French element, left Italy for Marseilles where they hoped to find transport to the Holy Land. Instead, immoral merchants duped them into boarding ships bound for Alexandria where some were drowned in shipwrecks and others were sold into slavery.[445] The remaining youth went to Rome where they asked Innocent III to release them from their Crusade vow. Those younger than fourteen and the elderly were granted their request, but participants not in those categories were still held to their vow.[446] Nicholas was last sighted in Brindisi looking for transport to the Holy Land. It is possible that he fulfilled his

Crusade vow by joining the Fifth Crusade and fighting in the Egyptian campaign of 1218–1221.[447]

The Legacy of the Children's Crusade

The Children's Crusade was the first, but not the last, of the "popular" Crusades, or those undertaken by the non-noble or military classes. A generation after the Children's Crusade, Christendom was witness to the Shepherd's Crusade (in 1251, with another one in 1320). Unlike the Children's Crusade, the other popular Crusades would be marked by violence as the participants attacked Jews and the clergy.

Despite its non-violent and deeply pious record, the assessment of the Children's Crusade by contemporary writers was quite negative. The main criticism was that the movement amounted to nothing, because as one chronicler suggested, "it was founded upon nothing."[448] Another chronicler focused on the fate of the participants, who "were ruined, died, or returned."[449] Perhaps the criticisms were harsh because medieval people wanted to believe in the youth movement or wanted to believe that the pure and humble of heart could indeed succeed where the rich and prideful had failed. Crusade failures were looked upon harshly because medieval people cared deeply about the Holy Land.

The mythistory of the Children's Crusade grew in the centuries after the movement as fourteenth-century chronicles recounted the event and added new fictitious and salacious details. Later chronicles maintained the mythistory while adding their own twists to the story; for example, the sixteenth-century German author, Johannes Bailius Herold (1514–1567) posited the outlandish tale that many of the "Children's Crusaders" were noble girls disguised as boys.[450] Pietro Bizzarri added the bizarre twist that the children believed the Mediterranean Sea would part so they could walk to Jerusalem dry-shod.[451] The mythistory of the "Children's Crusade" reached its height during the Enlightenment in the works of Voltaire who implicated the clergy and teachers of the youth in their ultimate demise:

This epidemic disease [i.e. the Crusading movement] spread even to children. Thousands of them, led by their schoolmasters and monks, left their parents' homes on the faith of these words: 'Lord, you have drawn your glory from children.' Their leaders sold some of them to the Muslims; the rest died of poverty.[452]

Like the Fourth Crusade, the Children's Crusade is one of modernity's most often recalled episodes of Crusading history. Critics of the Crusades paint pictures for modern audiences of horrible campaigns sponsored by the Church that involved even innocent children. In reality, the Children's Crusade was simply a movement of deeply pious medieval young people enraptured by the Crusading fervor of their time and the desire to reclaim the True Cross and liberate the Holy City of Jerusalem.

The Fifth Crusade

There were many lessons learned from the disaster of the Fourth Crusade, but the most important one, for Pope Innocent III, was the need for the Church to administer and centrally manage future expeditions to the Holy Land. Six months after the Children's Crusade, Innocent preached a new Crusade wherein he hoped "to accomplish what he had failed to achieve in 1202–1204, the destruction of Ayyubid Egypt, the recovery of Jerusalem, and the spiritual renewal of Christendom."[453] Innocent's Crusade bull, *Quia Maior,* promulgated in April 1213, along with the conciliar decree, *Ad Liberandum,* from the Fourth Lateran Council in November 1215, established the "rhetorical, legal, fiscal, liturgical, and administrative norms of official Crusading for the next century and a half."[454]

Innocent believed that participation in the Crusade should be extended to all Christendom, and he granted plenary indulgences to those who fought, as well as to those who sent proxies in their stead (and to the proxies themselves). Those who could not fight were exhorted to pray and fast for the success of the expedition and, if they had the financial means, they could finance a Crusader and through this "substitution payment" also receive the indulgence. Those without the financial means to pay the full expenses of a warrior on Crusade could donate a smaller amount to the Church for general Crusade expenses and through this "redemption payment" also receive the indulgence.

Innocent marshaled all of Christendom to participate in the Crusade in order to maximize the chance of success and to bring about a general spiritual awakening. In order to focus on the Holy Land campaign, Innocent suspended the indulgence for those fighting against Muslims in Spain and the Albigensian heretics in the south of France.[455] Although the Fifth Crusade was designed by Innocent to be centrally administered by the Church and involved a huge recruiting effort throughout Christendom, there was no effort to appoint central secular leadership. This lack of central leadership and the ambitious size of the project constituted serious deficiencies that eventually hampered the success of the expedition.[456]

Preaching the Crusade

Preaching the Fifth Crusade was a massive effort encompassing every diocese in Christendom over eight years. Innocent ensured that those who preached were specially trained, were forbidden to accept money, and were instructed to travel moderately and behave piously. Handbooks on how and what to preach were compiled and published to assist Crusade preachers. The pope personally oversaw preaching efforts in Italy, and demanded bishops remain engaged with the preaching efforts in their dioceses. One successful preacher who also joined the Fifth Crusade was Oliver of Paderborn, a teacher from the cathedral school at Cologne and later bishop. Oliver preached the Crusade in Germany, Flanders, and Holland and claimed that his efforts resulted in 15,000 warriors taking the cross throughout the Netherlands.[457]

The massive preaching effort also produced fruit in Austria, Germany, Hungary, and England. Unlike previous Crusades, participation was not high in France, primarily due to the ongoing Albigensian Crusade. Unlike the Fourth Crusade, major

secular rulers took the cross, including Frederick II, king of
Germany and Sicily, Duke Leopold VI of Austria, King Andrew
of Hungary, and King John of England. (Despite his vow, King
John never fulfilled his quest due to the eruption of civil war in
England that threatened his reign.) Innocent also called upon
the Venetians to fulfill their vow from 1202, since the Fourth
Crusade never accomplished the goal of liberating Jerusalem.[458]

While the preaching campaign was in full swing, and warriors throughout Christendom were taking the cross and making preparations for the expedition, the man who influenced and
supported the Crusading movement more than any other, Pope
Innocent III, died unexpectedly at the age of fifty-five in the
summer of 1216. The Crusade moved forward under the direction of his successor, Honorious III.

The Crusade Begins

The conquest of Egypt had been an objective for Western warriors since the First Crusade. Godfrey de Bouillon fought to
capture Ascalon in order to provide a base of operations against
the Fatimid caliphate in Cairo. Richard I tried unsuccessfully to
convince his army to campaign in Egypt during the Third Crusade, and Egypt was the true objective of the Fourth Crusade
before decisions pulled that campaign elsewhere. Egypt remained
a source of military power and material aid for the Muslims in
Outrémer, and a major threat to the Crusader States. Conquering Egypt would not only liberate ancient Christian territory but
would also provide a secure and important base of operations for
the eventual liberation of Jerusalem and the Holy Land.

The Fifth Crusade suffered from a lack of strong leadership.
No single Western lord stayed with the army for the duration of
the campaign. The absence of Holy Roman Emperor Frederick
II and his army, despite his repeated promises, was painfully
felt throughout the expedition. Not even the major local noble,
King John of Brienne, stayed throughout the campaign, even
though he was the nominal leader of the Crusade. Additionally,

the papal legates sent by the Church to oversee the operation exercised leadership that included questionable decision-making.

Two legates were sent: Cardinal Robert from England and Cardinal Pelagius from Portugal. Soon after their arrival in Outrémer, "Cardinal Robert died, and Pelagius lived, which was a great pity, for he did much evil."[459] The "evil genius" of the Fifth Crusade, Pelagius was "hard-hearted, intolerably severe with all men, ostentatious, insolent, holding himself out as invested with all the prerogatives of the papacy, bedecked from head to foot in red, even to the saddlecloth and bridles of his horse."[460] Pelagius was able to assume control over the Fifth Crusade not only due to the death of his fellow legate and the absence of major secular rulers but also because he controlled the money for the operation.

The Siege of Damietta

At first glance, the city of Damietta—two miles inland from the mouth of the main branch of the Nile River—did not seem to warrant the attention it received from the Crusaders. Regardless, the town of 60,000 inhabitants happened to lie on the most direct approach to Cairo, and so "for the next three and a half years, this narrow waterlogged region of flats, marsh, canals, and rivers remained the focal point for the thousands who joined the Crusade from the west, the longest static campaign in the history of the eastern Crusades."[461]

The Crusaders arrived in May of 1218 and quickly assessed the task before them. Damietta was a heavily fortified town with triple land and sea walls whose harbor defense consisted of the seventy-foot Chain Tower. A 300-man garrison was charged with defending the harbor and ensuring that the massive chain that stretched from the tower to the city did not collapse, allowing enemy ships to get close to the city.

The Crusaders began the siege of Damietta by using their fleet to blockade the city in order to cut off supplies with the hope that the city would surrender. Although this maritime maneuver was necessary for the successful prosecution of the siege, it alone would not guarantee success. The Crusaders knew they needed to besiege the city on land, but to do so required control of the harbor, which in turn required the conquest of the Chain Tower that guarded the harbor entrance.

Several attempts to take the tower failed. The Crusaders were frustrated and getting desperate when Oliver of Paderborn had an idea. He suggested the Crusaders take one ship and build a siege engine on the deck with a rotating scaling ladder. The modified ship would sail to the Chain Tower and soldiers in the siege engine could use the ladder to scale the tower. The contraption was similar to what the Venetians had built and used successfully at the siege of Constantinople during the Fourth Crusade. Oliver's idea worked, and they finally captured the Chain Tower in August of 1218, three months after their arrival at Damietta.

The siege of the city could now begin in earnest. Unfortunately, large groups of Crusaders left the army and returned home after the Chain Tower fell. During the height of the campaign the army consisted of 30,000 troops, but by the time the army marched to Cairo it contained only 1,200 knights, 4,000 archers and several thousand infantry.[462] Indeed, "the history of the Fifth Crusade is one of a fluid army defined by the constant arrivals and departures of soldiers. In part, this was the logical outcome of the new formulation of a Crusade as a papally sanctioned war against the enemies of the faith, rather than an armed pilgrimage to the land of Christ."[463] Soldiers leaving the campaign while it was still ongoing became a significant issue and prevented the troops from pressing their advantage and securing victory. "The transient fluidity of tours of service between 1217 and 1221 ensured that the best funded, most widely preached and professionally recruited Crusade to date failed to convert numerical popularity into lasting achievement."[464]

Diplomatic Negotiations

Desiring to rid himself of the Crusaders, the Muslim ruler al-Kamil offered a diplomatic solution. In return for the Crusader withdrawal from Egypt, al-Kamil offered to restore the previous territory of the Kingdom of Jerusalem except for a few important castles in the Transjordan. The offer was stunning; in effect, "al-Kamil offered to wipe away all of Saladin's conquests in Palestine for the Crusaders' lifting of one siege in Egypt."[465]

King John of Brienne urged acceptance of al-Kamil's offer, but the Templars and Hospitallers cautioned against it since it would be extremely difficult to defend Jerusalem without the Transjordan castles. Cardinal Pelagius weighed the opinions and ruled against accepting al-Kamil's generous offer. He earnestly believed the Crusaders were in a position of strength and would emerge victorious. In the mind of the cardinal, acceptance of a negotiated settlement while occupying a superior military position was foolish. Additionally, the German Crusaders were reticent to accept any offers of peace before the arrival of Frederick II.[466]

The specter of the emperor's anticipated arrival would continue to influence decisions during the Crusade. Ultimately, the failure of the Fifth Crusade did not hinge on the rejection of this (and subsequent) diplomatic overtures from al-Kamil, but on poor military decisions.[467]

The Saint Arrives

As the siege wore on, Crusaders continued to arrive and depart while the army awaited the arrival of Holy Roman Emperor Frederick II. Those remaining in the Crusader camp were greeted with a strange sight in the late summer of 1219, when a group of twelve men in tattered clothing arrived instead. These twelve companions had come to the Crusade to witness to Christ among the Muslims even to the point of martyrdom. Their leader was a man destined to be declared a saint by the Church: Francis of Assisi. He and his eleven friars had reached Damietta to convert al-Kamil and end the Crusade.

Despite modernity's sentimental view of St. Francis as a proponent of tolerant diversity, he "sought no accommodation with Islam, [but] rather its eradication through reasoned evangelism."[468] Francis discussed his desire to proclaim the gospel to al-Kamil with Cardinal Pelagius, who urged him to abandon such plans. St. Francis and Brother Illuminato left anyway.

Francis was confident of the Lord's protection, but Brother Illuminato was concerned about their reception among the Muslims. As they walked, Francis noticed two grazing ewes and said, "'Courage, Brother! Put your trust in him who sends us forth like sheep in the midst of wolves.'"[469]

When they reached the Muslim sentries they were taken into custody, beaten, and chained. Francis cried out to his captors, "I am a Christian. Take me to your master."[470] Brought before al-Kamil, Francis preached to him through an interpreter for several days. The sultan listened attentively and responded personally and warmly to Francis before telling him, "I am going to go counter to what my religious advisors demand and will not cut off your heads . . . You have risked your own lives in order to save my soul."[471] Although moved by Francis's words and holy life, al-Kamil told the saint he could not convert to the Catholic Faith without deeply alienating his people who would see the conversion as apostasy, which brings punishment by death in Islam. The sultan asked the saint to "remember me in your prayers, and may God, by your intercession, reveal to me which belief is more pleasing to him."[472]

The dramatic interaction between the Catholic saint and the Muslim sultan did not produce the hoped-for fruit of conversion, nor did it end the Fifth Crusade, but it was an episode that illustrated the spiritual purpose of Crusading. It was a bold and daring move worthy of remembrance, and it almost worked. St. Francis, although not a vowed Crusader, was nonetheless an authentic Crusader for he "embodied both the poor man and the knight, the two forces that had set out together in olden times along the road to the Holy Land and had retaken Jerusalem."[473]

After his return to Italy, St. Francis revised the Rule of the Order of Friars Minor to reflect his experience. An entire chapter of the Rule was now dedicated to relations with Islam, and how the friars could spread the gospel among the Muslims. In the Rule of 1221, Francis stressed the need for friars working in Muslim lands to live an authentic Christian witness, to proclaim the Word of God, and to be prepared for martyrdom, which occurred even during the lifetime of the saint.[474] Francis's mission to convert al-Kamil proved unsuccessful, but its potential success constitutes another one of the great "what ifs" of the history of the Crusades.

The Fall of Damietta

Eighteen months after the first Crusaders arrived at Damietta, the city fell. A group of Crusaders noticed one of the defensive towers on the wall was not manned, and they stormed it. From this foothold they were able to gain control of the wall and open the gate for the main body. The city was taken without a fight— an unexpected development—but the Crusaders soon discovered why the final assault was so easy.

Once inside the city, the Western warriors were appalled to discover corpses everywhere. Eighteen months of blockade and siege had dwindled the food supplies within Damietta to dangerous levels, resulting in the starvation of 50,000 people.[475] Oliver Paderborn described the macabre scene that greeted the Crusaders: "As we were entering [Damietta], there met us an intolerable odor, a wretched sight. The dead killed the living."[476]

News of the fall of Damietta reached al-Kamil who once again reached out to the Crusaders in an attempt to find a diplomatic solution. He offered the same terms as before, but this time sweetened the deal by promising restoral of the True Cross, captured by Saladin at the Battle of Hattin in 1187. Cardinal Pelagius once again refused.

The hindsight of history produces the analysis that "four years of Crusade had been wasted through the arrogant folly of a prince of the Church."[477] However, the situation at the time gives legitimacy to the decision of Pelagius to reject al-Kamil's second diplomatic advance. The Crusaders had just captured Damietta, without significant loss of combat strength, and the

Muslim army was not threatening offensive action. Pelagius had every reason to believe the situation was favorable to the Crusaders, dictating a militant rather than diplomatic posture.

As summer approached, the troops were idle and restless and in need of a campaign, so Pelagius ordered the army to move out in a combat operation to capture al-Kamil's stronghold of Mansourah, which was halfway between Damietta and Cairo. The army approached Mansourah and halted its advance in a precarious defensive position opposite the city and between the Nile and the al-Bahr-as-Saghir canal that linked the Nile to Lake Manzalah. The choice of encampment placed the army in a position that was surrounded by three waterways and provided a prime opportunity for an astute enemy to cut off their supply line, which is exactly the plan followed by the Muslim army. The Crusaders were faced with the dilemma of attempting a difficult advance on Mansourah separated from their line of supplies, digging in and waiting for reinforcements, or a tactical withdrawal. Since the army only had provisions for twenty days, Pelagius made the decision to withdraw to Damietta. The retreat from Mansourah placed the Crusade in jeopardy as the campaigning season came to a close, and the army's strength was not enough to launch another operation against Cairo.

The failed expedition to Mansourah had dangerously drained the effective fighting force of the Crusaders. This situation, coupled with the prospect of a long stalemate and uncertainty about when or if Frederick II's German army would arrive, forced Cardinal Pelagius to realize the only viable solution was diplomacy, so he sued for peace. Terms were reached on August 29, 1221: If the Crusaders would surrender Damietta and leave Egypt, al-Kamil offered an eight-year truce, a prisoner exchange, and a promise to return the True Cross. Pelagius agreed to the terms and the army left in September.

The failure of the Fifth Crusade was especially disheartening since it had been so close to succeeding. Unlike the failure of previous Crusades, however, which demoralized Christendom and negatively impacted the Crusading movement, the disappointment of the Fifth Crusade provided a learning experience that the Church and secular rulers took to heart. They learned "the lesson that their efforts needed to be more sharply focused in terms of logistic preparations, military organization, and religious commitments. The Fifth Crusade met military defeat for itself while securing institutional success for its cause."[478]

The Crusade of Frederick II

One of the factors that significantly contributed to the failure of the Fifth Crusade was the absence of Holy Roman Emperor Frederick II's army. Christendom and the warriors of the Fifth Crusade eagerly awaited the fulfillment of Frederick's vow, first taken in 1215. When these warriors returned home, the wait for Frederick II continued.

The son of Henry VI (d. 1197) and Constance of Sicily (d. 1198) was something of a spectacle. Described as a "polymath, intellectual, linguist, scholar, falconry expert, and politician of imagination, arrogance, ambition, and energy," Frederick had been raised as a ward of the Church after his parents died when he was four years old. Innocent III was his guardian.[479] Frederick's curious affinity for Islam and insatiable personal aspirations prompted contemporaries to refer to him as *stupor mundi*, the "wonder of the world." Indeed, his political policies, individualistic demeanor, and spurious religious convictions were ahead of their time in the medieval period. His upbringing in Sicily exposed him to Islamic culture, and he seemed to find himself more at ease in the company of Muslims than Christians. He spoke and wrote Arabic and traveled with a Muslim bodyguard.[480] After the death of his second wife, Isabella II, he instituted a harem stocked with Muslim women.

In 1221, Frederick met with his former tutor, Cencio Savelli, who had been elected pope five years before, taking the name Honorius III. He once again renewed his Crusader vow and set a departure date of the Feast of St. John the Baptist, June 24, 1225. Frederick was a "serial *crucesignati*" whose first vow was taken in

1215 during his coronation as King of the Germans at Aachen.[481] His second vow came five years later during his coronation as holy Roman emperor in Rome. His meeting with Honorius III came after the Fifth Crusade's retreat from Egypt, and he later publicly promised to go to the Holy Land in 1225 and 1227.

In the summer of 1225, as the departure date approached, Frederick was concerned by the lack of response from the German nobility. He asked Honorius to grant him another extension. The pope agreed to one final delay, but it came with stipulations. This time Frederick agreed to leave on the Feast of the Assumption, August 15, 1227, twelve years after his first Crusade vow. He also agreed to pay to maintain one thousand knights in the Holy Land for two years and provide earnest money of 100,000 ounces of gold that would be returned to him upon his arrival in Acre. Frederick acknowledged, too, that failure to keep these promises would lead to excommunication. Honorius was willing to grant leniency to Frederick due to their long-standing relationship, but his successor was not as patient with the emperor.

Pope Gregory IX

In the spring of 1227, Honorius III died and the fifty-seven-year-old Ugolino Cardinal Conti was elected as his successor, taking the name Gregory IX. He was the grandnephew of Pope Innocent III and a personal friend and supporter of Francis of Assisi. Gregory was a canon lawyer, Scripture scholar, and diplomat who reigned for fourteen years as "one of the greatest popes in the history of the Church, though curiously neglected by posterity (particularly post-medieval posterity)."[482]

Like his great uncle, Gregory IX was intensely supportive of the Crusading movement. While a cardinal in Italy he spent time preaching the Fifth Crusade, viewing the Crusades as a "unique instrument of ecclesiastical and specifically papal authority with wide application."[483] Consequently, he did not have the patience to wait for a preeminent Crusader like Frederick

II to delay fulfillment of his vow, a point he mentioned to the emperor in his first letter to him. Their relationship was stormy and bitter and has been described as "one of the most dramatic stories of all time."[484]

The "Crusader without Faith"[485]

As Frederick II made preparations to embark on his journey to Outrémer, al-Kamil sent an envoy, Emir Fakhr al-Din, to the emperor in 1226 bearing rich gifts. Al-Din was tasked by al-Kamil to offer Frederick a peace treaty that included relinquishing Jerusalem in exchange for Frederick's military aid in the war against al-Kamil's brother in Damascus.

Frederick needed time to consider the offer, so he sent al-Din back to al-Kamil with a noncommittal reply. While the negotiations were ongoing, Frederick and his army made preparations for their promised departure in August of 1227. Frederick planned his campaign to be limited in scope. The army was not large and the focus of the expedition had more to do with asserting Frederick's royal and imperial rights by exploiting the diplomatic opportunity presented by al-Kamil while at the same time fulfilling his political obligations to the papacy.[486]

As the troops assembled in Brindisi, the heat of the summer and squalid conditions in the camp produced a disease that ravaged the Crusader force. Many warriors died, including the husband of St. Elizabeth of Hungary, Louis IV of Thuringia.

Frederick arrived in the camp and was dismayed by the outbreak of the illness, yet he finalized preparations to depart. After setting sail on the Nativity of the Blessed Virgin Mary, September 8, 1227, the emperor and his retinue soon became ill. The fleet was directed to stop at Otranto on the Adriatic only fifty-four miles away. There the sick emperor decided to cancel his journey to Outrémer.

But, as with Philip II Augustus during the Third Crusade, illness was not an acceptable reason for failure to fulfill one's Crusade vow. This latest failure of Frederick II to fulfill his vow, now twelve years old, prompted Pope Gregory IX to issue the promised excommunication.

Frederick was undeterred by the ecclesiastical censure, and made preparations to travel east once healthy. Gregory IX then used the excommunication to engage in an armed contest to wrest control of Frederick's Italian land holdings. The situation was a "remarkable spectacle" wherein Christendom witnessed "an excommunicated Crusader sailing to restore Jerusalem, while the pope was organizing armies, one of which was led by the former king of Jerusalem [John of Brienne], to secure the Crusader's political overthrow in the west."[487]

In June of 1228 the excommunicated emperor left Italy despite the warnings of Pope Gregory IX. The "Crusader without faith" arrived in the Holy Land in September. Technically, this journey was not a Crusade since one who was excommunicated was not allowed to participate in Crusading but, true to form, Frederick II did not care what others imposed upon him.

Once in Outrémer, Frederick II was in a difficult situation. He insisted on taking the throne of the kingdom although he was only regent for his son Conrad, and al-Kamil's previous offer, although still on the table, was less palatable to the Muslim ruler since his brother, al-Mu 'azzam, the ruler of Damascus, had died in November 1227. Al-Kamil's need for Frederick had ceased, but the presence of Frederick in the Holy Land led both men to find a face-saving arrangement. Al-Kamil needed to settle with Frederick in order to free up his forces for use elsewhere, but he could not look weak in fulfilling his promises. Appearing to surrender to an inferior foe would place al-Kamil in a perilous political situation. The excommunicated emperor could not return west empty-handed, and he needed to avoid the appearance of being a supplicant to al-Kamil. The precarious position of both men provided for a delicate political process that Freidank, a poet and member of Frederick's army described as "watching two misers trying to divide evenly three gold pieces."[488]

On February 8, 1229, Fredrick and al-Kamil agreed to the division of the "gold pieces" and entered into the compromise

Treaty of Jaffa. The ten year truce called for the return of warriors from the Fifth Crusade languishing in Muslim prisons and gave Frederick the Holy City in exchange for Frederick's military aid to al-Kamil. Frederick agreed to not support any Christian war against al-Kamil, and even to assist him should Christian forces break the treaty. Jerusalem was recognized as a holy city for both faiths, though Christians were given control of most of it. The temple area, including the Dome of the Rock and the al-Aqsa mosque, remained in Muslim control, although Christians were allowed access. Bethlehem and Nazareth were also given to Frederick so that all the major Christian holy cities were once more in the hands of the followers of Christ.

The treaty was remarkable in its extent and in terms of how little it cost the emperor. As during the Fifth Crusade, al-Kamil proved himself to be generous in diplomacy. Jerusalem would remain in Christian control the next fifteen years. Frederick's unofficial Crusade had reaped significant dividends.

Now that Jerusalem was in his control, Frederick decided to travel to the Holy City to claim the throne of the kingdom. He arrived on March 17, 1229 and toured the holy sites in the company of local Muslim authorities, displaying his disdain for the Catholic Faith when he said he had come to Jerusalem "to hear the Muslims, at the hour of prayer, call upon Allah by night."[489]

This shocking admission was overshadowed by an even more outrageous comment to Fakhr al-Din concerning his reasons for negotiating for control of Jerusalem: "If I had not been afraid of losing my prestige in the eyes of the Franks, I would have never made the sultan yield up Jerusalem."[490] Perhaps the statement can be viewed as diplomatic small talk, but given Frederick's affinity for Islam and conflict with the Church, the comment provides insight into the man and validates the charge that he was the "Crusader without faith."

On March 18, 1229, Frederick entered the Church of the Holy Sepulchre for his coronation as king of Jerusalem. If not for his excommunication, this act would have fulfilled his Crusader vow. Because of his ecclesiastical censure, however, the crowd was sparse and no representative of the Church was present, so the emperor crowned himself king. In a sign he knew his actions were inappropriate, Frederick had Hermann von Salza read a statement justifying his actions and attacking his critics while the ceremony proceeded.[491]

Two days later, his "Crusade" complete with the accomplishment of his personal political goals, Emperor Frederick II returned to Acre where he stayed for the next several months until leaving for home on May 1, 1229. His departure was less than regal as recorded by the chronicler of the *Gestes des Chyprois*:

> His departure was a shabby affair. The emperor made the preparations for his passage in secret, and on the first day of May, without telling anyone, he set out before dawn, going through the butcher's quarter to reach his galley. Now, it came about that the butchers in these streets ran after him and pelted him shamefully with tripe and entrails. And in this way the emperor left Acre, hated, accursed, and reviled.[492]

Frederick's adventure in the Holy Land was a strange one. The sight of an excommunicated emperor going on Crusade, negotiating with a Muslim sultan for control of the Holy City and crowning himself king of Jerusalem was most assuredly one of the greatest spectacles of the medieval period. Yet despite his unorthodox behavior and methods, Frederick II's journey to Outrémer proved oddly successful, for "what Richard I had failed to win by force and the Fifth Crusade had rejected as unworthy or unworkable, Frederick achieved through dogged negotiation . . . The three holiest sites, Jerusalem, Bethlehem, and Nazareth, were restored to Christian hands."[493]

The excommunicated holy Roman emperor's expedition to the Holy Land indeed resulted in the return of Jerusalem to Christian control—but only for a decade. The Egyptian ruler, al-Salih Ayyub, the great-nephew of Saladin, desired to conquer Palestine to restore Saladin's empire and bring unity among the Muslim people. For help, he hired Khwarazmians, a Muslim people who in the 1220s had been driven from their lands in modern-day Iran by the arrival of the Mongols from the Asian steppe. Al-Salih Ayyub sent his new mercenary army to attack Jerusalem on August 23, 1244. The Khwarazmians captured the city, killed significant numbers of Christians, and desecrated the holy places. The loss of Jerusalem prompted the calling of another Crusade and motivated the king of France to take the cross.

8

The End of the Crusader States

If we are conquered, we shall be martyrs; if we triumph,
the glory of God and of France, and of all Christendom will be
exalted. This is God's cause; we shall conquer for Christ's sake.
He will triumph in us; he will give the glory, the honor,
the blessing, not to us, but to his name.

King St. Louis IX[494]

God is pleased! The Kingdom of the Cross has perished.

Abu'l-Tana[495]

The king was sick and near death. One attendant even believed
he had already died and moved to cover his body with the bed
sheet but was stopped by another nurse who "said he still had
his soul in his body." The king heard their debate and, although
previously mute, requested they bring him the cross—for he was
going on the Crusade.[496]

The Saintly King of the Franks

It was a bold and risky decision. Some believed the vow was not
binding since the king had taken it while ill and that impaired
his judgment. Yet when he had indeed recovered from illness,
in December 1244 the king took the cross again in a dramatic
manner by ripping the previously sewn cross from his garment
and handing it to the bishop of Paris. He then ordered the prel-
ate to give it back to him "so that no one can keep saying that he
took it without knowing what he was doing."[497]

The king's insistence on taking the cross and journeying to the Holy Land was an outgrowth of his deep faith and love for Christ. He yearned to see Jerusalem under Christian control once more. His desire was so great that he was prepared to risk his personal and royal fortunes on the expedition. He was sovereign of the wealthiest region in all Christendom and the king of the most populous Christian country.[498] There was much to lose by going on Crusade, but the "perfect Crusader," King St. Louis IX, knew that the eternal reward greatly outweighed the temporal risk.[499]

The thirteenth century was the "century of St. Louis," as no man more exemplified the tenor of the age than the saintly king of the Franks.[500] Louis was blond, slender, handsome, gentle though firm, decisive in policy and generous in charity. He was a devout and dutiful son and a loving husband and father. Along with Holy Roman Emperor Frederick II, Louis was the most important political figure of the thirteenth century and the central figure in Christendom.[501]

Those two men could not have been more opposite in all aspects of their lives. Frederick was the "Crusader without faith" whereas Louis was the "perfect Crusader." One man seemed to eschew all religious faith whereas the other embraced it and was declared a saint of the Church. Frederick kept a harem of Muslim women whereas, uncharacteristic of the age for monarchy, Louis was a monogamous husband. The two men can be easily distinguished by their ultimate dreams in life: "Frederick II thinking only of his imperial dream and Louis IX of his eschatological dream."[502] Louis was a product of his times but he also shaped the era in which he lived and his influence (and intercession) continues to the modern world. There was perhaps no greater king in the history of France. He governed his realm peacefully and justly for forty-four years and followed three principles as monarch: devotion to God, self-discipline, and affection for his people.

Louis's Family

The saint was born on April 25, 1214 at Poissy on the Feast of St.

Mark the Evangelist. His later biographer and personal friend, John of Joinville, who lived to the advanced age of ninety-three and wrote his life of Saint Louis thirty years after the king's death, noted the significance of Louis's birth, the celebrations performed on the Feast of St. Mark, and his two Crusades:

> On this day, people carry the cross in processions in many places, and in France they are called black crosses. So, this was like a prophecy of the great multitude of people who died on these two Crusades, the one in Egypt and the other when he died at Carthage for there was much great mourning over these in this world and many great joys that arise from them in heaven for those who died as true Crusaders on these two great pilgrimages.[503]

Louis was close to his brothers and sister. Robert, his most beloved brother, was only two years younger and they were constant companions.[504] He accompanied Louis on his first Crusade to Egypt and was killed in a battle with Muslim forces. Alphonse was born in 1220 and accompanied his saintly brother on both Crusades, dying on the return trip from Tunis in 1271. The youngest brother, Charles, became king of Naples and Sicily and died in 1285. Although he was close to his brothers, it was Louis's sister, Isabelle, who was most similar to the king. From her youth Isabelle was a deeply pious woman who took a vow of chastity and refused to marry Conrad, the son of Frederick II. Instead, "she lived at court, dressed modestly, and practiced exercises of remarkable piety."[505] Eventually, Louis built a convent for a group of Poor Clares in 1259, to which Isabelle retired in 1263. His devout sister never took the habit but lived a holy life as a laywoman. She died in 1269, right before Louis's departure on his second Crusade. Her sanctity of life was recognized by the Church centuries after her death and she is known as St. Isabelle of France.[506]

In spring of 1234, the twenty-three year old king married thirteen-year-old Marguerite of Provence. Their marriage was fruitful: Eleven children were born to the royal couple, the first in 1240. Louis was the ancestor of all subsequent kings of France, a fact recalled by the priest on the scaffold with Louis XVI in 1793 when he called the condemned monarch "a son of St. Louis."[507]

A Life of Faith

Even in an age of faith, the king's personal piety and sanctity stood out. He was concerned for his own salvation but even more so for the salvation of his subjects, which he considered "his highest duty."[508]

His personal piety involved wearing simple clothing, especially after his return from the Crusade, and a regimented prayer life. Louis awoke each night at midnight to participate with his royal chaplains in the Liturgy of the Hours and said fifty "Hail Mary's" each evening, kneeling and standing for each prayer.[509] Louis's prayer life was augmented by penitential practices including fasting, the wearing of a hair shirt, and the special personal practice of not laughing on Fridays. The king greatly enjoyed life and joking so the mortification of not laughing one day a week was a serious and difficult penance.[510] Louis recognized the need for grace to refrain from sin as well as the need to beg the Lord's mercy for committed sins, so he went to confession weekly and maintained both a daytime and nighttime confessor in order to receive the sacrament when needed.[511]

The First Crusade of King St. Louis IX[512]

Within two months of Louis's taking the cross in December 1244, Pope Innocent IV authorized Odo of Châteauroux to preach the Crusade in France. While Odo preached the Crusade and recruited warriors to join the king, Louis began the massive material preparations required. He entered into agreements with the Italian cities of Genoa and Venice to provide transports for his army while royal agents spent the following two years stockpiling food and supplies, especially in Cyprus.[513]

Continuing the practice of First Crusade warriors, King St. Louis IX prepared himself spiritually for his armed pilgrimage to the Holy Land. However, because he was king, he extended these practices to encompass his entire kingdom. In 1247 he appointed royal investigators to inquire throughout the realm about complaints against royal officials in order to settle any grievances before he left on the Crusade. He entrusted this task to mendicant friars whose duty was "to draw up a list of all the injustices committed by the agents of the king or in the name of the king in order to wipe them out and satisfy any royal subjects who had been wronged."[514]

Crusading was expensive, and financing the expedition was borne mostly by the king. Louis heavily subsidized his fellow Crusaders, including his later biographer, John of Joinville. Joinville's experience was typical and provides a picture of how important the king's financial contributions were to the campaign. Joinville took the cross for Louis's expedition, receiving the pilgrim staff from the Cistercians, and made his spiritual preparation by walking barefoot as a penitent touring local shrines before his departure.[515] He initially refused to swear fealty to the king, since he was not originally his vassal, and decided to travel independently to Outrémer. In order to finance his Crusade he heavily mortgaged his lands, but his funds were not enough and he ran out of money while in Cyprus. Desperate, he reached out to the king and entered into royal service upon which the king granted him 800 *livres tournois (l.t.)*. Louis's total expenditures on the Crusade would amount to 1.5 million *l.t.* or six times the annual royal income.[516]

The king left Paris on June 12, 1248 after receiving the insignia of a pilgrim and the oriflamme at St. Denis. Louis went as a penitent to the cathedral of Notre Dame, where he participated in Mass, and then walked barefoot to the abbey of St. Antoine-des-Champs. Recognizing the penitential nature of the Crusade and his desire to engage fully in the spiritual opportunities afforded from such a journey, the king changed his appearance. He eschewed rich and costly clothing and accouterments and dressed instead as a humble and simple penitent throughout the expedition.[517]

The king traveled from Paris to Lyons where he met with Pope Innocent IV, and then made way to Aigues Mortes, which was a man-made port in royal territory. Louis thus became the first French king to leave for the Crusade from his own soil.[518] His fleet departed on August 25, 1248 and sailed for Cyprus. They spent the winter on the island, and the delay, although understandable, "devoured supplies, sapped morale, and gave the Egyptians time to prepare their defenses."[519] The army left the island on May 30, 1249 en route to Egypt. Louis had decided to re-enact the Fifth Crusade and liberate Egypt in order to use it as a base of operations from which to liberate the Holy City.

Egypt

The French fleet arrived at Damietta on June 4, 1249 and once more the Muslim garrison prepared to fight Crusaders. The next morning the Crusaders undertook an amphibious landing with Louis in the lead. When warriors waded to shore the Muslim garrison commander, Fakhr al-Din, saw the strength of the Crusader army and decided to withdraw from the city to the sultan's camp several miles away.

The city, now emptied of its defenders, was soon occupied by the French Crusaders in a surprisingly easy undertaking, which was the opposite of the siege during the Fifth Crusade. Indeed, "Damietta had fallen in hours instead of the seventeen months it had taken in 1218–19."[520] Louis found stockpiles of food, equipment, and material that the Muslims left behind in their hasty retreat. The king decided to spend the summer in Damietta while waiting for his brother Alphonse and other Crusaders to arrive. As winter approached, Louis thought an attack on Cairo would give the Christians complete control of Egypt and finish the task left undone by the Fifth Crusade, so he gave the command to march there in late November 1249. He left a garrison and his five-months-pregnant queen in Damietta and ordered the fleet to shadow the army's movement offshore.

One of the main reasons for the eventual failure of Louis's expedition was the inability to learn from the mistakes of the Fifth

Crusade. Louis inadvertently made the exact same mistakes, one of which was the failure to build supply depots along the route to Cairo before the main army left Damietta.

The slow-moving Crusader army finally reached the outskirts of Mansourah in late December. Louis quickly ordered his troops to dig in and fortify their position. In order to capture Mansourah, the Crusaders needed to cross the Bahr as-Saghir river, but Muslim forces prevented them from building a causeway. After receiving intelligence about a ford upriver that offered an opportunity to surprise and outflank the Muslims guarding the town, Louis developed a carefully coordinated plan. It centered on an advance element under the command of his brother, Robert of Artois, capturing the ford during a surprise night attack and, once it was secured, awaiting the crossing of the main army before advancing on the town.

The Attack

The surprise attack on the ford occurred on February 7, 1250. It was successful but, in a fateful decision that ultimately doomed the entire Crusade, Robert failed to abide by the plan and instead advanced on the Muslim army camp without Louis and the main army.

Robert's initial attack on Fakhr al-Din's field camp was effective. The Crusaders easily surprised and overwhelmed the Muslim force. The surprise was so complete that Fakhr al-Din was killed during his morning washings, unable to defend himself from the onslaught of the Christian warriors.[521]

Some of the Muslim troops ran in haste to the safety of Mansourah, and Robert, flush with his stunning victory, pursued them in further violation of his orders. Robert's unit advanced into Mansourah, where the majority of the Muslim troops were quartered. The hasty decision led to his death and the slaughter of his 300 knights, most of whom were killed by defenders throwing blocks of wood from the windows of city houses.[522] It was a risky action undertaken in the heat of battle by a warrior raised and trained from an early age to ignore personal risk and seek glory and honor on the battlefield.

Louis was deeply grieved at the news of his brother's death and regarded it as martyrdom. Upon his later return from the Crusade, Louis petitioned the papacy to recognize his fallen brother as a martyr but the pope refused the request.[523] Louis's reaction was in keeping with most Crusade veterans who consistently believed their fallen comrades should be regarded as martyrs, but the Church never identified the dead warriors as such. Although they fought for Christ and his patrimony, their deaths in combat (or from disease and starvation) were not the result of persecution for the Faith.

The main body of the Crusade army crossed the river while Robert was engaged in his folly and, after his death, the Muslim army counter-attacked. The fighting was intense and lasted all day as hand-to-hand melees broke out across the battlefield. Joinville also recorded the intensity of the combat as he was hit by five arrows and his horse by fifteen during the struggle.[524] The Crusaders were finally victorious as the Muslim forces retreated into the town, but the victory was costly, It would also prove to be "the prelude to catastrophe."[525]

Time to Retreat

Although Louis's personal bravery during his Egyptian campaign cannot be questioned, his military strategy was deficient, and the discipline of his army (or at least that of his brother) proved an Achilles heel. His brother's rash advance resulted in high casualties, and now Louis did not have enough troops to attack Mansourah—let alone Cairo. He was faced with a critical decision: stay and try to press the attack or retreat immediately to Damietta to regroup and refit.

Unfortunately, the king proved the leadership axiom that a bad leader is not someone who makes bad decisions, but someone who makes no decisions. He opted to hold the army in place in an untenable tactical location surrounded by water in a virtual cul-de-sac. The Crusaders remained for almost two months from February 11 to April 5, their food supplies dwindling to a critical level and the Muslim forces gathering strength. The Egyptians knew the supply line to the Crusader army was the key to victory, so they attacked and captured relief convoys.

The situation became unbearable as disease, particularly scurvy and dysentery, broke out among the Crusaders, further weakening their military effectiveness. Even the king was afflicted to the point where the back of his trousers was cut open to deal with the nasty effects of dysentery.[526]

The king gave the order for a general retreat on April 5 and the army began the slow return march to Damietta. They never made it. "Hampered by enemy forces, illness, hunger, fatigue, difficult terrain, and collapsing morale, the shattered army on land, shadowed by a rag-bag navy increasingly vulnerable to enemy shipping on the Nile, effectively disintegrated."[527] The next day Louis sued for peace.

The Muslim army surrounded the pitiable Crusader host and immediately executed all the sick, wounded, and poor Crusaders. Louis and the French nobility were captured and sent to the prisons of Mansourah. The sultan of Egypt, Turan Shah, giddy at the capture of the noble French king, further humiliated him by sending his captured royal cloak to Damascus where it was paraded through the city as a war trophy.[528]

Having thus gloated, Turan Shah now needed to assess the reality of the situation. He was faced with the same decision as his grandfather al-Kamil was during the Fifth Crusade. The Crusader field army was defeated but the city of Damietta was still in Christian hands. Should he undertake a costly siege to recapture the city or find a diplomatic settlement?

He chose the latter and entered into detailed negotiations with the imprisoned king. After a few weeks, they reached a deal. Louis agreed to return Damietta and to pay 800,000 bezants , or more than three times the annual royal income, for his freedom. Turan Shah agreed to release the king after payment of half the ransom with the stipulation Louis remain onboard ship off the coast of Damietta until the second half was paid. Queen Marguerite worked tirelessly to collect the required funding and, after delivery of the 400,000 bezants, Louis was released.

His captivity had lasted a month during which time his captors tried to convince him to renounce his faith and embrace Islam. The saintly king had refused, telling his captors "You can very well kill my body, but you will never have my soul."[529] The king also maintained his honesty and integrity despite the harsh conditions and the humiliation of defeat. Despite his verbal agreement to remain on ship off the coast of Damietta until the second half of the ransom, his barons tried to convince him to leave without paying the second half; he steadfastly refused.[530] Once safely back among his remaining army, Louis learned the initial ransom payment was left purposefully short by 10,000 pounds. He was furious at the deception and immediately ordered it paid to Turan Shah.[531]

Ruling the Kingdom of Jerusalem

Upon his release from prison, Louis discussed his plans with his nobles. The king was determined to stay in the Holy Land but allowed those who wanted to leave to do so. Louis wrote a letter to his subjects explaining why he was remaining in Outrémer for an unspecified time. He told them he was staying in order that "something good, the deliverance of the captives, the preservation of the castles and fortresses of the Kingdom of Jerusalem, and [of obtaining] other advantages for Christendom" would result.[532] He urged his subjects to take the cross and journey to the Holy Land to join him in these endeavors.

The king of Jerusalem was Conrad II (IV of Germany), the son of Frederick II, but he lived in Europe and so the kingdom suffered from an absent monarch. Louis filled the vacuum by taking command of the Christian areas in the kingdom. Although he had no legal authority to act as the king, he had a *gravitas* that was recognized and welcomed by the Christians of Outrémer.

The saintly king spent his time building up the kingdom's coastal city defenses, feeling duty-bound to provide as best he could for the needs of the local Christians. During his stay Louis received a letter from the sultan in Damascus offering him safe conduct to visit the Holy City as a pilgrim. Louis wanted to go but knew he could not. Instead he followed Richard the Lion-Hearted's lead and refused to set foot in Jerusalem while it was still occupied. He understood that "he must renounce seeing Jerusalem in order to sustain the will and the hope of holding it and possessing it."[533]

Louis's presence in the Holy Land for six years had been a pivotal time in the history of the Kingdom of Jerusalem, during which he "restored . . . cohesion, unity, and the idea of a state" to the Christian inhabitants of Christ's patrimony. However, the time was at hand to return to his beloved France.[534]

The Return to France

In the spring of 1253, Louis received news that his mother, Blanche, had died on November 27, 1252. The news prompted Louis to make arrangements to leave Outrémer and return home. Despite the king's preparations and best intentions, his first Crusade had been a catastrophe, resulting in his brother's death and his own imprisonment. He repeated the mistakes of the Fifth Crusade by failing to secure his rear areas and supply lines, made poor tactical decisions, and commanded an ill-disciplined army that collapsed when his brother foolishly charged into the town of Mansourah unsupported. Louis's Crusading career was not over but it would take another fifteen years for the king to ride once more unto the breach.

Baybars the Merciless

In the fall of 1260, a large Mongol army under the command of Kitbogha left Damascus on a campaign to conquer Egypt. The Egyptians responded with an army commanded by a general named Baybars. The forces met at Ain Jalut in Galilee on September 3, where the Mongols were decimated in a decisive victory for

Baybars and the Egyptians. The battle marked the first time the Mongols were overwhelmingly defeated on the battlefield.

Baybars, a blue-eyed Russian Turk, was a "savage and treacherous wild beast but a soldier of genius and an incomparable administrator."[535] After his victory the Mamluk warrior installed himself as sultan of Egypt and Damascus and effectively reestablished Saladin's empire. He was a great warrior, better than Saladin, and the scourge of Christians in Outrémer, primarily because he was a man with "a complete absence of scruples."[536] Baybars began a campaign of *jihad* to eradicate the Christians in the Holy Land, providing a "means to consolidate his power as well as establish his credentials as a worthy Islamic ruler."[537]

Baybars engaged in a scorched-earth policy to compel the elimination of the Christian presence from Outrémer. He ordered the destruction of all captured Christian cities in order to prevent their liberation and resettlement. His preferred methods in dealing with Christian populations were massacre and enslavement. The campaign was swift and deadly, and the prospect that the entire Kingdom of Jerusalem could fall into the Mamluk's hands looked promising.

Urgent appeals were sent to Europe for another major Crusade. Meanwhile, Baybars sacked Jaffa in 1268 and, in the spring of 1271, captured the previously impregnable fortress of Krak des Chevaliers, the Hospitaller stronghold that not even Saladin had been able to conquer. Panic reached a heightened state after the merciless Baybars sacked the city of Antioch after a four-day siege. His troops killed every Christian in the city, including all the women and children. It was the single greatest massacre in Crusading history. Baybars ensured the remembrance of the massacre by sending a description of it to the absent ruler of Antioch, Bohemond VI:

> You would have seen the crosses in your churches smashed, the pages of the false Testaments scattered, the patriarch's tombs overturned. You would have seen your Muslim enemy trampling on the place where you celebrate the Mass, cutting

the throats of monks, priests and deacons upon the altars . . . You would have seen fire running through your palaces, your dead burned in this world before going down to the fires of the next.[538]

The ancient Christian city would never be recovered. The Principality of Antioch, established after the First Crusade, 170 years previously, was no more. The scourge of Baybars the Merciless demanded a response, and once more the saintly Crusader of France took up the cross.

The Second Crusade of King St. Louis IX

News of Baybars's raids and destruction of Christian territory in Outrémer and the unfinished business of his first Crusade prompted Louis to take the cross on the Feast of the Annunciation, March 25, 1267. The decision was somewhat of a surprise, as Louis was now in his fifties. He left Aigues Mortes on July 2, 1270 with a similar sized army as in his first Crusade: 325 knights and between 10,000 to 15,000 infantry.[539] After his departure Louis announced that his initial objective was Tunis on the African coast opposite Sicily.

Through the centuries historians have tried to answer why Louis chose Tunis as the object of the Crusade. Some authors have argued that he was motivated by political reasons, since conquest of Tunis would help his brother Charles I, king of Sicily. Others have written that Louis believed Tunis was an ally of Egypt and would provide a secure base of operations for the Crusaders to attack Egypt, a long-time objective of Crusade armies.

These speculations derive from those living centuries after the king and are inadequate. The contemporary confessor of Louis, Geoffrey of Beaulieu, provides a better explanation and one in keeping with the saintly Crusader's spiritual emphasis. He indicated that Louis desired to convert the Muslim ruler of Tunis, who had said he would embrace the gospel if a strong Christian army came to his realm.[540] A Tunisian embassy who

visited Louis's court in 1269 before the king's departure may
have influenced his decision. There was also a very good logistical reason for choosing Tunis, as every Crusader fleet needed a
muster port before sailing on to the Holy Land. Embarkation
to Outrémer usually occurred in late summer or early fall and
every Crusade army since the Second Crusade wintered over
somewhere. Louis had previously used Cyprus as his staging area
before sailing on to Damietta but "Tunis was within easier and
safer sailing distance than Cyprus."[541] A combination of evangelization and logistics, therefore, motivated Louis's decision to
attack Tunis in the summer of 1270.

The Death of the King

Louis spent two weeks at Tunis before advancing to Carthage
in order to await the army of his brother, Charles I, en route
from Sicily. Unfortunately, the wait at Carthage proved fatal.
The "high summer, poor diet, and water contaminated by the
immobile army soon stoked the outbreak of virulent disease,
probably typhus or dysentery."[542] The Crusaders began to die.
Louis's son, Jean Tristan, born at Damietta in 1250 during Louis's first Crusade, died, followed soon thereafter by the papal
legate. Then the saintly Crusader became sick and bedridden.
After a month of sickness, the king finally succumbed and died
on August 25, 1270 at the age of fifty-six. He died at the hour of
mercy while lying on a bed of ashes mouthing the words, "Jerusalem, Jerusalem."[543] St. Louis was the last monarch of Europe to
go on Crusade to the Holy Land and even with his dying breath
his last thought was the liberation of the Holy City; he was truly
the "perfect Crusader."

A few hours after Louis's death, his brother Charles of Anjou
arrived at Carthage with his army. The next few months witnessed minor skirmishing between the Crusader and Muslim
forces that ended when Charles negotiated a peace with the emir
of Tunis in November that included an allowance for Christian
evangelization and worship in lands controlled by the emir.

Charles's return trip to France was marked by disaster and death. On November 15–16, the French fleet struck a storm that destroyed forty ships, including eighteen large transports. Thousands of souls were lost.[544] The survivors reached land and began the march home but by then "it was not an army but a funeral procession which returned to France" as Crusaders continued to die, including Isabelle of Aragon, the wife of Louis's son Philip III.[545] The pregnant Isabelle fell off her horse while crossing a river, which induced premature labor and resulted in a stillbirth.[546] Saint Louis's brother, Alfonso of Poitiers and his wife, Jeanne, also died in Italy on the way home from the Crusade.

Louis's second Crusade was a costly endeavor with little temporal gain. Pope Boniface VIII, whose relationship with Louis IX's grandson Philip IV "the Fair" was notoriously bad, canonized the saintly Crusader on August 11, 1297, twenty-seven years after his death on his second Crusade in the desert of North Africa.

The End of the Crusader States

As the thirteenth century came to a close, Christian territory in Outrémer occupied only a very narrow coastal strip. The area was, however, extremely fertile and rich. The annual revenue of Acre, the major Christian port in the Holy Land, was more than that of the English king. The material wealth of the kingdom and its role in the Holy Land economy gave the Christians there a false sense of security, as they believed their economic importance provided a defense against Muslim attack. There was not much else the Christians could depend on, as their own military forces were woefully inadequate. Their military strategy centered on diplomacy with their Muslim neighbors and Western assistance in times of crisis. After the fall of Tripoli in 1289, King Henry II of Jerusalem entered into a ten year truce with the Mamluk sultan of Egypt, al-Mansur Qalawun. Henry hoped the truce would safeguard the remaining Christian cities and avoid the fate of Tripoli. His hope proved futile.

In the summer of 1290, Muslim merchants from Damascus arrived in Acre and were attacked by Christians. No one is exactly certain why the merchants were attacked. Some believe drunken revelers from a party lost control and set upon the Muslims. Others said a local Christian discovered his wife in bed with one of the Muslim merchants and killed him.[547] Regardless of the reason, the killings gave Qalawun an excuse to break the treaty and launch an attack on the major Christian city.

In early November the Mamluk army left Egypt bent on the conquest of Acre. Six days into the march, Sultan Qalawun died. He was replaced by al-Ashraf Khalil, who also ordered Syrian forces to mobilize and join the Egyptians at Acre. The Christians were soon to be descended upon by a large, united Muslim force.

Khalil set a muster date of March of 1291 for the combined army and initiated a campaign aimed at raising enthusiasm for the *jihad* against the Christians. A week before the main army set out, the Qur'an was recited publicly in Cairo and a call went out for general volunteers, who would be used as cannon fodder, to join the army.[548] Baybars al-Mansuri, the emir of Karak, best expressed the mood within the Muslim community when he wrote, "My soul had a strong desire for *jihad*, a desire for it like the earth thirsts for delivering rain."[549]

In order to stem an attack on the city, Acre sent the ambassadors Philip Mainboeuf, an Arabic scholar, Bartholomew Pizan, a Templar knight, and George, a Hospitaller secretary, to Khalil. He refused to see them. Instead, he had them arrested and put in prison, where they later died.[550]

Nothing could convince Khalil to change his mind. He was determined to wrestle control of Acre away from the Christians. It was a holy city in the eyes of Islam and the time had come for its conquest through *jihad*.[551]

Amalric, the brother of King Henry II, was deeply concerned. In charge of the defenses of Acre, he knew there were not enough men to combat the massive Muslim army bearing down on the city. There was some comfort in the fact that the

Templars, Hospitallers, and Teutonic Knights augmented his forces, and each order had sent summons to Europe for all available men to make haste to Acre. All three grand masters of the military religious orders were already present.

Those who could afford it began to leave the city for Cyprus. As the calendar turned to 1291, Christian forces from other towns were pulled to defend Acre. Despite this extreme measure the Christians were vastly outnumbered. The combined Muslim forces included 160,000 infantry and 60,000 cavalry; a force that quadrupled the population of Acre.[552] Christian forces numbered only 15,000 with 1,000 knights, 14,000 foot soldiers and a contingent of crossbowmen first provided to the city by King Louis during his sojourn in Outrémer.

The disparity in numbers influenced Christian strategy. "Their only realistic chance of survival lay in disrupting the Muslims by inflicting unexpected or unacceptable casualties."[553]

The Last Stand

Khalil's army arrived at Acre in early April 1291. The sultan knew he had superior numbers but he also knew that fact alone would not ensure victory. Acre was a well-fortified city, with double walls that would need to be breached. Situated with its back to the sea, the city afforded a limited landward position for maneuver. Khalil had no fleet and could not command the sea, so he was forced to concentrate all his forces on a smaller area, which limited the numbers of troops he could commit to battle at any one time. Access to the sea kept the defenders supplied and provided a gateway for reinforcements as well as an escape plan for those who could get on ships. Khalil knew success demanded the destruction of the walls, or at least a part of them, so he planned a massive artillery bombardment of the city. The siege of Acre was to "be a contest of throwing machines."[554]

The Muslims brought more than a hundred siege engines to the contest. This included one particularly massive engine that had been captured at Krak des Chevaliers in 1271 by Baybars.

It took a hundred carts and thirty days to travel the 125 miles to Acre.[555] The number of machines was astounding, and unprecedented in Muslim military history.[556] The Templar of Tyre recorded that several of the siege engines were given names and he noted their dispositions during the battle:

> One of these engines was called Ghadban, that is to say Furious, and it was set up in front of the Templars' section. Another which shot at the Pisans' section was called al-Mansuri, that is to say Victory. Yet another, very large, whose name I do not know, shot at the Hospitallers' section, and a fourth engine shot at the great tower called the Accursed Tower.[557]

The first week of the siege saw limited skirmishing as each side tested the strengths of the other. The Master of the Templars, William of Beaujeu, led a surprise raid on April 15 with both regular and Templar knights. The raid began promisingly, catching the Muslims completely unawares, but then disaster struck, as described by the Templar of Tyre:

> [B]oth brother and secular knights went so far in amongst the tents that their horses got their legs tangled in the tent ropes and went sprawling, whereupon the Saracens slew them. In this way we lost eighteen horsemen that night . . . though they did capture a number of Saracen shields.[558]

One unfortunate knight fell into the emir's latrine, where he was killed.[559]

The Christians launched additional raids from April 18–20 but they did not achieve any lasting success. Eventually the raids stopped as the defenders became concerned about the number of troops available for wall defense. In early May, the Christians received a huge morale boost as King Henry II arrived in forty ships with 100 knights and 2,000 infantry from Cyprus.[560] He assumed command of the defense and quickly surmised the situation was militarily hopeless.

Henry decided to seek a diplomatic solution and sent envoys to Khalil on May 7. If the envoys had hopes of striking a negotiated settlement, these were quickly dashed as Khalil greeted them with a question: "Have you brought me the keys of the city?"[561] Despite the cold reception, the envoys pressed forward with the negotiation and managed to get Khalil to agree to let everyone in the city live if the king surrendered.

The envoys needed to receive the king's consent before they finalized the deal. As they were leaving the sultan's tent, a huge catapult stone from the city crashed near it. Khalil was furious the Christians would continue to fire on his army with their envoys present in the camp and he threatened to kill them. He relented and allowed them to go but he reneged on the deal. Acre would either hold or be destroyed.

The End of Acre

Two weeks after King Henry's arrival, Khalil launched the final assault on the city. It began with a thunderous barrage of noise from 300 camel-mounted drummers.[562] After more than a month of bombardment, the Muslims finally breached the walls and entered the city. The chronicle of the Templar of Tyre captured the scene of the Muslim army pouring in:

> In front came men carrying tall shields, and after them came men who threw Greek fire, and after them came men who hurled javelins and shot feathered arrows . . . At this the Saracens . . . took two routes, since they were between the two walls of the city . . . Some of them entered by a gate of that great tower called the Accursed Tower, and moved toward San Romano where the Pisans had their great engines. The others kept to the (main) road, going to St. Anthony's Gate.[563]

All remaining women and children fled to the harbor to board escape ships. Meanwhile, the Hospitallers, Teutonic Knights, and Templars continued the battle within the city. The fighting was intense, and casualties, both military and civilian, were high.

Eventually Christian resistance collapsed, and Muslim warriors rampaged through the city slaughtering everyone in their way. Jean de Villiers, the grand master of the Hospitallers, was gravely wounded from a spear that struck his back and he was carried from the scene by his confreres.[564] William of Beaujeu, the master of the Templars, was mortally wounded at the hour of mercy;[565] not in full battle armor at the time, he was struck by a spear.[566] The master and the order's standard-bearer left the battlefield, which prompted shouts from the nearby troops who thought he was fleeing in the face of the enemy. He shouted to them, "I am not fleeing, I am slain: You can see the stroke!"[567]

The entire city, except for the citadel and the fortified compounds of the military religious orders, was in Muslim hands. King Henry II and Jean de Villiers hurried to the harbor where they boarded ships. The patriarch of Jerusalem tried to leave as well but was drowned in the attempt. Several stories exist as to how he drowned. One version indicates he slipped trying to get into a boat; another is that out of pity for the fleeing inhabitants of the city he allowed too many to board his ship and the vessel capsized.[568]

The last bastion of Christian resistance in Acre was now the Templar Tower, which was a heavily fortified castle at the end of the city. It was built on the tip of the landmass that jutted into the Mediterranean, "so close to the sea that the waves broke against it."[569]

The Muslims tried to force the Templars and refugees out of the Tower but to no avail. Ten days after the final assault, the Templars recognized the situation was hopeless and offered to surrender the citadel if the sultan granted them safe conduct out of the city. Khalil agreed and sent a unit of troops into the Tower to oversee the surrender of the Templars.

Once inside the compound the Muslim troops could not restrain themselves from harassing the Christian civilians who had sought refuge with the Templars. They tried to take possession of the men for slaves and of the women to satisfy their sexual

Muslims go back on word

desire. The Templars reacted by grabbing their weapons and slaughtering the sultan's troops. They shut the gates to the citadel and made up their mind to fight to the death.

Khalil sent word to the Templars that he did not harbor ill will toward them for the death of his men since they had acted foolishly. He reiterated his terms and asked them to open the gates. Peter de Sevrey, the marshal of the order, and several other Templars left the fortress and walked toward the waiting sultan. They were apprehended and beheaded.

Muslims go back on word

After Khalil's treachery the remaining Templars and civilians in the tower once more pledged to fight to the end. But when the Muslims began a mining operation to destroy the tower and with no means available to stop it, the Christians realized they had no choice but to surrender.

Khalil sent a force of 2,000 cavalry into the tower to accept the Templars' capitulation. While overseeing the withdrawal, the mine underneath gave way and the tower collapsed killing the remaining Templars and the Muslim cavalry.[570] It was a costly end to a costly siege that had killed nearly 30,000 Christians in five weeks.[571] Khalil, following the example set by Baybars, ordered the city razed. Acre had fallen, a hundred years to the day of its capture by the forces of the Third Crusade.

News of its fall prompted outbursts of shock and dismay in Europe. It was inconceivable that the Kingdom of Jerusalem was no more. Although there were small pockets of Christian territory remaining in Outrémer, they soon surrendered and by the end of the summer of 1291, the Crusader States were gone.

Changes in the Crusading Movement

By the end of the thirteenth century, the Crusades were not simply armed pilgrimages to the Holy Land. They had become a way of life that encompassed a worldview shaped by the teachings of the Catholic Church. Despite the eradication of the Crusader States, pilgrimages continued to the Holy Land and a Christian presence at the holy sites in Jerusalem was guaranteed by the Franciscans, *mamluk: owned slave of the king. Arab designation for slave.*

who, by the mid-1330s, were granted a license by the Mamluks to oversee the Latin sectors within the Church of the Holy Sepulchre, the Upper Room, and the Grotto of the Nativity in Bethlehem.[572]

The reign of the Crusader States was short, lasting less than 200 years. But although the fall of Acre meant the end of Christian control of Outrémer, it did not produce the decline of the Crusading movement. The Crusades continued, but their focus changed.[573] The movement received fresh impetus with the arrival of the Ottoman Turks, who in the fifteenth and sixteenth centuries threatened the very existence of Christendom.

9

Defending Christendom

Mehmet will never lay down arms except in victory or total defeat.
Every victory will be for him a stepping-stone to another, until, after
subjecting all the princes of the West, he has destroyed the gospel of
Christ and imposed the law of his false prophet upon the whole world.

Pope Pius II[574]

It's an extraordinary thing how the very mention of the
Turks is so horrifying and terrible to the Christians that it makes
them lose not only their strength but also their wits.

Jérome Maurand[575]

Warning bells rang out from the church, and people rushed to
their homes. Men took up arms to defend their families and
fellow townspeople. The town of Otranto had fallen into the
crosshairs of the mighty Ottoman Empire.

Sitting on the heel of Italy near the Adriatic Sea, Otranto
provided a strategic base of operations for an invasion of Italy,
and the ultimate destruction of Christendom. The Muslim invasion force was ruthless and unmatched in its savagery. Turkish
warriors massacred more than half of the town's residents, and
martyred the archbishop, who was seized during Mass, taken
outside the cathedral, and sawed in two.[576]

As an example to the rest of the townspeople and to all inhabitants of Italy, the Muslim commander, Pasha Ahmet, arranged to have 813 men put to death. Before the execution,
they were exhorted to convert to Islam; a tailor named Antonio
Primaldi replied that he was willing to die a thousand deaths for

Christ.[577] His brothers in Christ, moved by his faith, also agreed to remain steadfast.

The next morning, on the Vigil of the Assumption, the men were led to the hill overlooking the city. Pasha Ahmet ordered the executioner to strike the neck of Antonio Primaldi first. Upon his decapitation, Antonio's body miraculously stood up and could not be moved. It remained standing throughout the executions. One executioner was so moved by the faith of the martyrs that he converted to Christ on the spot and then joined the ranks of the martyrs.[578]

The Church recognized the brave witness of these men when they were officially declared martyrs by Pope Benedict XVI in July 2006, and then canonized as saints by Pope Francis in May 2013.

The Rise and Advance of the Ottoman Turks

In the late thirteenth century, a Turkish emir known as Osman established a strong government bolstered by an efficient and ruthlessly effective military. After winning dominance over other Turkish tribes, Osman pushed westward, expanding his Ottoman Empire, and engaged the Byzantine Empire in the first of a long series of conflicts that would eventually culminate in the total destruction of the Byzantines. By the late fourteenth century the Ottomans were making incursions deep into imperial territory in the Balkan states. Military victories were the foundation of the Ottoman Empire, and the goal of its every ruler was expansion, conquest, and world domination. During his reign every Ottoman sultan was expected to bring at least one foreign state under Islamic rule.

The rise and advance of the Ottoman Turks necessitated an evolution in the Crusading movement. Previously, the movement had focused on wars to liberate ancient Christian territories from the forces of Islam. With the Turks, however, the Crusading movement focused on defensive wars to protect the European homeland, and to survive. The war against the Ottomans would be a long "war of self-defense waged by a European community that was both Christian and civilized, against an implacably aggressive and uncivilized Islamic power."[579]

A New Weapon

A man called the "Blood-Drinker" for his cruelty became sultan of the Ottoman Empire in 1451 at the age of nineteen. Mehmet II was "deeply secretive and suspicious of others; self-reliant, haughty, distant from human affection, and intensely ambitious . . . astute, brave, and highly impulsive—capable of deep deception, tyrannical cruelty, and acts of sudden kindness . . . a personality of paradox and complexity."[580]

Mehmet embarked on a policy of total domination and victory over the Byzantine Empire. He knew the key to destroying Byzantium was the conquest of Constantinople. He had begun his studies of the city and its defenses and started planning his conquest at the age of thirteen.[581] Conquering Constantinople "would unite his empire, remove a potentially troublesome base for hostile troops and help define a universalist imperial ideology."[582] Intelligence reports arrived in Constantinople informing the Byzantines of Mehmet's plans, so Emperor Constantine XI sent envoys to Mehmet to negotiate a treaty. Mehmet had them beheaded. War was imminent.

Mehmet knew that his army was superior to the Byzantine army in terms of numbers of men, quality of officers, and expertise in siege tactics; however, he had also studied and learned from past Ottoman failures at Constantinople. Those armies had failed because they could not find a way past the massive Theodosian defensive walls. But Mehmet had something in quantity and quality those previous Ottoman armies did not: cannon. He designed a siege that focused on destroying the walls using gunpowder, but he also knew that available cannons were not strong enough to destroy the walls themselves. He needed a bigger gun.

A year before the siege, he met a Hungarian engineer named Urban who was looking for work. He had recently offered his services to the Byzantine emperor who had no use (or funds) for his skills, so he went to the Ottomans.[583] Mehmet ordered Urban to begin work on a super gun that would bring Constantinople to its knees.

It took Urban three months of hard work, but he produced the largest bronze cast cannon in the world. It was twenty-seven feet long with a barrel surrounded with eight inches of solid bronze, and measured thirty inches across the muzzle.[584] The cannon fired a solid shot eight feet in circumference, weighing fifteen hundred pounds, a full mile.[585] The cannon was so large it required sixty oxen and 200 men to move it and could only travel two and half miles a day.[586] Firing the gun was so complex and labor-intensive that it could only be done seven times a day.[587]

Mehmet now had a weapon that would demolish the walls of Constantinople.

The Attack

The Ottoman force left the capital of Erdine on Friday, March 23, 1453 and arrived outside Constantinople on Easter Sunday (April 1). In accordance with the rules of war at the time, the city was asked to surrender, and it refused.

The emperor, Constantine XI, was a fighter more than an administrator, and it was providential he "held the purple" during Constantinople's most desperate hour. Born of a Serbian mother named Helena and a half-Italian father, Constantine was "capable and trustworthy, 'a philanthropist and without malice,' imbued with resoluteness, courage, and a deep patriotism."[588]

Mehmet's strategy was one of attrition, since he had soldiers to spare. He also gave orders to "batter the walls day and night with artillery fire and to launch unpredictable skirmishes to wear down the defenders and to make a major breach for a final assault."[589] The bombardment began in earnest and continued non-stop from April 12 through April 18. The sixty-nine guns in the Turkish artillery fired 120 shots a day.[590] Urban's super gun hammered the Theodosian walls and caused extensive damage, but it developed cracks and ruptured early in the siege, robbing Mehmet of his special weapon.

The Time Is Near

A month into the siege, the situation was desperate for the defenders. Food was scarce, supplies were dwindling, and the constant Turkish artillery barrage and assaults had taken their toll. Many soldiers left the wall to find food for their families, further weakening the defenses. A major council of war recommended Constantine leave the city for the Peloponnese, gather new troops, regroup, and strike the Turks from the rear. But Constantine refused to leave the city in its hour of desperation.[591]

As the siege approached its second month, both sides were eager for it to end. Mehmet sent a proposal of surrender to the city that stipulated an annual tribute payment of 100,000 bezants and abandonment of the city. Constantine rejected the offer.

On May 29, Mehmet ordered a general assault. The Byzantine clergy prayed, blessed the city, and carried icons along the walls for help and protection. The Ottomans kept coming, and at one point, a stone from one of Mehmet's big guns opened a breach in the inner enclosure.

Almost immediately, 300 Muslim warriors poured in through the gap, but were met with fierce Byzantine resistance. The defenders had been fighting for nearly four hours and were exhausted, but the Turks were unyielding as Mehmet ordered 5,000 Janissaries forward.[592] The crack troops gave out such a yell that it was heard five miles away.[593]

Once more the beleaguered Byzantine defenders beat back the Ottoman attack, and the tide appeared to turn in their favor. Constantine could sense it, and urged his warriors: "Brave soldiers, the enemy's army is weakening, the crown of victory is ours. God is on our side—keep fighting!"[594]

In war, however, victory can be elusive and defeat sudden. Some Ottoman troops found a postern gate near the Blachernae Palace unguarded. In a repeat of the action that led to the Crusader victory in 1204, they opened the gate and tore into the city's defenses. Soon they infested the wall and tore down the Christian banner and replaced it with the Ottoman standard.

Ottoman troops poured into the city surging past the defenders. Within fifteen minutes, 30,000 Muslim warriors were in the city.[595] Horrified at the sudden change in the situation, Constantine rushed to the wall:

> Constantine XI, last of the Roman emperors, tore the purple cloak from his back and raised his sword to catch the morning sun upon its blade . . . he plunged into the melee at the breach, to die fighting as a common soldier against the triumphant infidel. Turbans and scimitars overshadowed him. He vanished from sight. He was never seen again. His body was never recovered.[596]

The sultan had triumphed; the emperor was dead and his empire with it. "A Constantine, son of Helena, had built this city more than 1,000 years ago; another Constantine, son of another Helena, had now lost it forever."[597]

The Sack

The Muslim troops ran through the undefended city slaughtering the inhabitants, stopping just long enough to take the pretty women and children for slaves before dispatching the rest. Women (including nuns) and boys were savagely raped.[598]

A large group of citizens trying to escape the Ottoman horde ran to Hagia Sophia, the sixth-century church built by Justinian the Great and the largest church in Christendom. When news reached Mehmet that his troops were in the city, he rode straight for Hagia Sophia, entered, and declared it a mosque. It would remain a place of Muslim worship until 1935, when it was turned into a museum.[599]

In the end, 4,000 Christians were killed in the sack and 50,000 seized, of which 30,000 became slaves.[600] The Queen of

Cities was now in the hands of Islam. The "bone in the throat of Allah" had been dislodged.[601]

The Crusader-Pope

Five years after the loss of Constantinople saw the election of a new pope who would play a central role in "shaping the character of Crusading against the Ottoman Turks."[602] Aeneas Sylvius Piccolomini took the papal name Pius II at his election in 1458. He was completely dedicated to the Crusading ideal and made his primary papal goal the liberation of Constantinople.

Pius II called the temporal rulers of Western Europe to gather at a congress in Mantua in 1459 to discuss plans for the new Crusade. This idea of an international meeting to discuss the Turkish threat preceded Pius, but he implemented it. Unfortunately, the response was less than enthusiastic. None of the major rulers—more concerned with their national interests—came to Mantua. Pius II gave a speech at the congress in which he blamed the conquest of Constantinople on the lack of Western response to the city in her hour of need, and he reminded his listeners of the savagery of the Turks.[603] Pius also recalled the heroes of the First Crusade in an effort to shame and motivate the absent secular leaders to take up arms in the cause of Christ: "Oh, that Godfrey, Baldwin, Eustace, Hugh, Bohemond, Tancred, and those other brave men who re-conquered Jerusalem were here! Truly they would not need so many words to persuade them."[604]

While exhorting the warriors of Christendom to awake from their slumber and take back Constantinople, Pius also engaged in evangelization in the hope of converting the Ottomans. In 1461, he sent a personal letter to Mehmet the Conqueror urging him to abandon the false religion of Mohammed and to embrace the true light of Christ. His request was denied.

After several years of fruitless cajoling, exhorting, and pleading with the secular rulers of Christendom to take the cross, Pius decided to take the cross himself. He addressed his reason for taking the cross, an unprecedented action for a pope, in a letter:

Our cry, Go forth! Has resounded in vain. Perhaps if the word is, Come with me! It will have more effect. That is why we have determined to proceed in person against the Turks, and by word and deed to stir up all Christian princes to follow our example. It may be that, seeing their teacher and father, the Bishop of Rome, the Vicar of Christ, a weak and sickly old man, going to war, they will be ashamed to stay at home.[605]

Pius believed his personal example of taking the cross would be the impetus for others to do likewise. He knew that "zeal for the faith will bring some, greed for glory others, that and curiosity to see great events."[606] Pius's plan began to come to fruition as the rulers of Hungary, Venice, and Burgundy entered into an alliance with the Papal States to fight the Turks. The pope traveled to the muster site at Ancona in August of 1464 to await the arrival of other Crusaders.

Unfortunately, the pope's expectation for large numbers of Crusaders did not materialize, and those troops who did show quickly broke into quarrels along national lines. As was common with large groups of soldiers gathered together in close quarters during the summer, disease broke out, and many Crusaders died. Pius II, too, contracted the plague and died, and so ended his Crusade.

Ultimately, Pius's Crusade failed not because of his death, but because the political realities of Christendom had radically changed. Although it was true that "Christian Europe shared certain religious and cultural values, it was no longer possible to translate these into collective military action under the papal aegis."[607] Despite this reality, popes continued to try, because the very survival of Christendom depended on it.

Suleiman the Magnificent

When Selim I (1512–1520) died, the sultanate passed to his surviving male heir, Suleiman. Signs marked Suleiman's ascendancy: He was the tenth sultan in the history of the empire; he was born in the tenth year of the tenth century of the Muslim era. Ten is considered the number of perfection in Islam as there are ten parts to the Qur'an and there were ten disciples of Mohammed.[608] There was great expectation placed on the shoulders of Suleiman.

This grandson of Mehmet the Conqueror was a very effective, and at times, cruel ruler—he had one of his sons strangled in his presence. He also had a dream. Every sultan was required to add a new piece to the Ottoman Empire, but Suleiman was not content to add one or two territories—he wanted to rule the entire world. During his forty-six-year reign the Ottoman Empire achieved the height of its power. Suleiman's forces conquered Baghdad, Belgrade, Budapest, and Rhodes.

Naturally, the sultan desired control of the Mediterranean Sea as well. During his reign, the Ottomans controlled the eastern end, but the Hapsburgs of Spain controlled the western. For the next fifty years, a vicious fight would ensue for control of this strategic body of water. "On this terrain was played out one of the fiercest and most chaotic contests in European history: the struggle . . . for the center of the world."[609]

Malta—the Ravelin of Europe

As Suleiman the Magnificent neared the end of his life, one regret from his youthful days still haunted him: letting the Knights Hospitallers leave Rhodes in 1522 instead of annihilating them when he had the chance. It was a mistake he wanted to rectify.[610] Revenge was not the only reason to attack Malta, as the Knights used the strategic island in the middle of the great contested sea as a base of operations to hamper Turkish shipping, including pilgrim traffic to Mecca. Suleiman knew that "Malta was simply too central, too strategic, and too troublesome to be ignored indefinitely."[611]

He assembled an army of 40,000 warriors, 100 artillery pieces and 100,000 cannonballs to attack the little island in the middle of the Mediterranean.[612] He was certain of victory, but once again the Knights proved their mettle by pushing back against the Ottoman horde.

The Knights Hospitallers had used Malta as their base of operations for almost forty years when the great Ottoman invasion fleet arrived. The island's defenders were meager, with only 500 Knights and 8,000 Maltese militia and mercenaries from Spain and Italy.[613] As in previous engagements with the Ottomans, the Knights were woefully outnumbered. The master general of the order, Jean de La Valette, a veteran of the siege of Rhodes, knew the situation was desperate, so he sent a summons to all the Knights in Christendom to come to the island's defense.[614]

Jean de La Valette had been elected master general in 1557 and was a very pious and resolute warrior. Captured by the Ottomans in 1541, La Valette had suffered a year in horrible conditions as a galley slave chained to the oars. At the siege of 1565, the master was seventy years old and had spent fifty of those years as a Knight. He was "one of the greatest warriors in Christian history . . . a man tough as nickel steel."[615] He was "the rarest of human beings, a completely single-minded man."[616]

His singular vision in 1565 was the defense of Malta. He knew the island must hold out and defeat the Ottomans. Failure to do so would give the Muslims a strategic base to launch an invasion of Sicily and ultimately Italy, threatening Rome and the very heart of Christian Europe.

The Turks Arrive

Although the defenders of Malta were outnumbered, they took solace in their brilliant and formidable leader, and at the news that Pope Pius IV had granted a plenary indulgence to anyone who died in the defense of Malta.[617] They were fighting in the great Crusade to stop the advance of the Ottomans, and to save Christendom.

The Ottomans arrived on Malta in May of 1565, but from the beginning their time on the island was marked by division and difficulty.

Suleiman had divided command of the operation between two commanders, Mustapha Pasha and Piyale. Mustapha Pasha commanded the army. He was a veteran of the Persian and Hungarian campaigns, and as a young officer participated in the siege of Rhodes. He was "an experienced general but possessed an explosive temper and a streak of cruelty—and a particular hatred of Christians."[618] Piyale was admiral of the 180-ship fleet, and was an inexperienced commander. The commanders did not like each other, and their competition for glory and the sultan's favor caused friction in their relationship and handicapped the campaign.

The Ottoman landing was unopposed, and forces soon arrived at the main harbor where La Valette had placed his troops in several forts. Mustapha Pasha arranged his camp in a crescent shape per Ottoman custom.[619]

The Christian defense of the harbor centered on two linked peninsulas named Birgu and Senglea, which jutted into the Grand Harbor. Birgu was home to the main Hospitaller fort of St. Angelo and contained La Valette's command post. Senglea was home to Fort St. Michael the Archangel. The largest peninsula contained Mount Sciberras along its length and ended with Fort St. Elmo at the tip. Ft. St. Elmo controlled the harbor passes, and was the most strategic place on Malta.

Mustapha Pasha and Piyale agreed on the need to capture Fort St. Elmo, since no Ottoman ship was safe attempting to sail into the harbors as long as the Knights controlled the fort. If the "key to Europe was Malta, the key to Malta was Saint Elmo."[620]

The Fight for Fort St. Elmo

La Valette was pleased that the Ottomans had planned a focused assault on St. Elmo. That fateful decision bought him time to finish his defensive preparations at Birgu and Senglea, and, he hoped, time for a Spanish relief army to arrive.

The fight for Fort St. Elmo began on May 25, 1565. Ottoman engineers believed the fight would be short: four or five days.[621] But Christians held their ground and made the Ottomans pay dearly for every inch; by May 29, the date the Turkish engineers believed the fort would be in their hands, the Ottomans had only captured the outer trench.

As the fight for Fort St. Elmo slogged into June, both sides engaged in intense hand-to-hand combat and heavy sniper activity. Turkish artillery continued to pound the fort, lobbing 6,000 cannonballs per day. On June 18, the Ottomans once again launched a major attack that, over six hours, resulted in the deaths of 1,000 Turks and 150 Christians.[622] Although the defenders fought bravely, it was only a matter of time before the fort would fall into Ottoman control. The defenders knew that time was near when on the twenty-sixth day of the siege a cannonball decapitated the fort's commander.

The remaining Knights and soldiers knew they could withstand only one more attack, and it came on June 23, the vigil of the Feast of the Nativity of St. John the Baptist, the patron of the order. Only sixty defenders were left, and the senior officers in charge were unable to stand due to their wounds. They sat in chairs in the breach to fight, and were both shot dead in the final assault.[623] As the Turks poured into the fort, they made quick work of the remaining defenders. Only five Maltese soldiers were known to survive the final assault, by running down to the shore and swimming across the harbor.[624] Some soldiers tried to surrender to the Turks to save their lives, but they were lined up on a wall and shot. The bodies were then hung upside down where the heads and chests were split open and their hearts ripped out.[625]

The thirty-one-day siege had paid a heavy price to the Grim Reaper, with 4,000 Turks and 1,500 Christians killed.[626] Although the Turks could absorb the losses better than the Christians, it was still a heavy price to pay for such a small (albeit strategic) fort. Mustapha Pasha, while looking across the harbor to the main fortress of St. Michael the Archangel on Senglea, remarked, "Allah! If so small a son has cost us so dear, what price shall we have to pay for so large a father!"[627]

Mustapha Pasha hoped to demoralize the remaining Christian troops across the harbor so he ordered some of the bodies of the Knights stripped of their armor, their hearts ripped out and heads cut off. Each headless corpse was then marked with a cross cut into its chest and finally nailed by the hands and feet to a wooden crucifix that was placed into the water to float across the harbor to the Christian defenses.[628] La Valette responded to the Ottoman atrocity by beheading captured Muslim soldiers, loading the heads into his cannons, and firing them into the Muslim camp. This nasty exchange illustrates the fact that both sides knew this was a fight with enormous stakes for both Islam and Christendom, and a fight to the death.

The Fight for Birgu and Senglea

Those who died at Fort St. Elmo had given the other defenders of Malta time to consolidate and reinforce their positions, but the reprieve was now over. Mustapha Pasha ordered the attacks on Birgu and Senglea to begin on July 15.

The siege dragged on, and in early August, Mustapha Pasha ordered a heavy artillery bombardment that could be heard in Sicily.[629] The defenders kept their heads down in the trenches and on the walls as the Turkish infantry advanced.

Eventually the Christians noticed something odd about the artillery attack; they were suffering no damage. They soon realized the Turkish guns were firing blanks in the hopes of keeping the defenders hunkered down long enough for the infantry to reach the defenses. It did not work, and the assault was repulsed.

On August 7, Mustapha Pasha once more ordered a general assault, a combined attack on both Birgu and Senglea. The fighting was very intense at Birgu, and it appeared the Christian line might break. On hearing the news, the aged La Valette grabbed a helmet and pike and shouted, "Come, my knights, let us all go and die there! This is the day!"[630] He ran into the breach, grabbed a fallen arquebus, and began firing. A Turkish grenade exploded near him, and shrapnel wounded his leg. He refused to leave the line, telling those who were urging him to get to safety, "How can it be possible for a man of my age to die more gloriously than among my brethren and my friends in the service of God, in defense of our holy religion?"[631]

The hour was so desperate that even Maltese civilians, including women and children, manned the walls to push back the Turks. With victory almost in reach, something odd happened in the Turkish assault. Rumor quickly spread that the long-expected Spanish relief force had finally arrived. Although this was not true, the Ottoman soldiers thought it was, and their attack faltered. In reality, what had occurred was a small Maltese militia cavalry force had swept into the unguarded Turkish camp stealing away with supplies and killing rear echelon soldiers. This very timely disruption caused the panic that stopped the Turkish assault, which had been on its way to securing victory.

The remaining days of August were filled with intense trench combat that produced a stalemate. Disease broke out in the Ottoman ranks, further thinning Mustapha Pasha soldiers. Casualties on both sides throughout the month were heavy. La Valette tried to keep morale high by praising "the dead so as to put courage into the living."[632] As the calendar turned to September, the Christian defenders received the blessing of great news on the Feast of the Nativity of the Blessed Virgin Mary as 10,000 Spanish troops, the long awaited relief force from Sicily, arrived in eighty ships.[633]

The Spanish reinforcements began their march toward the harbor to relieve La Valette's troops on September 11, 1565. Mustapha Pasha knew defeat loomed on the horizon, but in order to stave it off, he tried a risky attack against the Spanish army. The fresh Spanish forces easily routed his troops, who were weary from four months of heavy fighting. The Ottomans retreated full bore to their awaiting ships in St. Paul's Bay, the famous site of Paul's shipwreck 1,500 years previously. They boarded their ships and sailed home.

Malta was saved. It had "survived through a combination of religious zeal, irreducible willpower—and luck."[634]

The siege of Malta was an epic struggle for the center of the Mediterranean, and it proved costly to both sides. The Turks lost half of the fighting strength of their invasion force, and La Valette lost half of his Knights and 2,500 Maltese troops.[635] An additional 7,000 Maltese men, women, and children also died during the siege.[636] Pope Pius IV offered La Valette the cardinal's hat for his valiant and brilliant defense of Malta, but the humble warrior refused the offer. He would live another five years, finally dying from a stroke suffered during the summer heat when returning from a hunt. He was buried on the island he had so gallantly defended.

Pope St. Pius V and the Holy League

Although the Ottomans faltered at Malta, they remained a strong force. Selim II (r. 1566–1574), the successor of Suleiman the Magnificent, conquered Cyprus in 1571, but his sights were on a much more impressive prize, one worthy of his great-grandfather, Mehmet the Conqueror: Selim dreamed of conquering Rome. He called the Eternal City the "red apple" that he believed was ripe for plucking. A massive fleet would be required for such an invasion, and so Selim set about building one. By the fall of 1571, it was ready.

Pius V had been elected pope in 1566. As a Dominican monk he was known for his orthodoxy and hatred of heresy, serving as the head of the Holy Office of the Inquisition under Pope Paul IV. Pius was very aware of the Turkish threat to Rome and Christendom, so he wrote letters to the major European secular rulers pleading with them to unite against it.

Most of them ignored the papal exhortation. Europe in the late sixteenth century "was a ferment of violent passions, torn apart by different interests, imperial dreams, and religious tensions."[637] Despite the lack of response, Pius kept pressing for an alliance to mitigate the Ottoman threat and, eventually, the persistent pontiff succeeded. A Holy League alliance between Spain, Venice, and the Papal States was formed on March 7, 1571.

The Battle of Lepanto

Selim II's naval campaign to rule the Mediterranean Sea began with the crafting of large numbers of oared galleys.[638] These galleys were ships with limited range that operated in the littoral areas near the shore. They rarely ventured into open ocean and could only do so for short periods of time, primarily because they required vast amounts of potable water for the oarsmen. Initially volunteers manned the oars for these ships, but by the sixteenth century, chained slaves—especially Christian slaves captured by Muslim pirates—and conscripts provided the manpower. Life as a galley oarsman was akin to servitude in hell: "[T]he galley was an amoebic death trap, a swilling sewer whose stench was so foul you could smell it two miles off."[639] In fact, galleys were periodically sunk just to cleanse the filth.

As the deployment season of 1571 came to a close, the Ottoman fleet sought anchorage in their fortified port of Lepanto at the mouth of the Gulf of Corinth. Lepanto was a strategic location, as the prevailing Mediterranean wind favored the defender. An attacker would waste valuable energy and time trying to row against the wind to get into the gulf while the defender sat and waited to attack until exhaustion took the enemy fleet out of action.

Ali Pasha commanded the Ottoman fleet in 1571. Ali Pasha was "brave and generous, of natural nobility, a lover of knowledge and the arts; he spoke well, he was a religious and clean-living man."[640] He was in charge of a substantial fleet of 300 war galleys, 100,000 men, and 14,000 Christian galley slaves. It was a fleet bred for one purpose: the invasion of Rome and the conquest of Christendom. His flagship flew a large green standard known as the banner of Mohammed. The flag was covered with verses from the Qur'an, and had the name of Allah embroidered 28,900 times in gold calligraphy. The banner had never been captured by enemy forces and always seemed to bring luck and victory to the Muslim force that raised it in battle.

The Holy League fleet had assembled in Naples in August. Don Juan of Austria, the twenty-four-year-old illegitimate son of Holy Roman Emperor Charles V, commanded the 208-ship fleet. Half-brother to Philip II, king of Spain, Don Juan was "good looking, dashing, intelligent, chivalrous, and daring, driven by an unquenchable appetite for glory."[641] Pius V sent

Cardinal Granvelle to Naples to consecrate Don Juan as commander of the Holy League, presenting him with a twenty-foot blue battle pennant that contained an image of the cross with the linked coat of arms of Spain, Venice, and the pope.

The cardinal also passed on the pope's exhortation to Don Juan to demand virtuous living from his sailors and soldiers. The notion that warriors would embody Christian virtues while preparing for and participating in combat was a mainstay of the Crusading movement, and Pius V clearly saw his Holy League as the newest chapter in Crusading history.

Among the 26,000 Holy Leaguers who were asked to live virtuously and pray the rosary (each man was given one), was the Spanish author, Miguel Cervantes. The later writer of *Don Quixote* fought well in the battle, was wounded, and lost the use of his left hand for the rest of his life. Despite his wound, Cervantes later wrote that the battle was "the greatest day's work seen for centuries."[642]

The Cross and the Crescent

The sound of the liturgy wafted across the water on the morning of October 7, 1571. The chaplains scattered throughout the fleet blessed the troops and granted them general absolution. Every man knew the next several hours would be filled with smoke, noise, confusion, death, and destruction. Each prayed that death would not find him.

They were one part of the largest assemblage of galleries in history. Combined with the Ottoman fleet in safe anchorage at Lepanto, they numbered 140,000 men and 600 ships, or 70 percent of all oared galleys in the Mediterranean.[643]

Don Juan left his flagship, the *Real*, to his staff with the words "Very well, let's fight!" and sailed in a light frigate past the galleys in the fleet.[644] Carrying a crucifix, he urged his men on, telling them, "You have come to fight the battle of the Cross— to conquer or to die. But whether you die or conquer, do your duty this day, and you will secure a glorious immortality."[645]

The Christian oarsmen were hard pressed as they sailed against the prevailing wind to the mouth of Lepanto. Don Juan decided to form his galleys in the shape of a cross, a formation that took three hours to complete, due to its intricacy and the sheer number of vessels.[646] Don Juan was anxious for the battle to start, and once his ships had formed up, he danced a jig on the deck of the *Real* in anticipation.[647]

Aware that the Christian fleet was outside the gulf and eager for battle, Ali Pasha made the decision to leave the sheltered anchorage and venture forth to win victory for the sultan, forming his galleys into the shape of a crescent. It was symbolic, but it also effectively served the Islamic strategy of encirclement and annihilation. On the morning of Sunday, October 7, 1571, the cross and the crescent literally clashed for control of the center of the world.

Despite being outnumbered, Don Juan was confident of victory. He trusted in the Lord, and also had special weapons that he believed gave his fleet the advantage. The Venetians had outfitted six large transport ships called galleasses with side-mounted as well as bow-mounted cannons; fifty guns in total. Contemporary naval convention used only bow-mounted cannon on galleys, which limited the number of pieces. The galleasses were towed into position by other ships, and did not need oarsmen, so the extra room on the deck was filled with 500 sharpshooting arquebusiers. Don Juan's use of these special ships revolutionized naval warfare, and soon side-mounted cannon became the naval norm.

Don Juan also relied on spiritual weapons, too. Each man was asked to use the rosary he had been given to pray to our Lady for victory in the battle.

Winds of Change

The galleasses wreaked havoc with the Ottoman fleet right at the beginning of the battle, devastating the center formation of Ali Pasha's ships. The Turks could not quickly overcome the shock, and the tide of battle initially favored the Christians. Later, though, the right wing of the Christian fleet under Admiral Doria found itself in trouble. His flagship was under heavy assault, and his force was greatly outnumbered. Fierce fighting waged across the ships. On one of the ships, Federico Venusta was attempting to throw a hand grenade at Turkish soldiers when it prematurely exploded, severely wounding his left hand. He ordered a galley slave to cut it off, but the man refused. Venusta cut off the injured limb himself, and then ran to the mess where he ordered the cook to put a chicken carcass over the stump. Armed with a dead chicken as his hand, he ran back into the fight yelling at his right hand to avenge his left! Another soldier was struck in the eye with an arrow. He plucked out the damaged eye, tied a bandage around his head and kept fighting.[648]

Despite these examples of bravery and heroism, the fight was going against the Christians. The wind prevented Admiral Doria from using his sails and releasing his oarsmen to join the fight. The situation seemed desperate when, miraculously, the prevailing wind changed direction, allowing the release of the Christian oarsmen from their rowing.[649] This permitted Admiral Doria to engage the enemy with additional troops and win the fight. There was no natural explanation for why the wind changed direction as it did, but on Admiral Doria's flagship was a special spiritual weapon: a copy of the image of Our Lady of Guadalupe. The Archbishop of Mexico, Don Fray Alonso de Montufar, aware of the Ottoman threat to Christendom, commissioned a small reproduction of the sacred image. It was touched to the real *tilma* of St. Juan Diego, and sent to King Philip II with instructions to give it to the Holy League. It is no coincidence that at the moment of direst need, our Lady came to the rescue of Admiral Doria's flotilla and saved the day at Lepanto.

After four hours the Battle of Lepanto ended in an overwhelming victory for the Christian forces of the Holy League. The final tally was 225 Turkish galleys destroyed or captured, and 25,000 dead Ottoman troops. The Holy League fleet lost only twelve ships with 15,000 Christian sailors and soldiers killed. Twelve thousand Christian galley slaves in Ottoman service were freed.[650]

Our Lady of Victory

While Don Juan was assessing his grand victory, and before news reached Rome, Pope St. Pius V was meeting with his treasurer when he suddenly stood up, went to the window and said, "This is not a moment for business; make haste to thank God, because our fleet this moment has won a victory over the Turks."[651] In commemoration of the salvation of Rome and Christendom through victory at the Battle of Lepanto, Pius V established the annual celebration of the Feast of Our Lady of Victory in 1572. A year later, his successor Gregory XIII changed the name to the Feast of Our Lady of the Rosary to highlight the important role played by that spiritual special weapon in the victory over the Ottoman Turks. It is a feast still celebrated on the Catholic Church's liturgical calendar.

Don Juan of Austria was the celebrated hero of Christendom, but he was not able to enjoy the accolades showered upon him. He was sent by his half-brother Philip II to the Netherlands to put down a violent Protestant rebellion, and appointed governor-general in 1576. Two years later, at the age of thirty-one, the valiant, dashing, and handsome victor of Lepanto was dead of typhoid.

The memory of Lepanto lived on after Don Juan's death, celebrated in books, paintings, and music throughout the remaining years of the sixteenth century and beyond. In 1911 the English author G.K. Chesterton recalled the great victory through a poem ("Lepanto") written on the 340th anniversary of the battle. Despite Chesterton's popularity among modern Catholics, that poem remains shamefully obscure. Dale Ahlquist, president of the American Chesterton Society, speculates why:

> This poem is more than just a poem. It is a rousing encounter with history, a pivotal event in history that some people would rather ignore . . . [T]the problem with the poem is that it is a defense of the Catholic Church, of the Crusades, and of war: three things not generally looked kindly upon in today's English literature class. Hardly anyone knows of the

poem. It suffers in obscurity because of a combined prejudice against rhyme and meter, against Catholicism, and against G.K. Chesterton.[652]

victory of Christian Europe over Turkish enemy

Hilaire Belloc, who was Chesterton's friend and the editor of "Lepanto," had even stronger words for those who ignore Chesterton's masterpiece celebrating the great Christian victory over the Turk. "People who cannot see the value of *Lepanto* are half-dead. Let them remain so."[653]

Christendom Threatened—Christendom Saved

After Lepanto the Turks solidified their hold on the Balkans and built up strength for an attack on the gateway of Europe, the cultured and strategic city of Vienna. Ottoman forces had besieged the capital city in 1529, when Holy Roman Emperor Charles V was dealing with heretical rebels in Germany. Suleiman the Magnificent had marshaled 120,000 soldiers to besiege a city of only 12,000 defenders, and was confident the siege would prove swift and victorious; he was wrong. The Viennese defenders proved their mettle as they beat back wave after wave of Muslim warriors. The siege dragged on into winter and with extended supply lines and heavy casualties, Suleiman made the prudent military decision to retreat. He hoped one day to return, but it would be more than a century before another Ottoman army arrived at the gates.

Holy Roman Emperor Leopold I (r. 1658–1705) was "highly educated, dignified, [and] he liked to take part in religious ceremonies, to hunt, and read . . . he never neglected the affairs of state; and he had strong general convictions; such as deep piety."[654] The emperor was a good man, but he had a fatal flaw: he was "infinitely susceptible to contradictory counsels, he was betrayed into excessive caution and only too often the results were inaction and delay. He foresaw but never anticipated."[655]

This flaw would prove problematic once the Turks invaded his lands and were at the very gates of his capital city. The forty-three-year-old emperor had pursued a diplomatic policy of appeasement with the Ottomans because he was more concerned about his belligerent neighbor, Louis XIV, the king of France. Some of Leopold's advisers believed the once-mighty Ottoman military was weak and ineffective compared to the large and strong standing army of the Sun King. Concerned with French intentions and military might, Leopold entered into a peace treaty with the Ottoman Turks in 1665. Despite the treaty, Muslim and Christian warriors fought frequent, but not large or decisive, border clashes. Hedging his bets, Leopold also entered into defense treaties with other European nations, including Poland, to come to his aid should the Turks invade. By 1684 the treaty was set to expire in another year, but the emperor was confident it could be extended. Unbeknownst to him, though, the Ottomans had decided a year earlier to break the treaty and invade Austria.

Mehmet IV (r. 1648–1687), the son of Ibrahim the Debauched and a Russian concubine, became sultan of the Ottoman Empire at the young age of seven. Mehmet had given executive powers to his grand viziers since his desire for outdoor sport (his nickname was "the Hunter") precluded his attention to political, military, and diplomatic affairs. At a meeting on August 6, 1682, his advisers persuaded Mehmet that the time was right to break the treaty with Leopold and invade imperial territory. The invasion would commence in 1683 with an army of 100,000 men under the command of Grand Vizier Kara Mustapha (1634–1683).

Kara Mustapha was a veteran of numerous military campaigns, but was not beloved by his troops since he was known to accept large casualties to accomplish the mission. He lived an ostentatious lifestyle with thousands of concubines in his harem, and numerous slaves and eunuchs to tend to his needs.[656] Kara Mustapha also hated Christians, and was looking forward to the campaign. He was overly confident of victory, and openly bragged he would stable his horses in St. Peter's Basilica.[657] The Ottoman army crossed the frontier in late June 1683, rampaging and pillaging as they marched.

The Siege of Vienna

Vienna was not prepared for a massive siege. The outer defensive fortifications had not been well maintained over the years, and extensive suburbs had been built near the main defensives, limiting effective fields of fire on an advancing army.

Rüdiger Starhemberg was appointed commander of Vienna's defenses, and he quickly recognized the difficulty of his task. There was no professional garrison in the city since the plague that decimated the ranks in 1679. Instead, a militia of only 13,000 able-bodied men—more a civil police force than a professionally trained army—was all that stood between the Viennese and the Ottoman Turks. The best Starhemberg could hope for was to hold out long enough for allies' relief forces to reach the city.

The Ottoman warriors arrived at the city on July 14 and once more arranged their camp around the city in the shape of a crescent.[658] Kara Mustapha's plan was first to encircle the city and cut if off, which he accomplished in short order. The Ottoman army musical corps "bombarded" the Viennese with music throughout the siege as a form of psychological warfare. The residents of the City of Music returned the favor so that at times over the din of gunfire one could hear a melodious tune wafting over the siege lines.[659]

As soon as news had reached Leopold I that the Turks were on the move, he had reached out to his allies and begged them to come to the aid of Vienna. Jan Sobieski (r. 1676–1696), the king of Poland and a devout Catholic, responded to his treaty obligations and raised a relief army. He had been the Polish envoy to the Ottoman court, and had studied their military tactics and learned the Tatar language. Sobieski was "the model warrior hero for his time, spiritually sharp with a strong Catholic faith, and a decisive and vigorous man."[660] He left Warsaw with an army of 20,000 men, mostly cavalry, on the way to Krakow where the rest of his troops were ordered to assemble. Along the march, Sobieski stopped to pray at the shrine of Our Lady of Czestochowa.[661] Entrusting the success of his military efforts to the intercession of the Blessed Mother, his army began the march to Vienna on the

Solemnity of the Assumption, August 15, 1683. His forces were buoyed by the knowledge that Pope Innocent XI (r. 1676–1689) had granted the Crusading plenary indulgence to all who fought for the defense and relief of Vienna.[662]

Starhemberg and his valiant defenders had fought bravely for a month, but by the end of August and into early September food was scarce in the city. Flour supplies were running low, so bakers ceased making full loaves of bread, instead forming smaller pieces in the shape of a crescent to remind the inhabitants of the reason for their meager rations.[663] Disease was also rampant, and out of the original complement of 13,000 troops Starhemberg's effective defenders had dwindled to 5,000. It was only a matter of time before the Ottomans broke into the city.

The allied relief army assembled in the Viennese woods, and appointed Sobieski supreme commander. They marched together toward Vienna, drawing near on September 9. Their scouts confirmed the unthinkable: The Turks had not secured the approaches to the city. In fact, they had not even posted sentries to warn Kara Mustapha of the approach of the relief army. It was a foolish and deadly mistake by the grand vizier, who was focused solely on his siege.

Sobieski developed his battle plan and prepared to attack the Ottomans using the high ground of Kahlenberg Mountain on the outskirts of Vienna. The battle began on September 11, 1683 as Kara Mustapha ordered his troops to attack the Christian forces in the hopes of disrupting their positioning maneuvers.

Fighting was intense, and the unseasonal heat of the day increased the suffering of the soldiers. Both sides were so exhausted by midday that they stopped fighting to regroup and rest. Fighting resumed and continued through the day until about five o'clock in the evening when Sobieski unleashed his famed Winged Hussars for a cavalry charge that demolished the Ottoman line. The rout was complete, and the Ottoman army fell into disarray. Kara Mustapha was captured, and later executed on December 25.[664]

Polish troops were first into the city and were greeted with cheers and prayers of thanksgiving by the beleaguered defenders.

Sobieski sent a victory message to Pope Innocent XI that echoed the report of Charles V after his defeat of a Protestant army at the Battle of Mühlberg in 1547: "We came, we saw, God conquered."[665] The pope credited the Christian victory over the Ottomans and the salvation of the city to the intercession of the Blessed Mother, and established the Feast of the Most Holy Name of Mary as a result.[666] Truly, the day of Vienna's salvation, September 11, 1683, "ought to be among the most famous in history."[667] It was the high-water mark of Islamic incursion into the Christian West.

The Ottoman campaign to capture the gateway to Europe and destroy Christendom was a risky operation. Its success would have ensured Ottoman hegemony over Eastern Europe and opened up the approaches to Western Europe. Instead, its failure began the empire's decline and ruin. Through the intercession of the Blessed Mother and the military genius of the Polish king Jan Sobieski, Christendom was saved. But the price was high. 50,000 Christian soldiers and civilians were killed during the siege of the great city of Vienna, and another 500,000 were killed as a result of the Turkish marches through Hapsburg lands.[668]

From its beginning Islam had been a violent, imperialistic movement bent on conquest. Muslim armies throughout Islamic history had proved the better of their opponents in significant clashes, which helped to spread the beliefs of Mohammed. At the end of the seventeenth century, however, a Muslim army finally met its match, and its defeat stopped the advance of the Ottoman Empire. The Hapsburgs would rally from the great victory at Vienna and begin the long process of liberating the Balkans from Ottoman rule. In two more centuries, the Ottoman Empire was the "sick man of Europe"—an empire in name only. The Turks allied with the Kaiser in the First World War, declaring their participation a *jihad* in the name of Allah, but they chose the wrong side, and in 1918 the victorious Allied powers finally disbanded the Ottoman Empire with the sweep of a pen.[669]

10

The Crusades and the Modern World

Lord, take me from wars between Christians in which
I have spent much of my life; let me die in your service so
I may share your kingdom in Paradise.

Josserand of Brancion[670]

I have decided to kill Pope John Paul II,
supreme commander of the Crusades.

Mehmet Ali Agca[671]

The Crusading movement was launched by the papacy, and its fate remained intertwined with that of the Roman pontiffs. As their role in European politics changed, so too did the movement's. As Western Europe moved toward the modern world, secular rulers became more independent, and focused more on internal policies.

The scandal of the Avignon papacy and the Great Western Schism in the fourteenth century severely weakened the papacy, which the Protestant Revolution then completely undermined in the sixteenth. As the pope's ability to influence Western secular rulers declined, so too did the Crusading movement. Warfare became the province of secular rulers who marshaled their forces solely for personal and national aims rather than for the good of Christ, the Church, and Christendom. Although there were moments of unity during the fight against the Ottoman Turks, the overall response was limited. All in Christendom reveled in the glory of victory, but few endeavored to sacrifice to achieve it.

The Crusades did not end because modern man saw the folly of the campaigns, as Enlightenment thinkers and modern critics suppose. Indeed, the Crusades remained extremely popular. Both rulers and subjects continued to like the idea of the Crusades, but over time their desire to plan, spend resources, and actually take the cross gave way to other priorities. Ultimately, "the Crusade did not disappear from European culture because it was discredited but because the religious and social value systems that had sustained it were abandoned."[672]

Why Islam Hates the West

Myths about the Crusades began during the sixteenth century, as Protestant revolutionaries attacked what they viewed as papal campaigns designed to increase the wealth of the Church. The creation of myths about the Crusades continued throughout the time of the Enlightenment until the present day, when the most prevalent myth concerns the Crusades and Islam. Arab nationalists and Islamic terrorists use the Crusades as propaganda to produce recruits for *jihad* against the West; Western intellectuals use it to attack the Church. Both groups profit by fostering the falsehood that the Crusades are the source of the modern-day tension between Islam and the West.

Those who embrace this myth believe that the Crusades have long been remembered in the Islamic world. Akbar Ahmed, chair of the Ibn Khaldun Islamic Studies at American University in Washington, D.C., summed up this claim when he commented, "The Crusades created a historical memory which is with us today—the memory of a long European onslaught."[673] Karen Armstrong, a former Catholic nun and self-described "freelance monotheist," asserts that the Crusades are "one of the direct causes of the conflict in the Middle East today."[674]

The historical reality is far removed from the picture painted by Ahmed, Armstrong, and their supporters. The Crusades were largely ignored as an important part of Islamic history soon after the fall of Acre in 1291, and were then forgotten in the Islamic

world until the late nineteenth century, only receiving promi-
nent attention in the twentieth.

A "Remembered" History

The Arabic word for the Crusades, *harb al-salib*, was introduced in
the mid-nineteenth century, and in 1899 the first Arabic history
of the Crusades was written by the Egyptian Ali al-Hariri.[675] It
was a time when the Ottomans were forced to recognize the independence of most of their former Eastern European territory.
Seeking to find a rationale for the disintegration of the once-
mighty Ottoman Empire, al-Hairi, in his book, placed blame
not on the internal failings of the sultans and their policies, but
rather on the historical "boogeyman" of the Crusades.[676]

It is easy to understand why for hundreds of years Muslims did
not remember the Crusades, since they represented a small and in-
significant portion of Islamic history. The Holy City of Jerusalem
was only in Christian hands for eighty-eight years (from 1099–
1187), and the Crusader States survived for less than two centuries.
The goal of the Crusades—the permanent liberation of Jerusalem
and recovery of ancient Christian territory—was not successful,
and therefore Islamic historians neglected the Crusades.

The modern Islamic attitude toward the Crusades began in
the twentieth century as a reconstructed memory of these events
and was presented to Muslim communities that had been impacted by European colonialism. Ironically, then, it was the European colonial powers—especially the "nineteenth-century French
vision of the Crusades as proto-colonizing expeditions"[677]—that
laid the foundation for the modern Muslim interpretation of the
movement. Through Western colonization, Enlightenment intellectuals from the very nations that once took the cross birthed
the modern Arab re-remembering of the Crusades.

Arab nationalists thus used the Crusades as a scapegoat for the
ills in the twentieth-century Islamic world. The Crusades were
presented as the first European colonial efforts, and modern
Middle Eastern poverty, corruption, and violence were blamed

on these initial European "invasions." The modern state of Israel was likened to the Crusader Kingdom of Jerusalem, a foreign presence in the midst of Islam. Cultural traditions rooted in this false narrative of the Crusades were reinforced through education in Muslim schools, as "generations of Arab school children have been taught that the Crusades were a clear case of good versus evil," and the myth that "rapacious and zealous Crusaders swept into a peaceful and sophisticated Muslim world leaving carnage and destruction in their wake" was reinforced.[678]

The Forgotten "Hero"

A perfect example of this Muslim neglect and "re-remembrance" via Western European assistance can be found in the figure of Saladin, the Muslim general who united the Abbasid and Fatimid caliphates and conquered Jerusalem in the twelfth century. Despite his achievements, in the Islamic world Saladin was mostly forgotten in the centuries after his death. Instead, the great Muslim military hero against the Christians was the Egyptian Mamluk sultan Baybars the Merciless. Baybars succeeded in stopping the Mongol advance, and he fostered the destruction of the Crusader States by sacking the city of Antioch. His complete destruction of Antioch, and the killing of the city's inhabitants, was the worst massacre in Crusading history. His efforts ultimately led to the razing of Acre in 1291, and the end of the Crusader States. In Islam, Baybars was remembered and Saladin forgotten, but in the West it was the opposite.[679]

Saladin was remembered almost with fondness in Christendom through popular literature, especially in the works of Sir Walter Scott; he was presented as the "perfect heathen."[680] He was seen as a man of virtue and military brilliance, akin to great Christian monarchs such as Richard I the Lion-Hearted. Saladin's name was even a popular choice for the parents of boys in medieval Venice.[681]

His reemergence in the Islamic world came about through the visit of a European ruler to the city of Damascus at the end of the nineteenth century. Kaiser Wilhelm II of the German Empire was an admirer of Saladin's. Raised with stories of Saladin since his boyhood, the kaiser earnestly desired to see the tomb of the great general during his Syrian journey in 1899. He was shocked by what he saw. He expected to find a huge ornate tomb to the greatest Muslim general, but what he found was a dilapidated structure in a state of extreme disrepair. He laid a wreath at the tomb with a banner that read "to the Hero Sultan Saladin." He also provided funds for the complete restoration and upgrade of the tomb with a bronze wreath emblazoned with the words, "From one great emperor to another" to show his admiration for Saladin and to commemorate his involvement in the project.[682]

The kaiser's visit to Damascus and Saladin's tomb stirred interest in the Muslim general in the Islamic world. Within twenty years of the German emperor's visit a university opened in Jerusalem bearing the name of Saladin. As the twentieth century came to a close, the remembrance of Saladin, and his appropriation by Arab nationalists, was in full swing.

Hafez Asad, ruler of Syria, commissioned a huge equestrian statue of Saladin in 1992 that displayed Christian warriors groveling at the feet of the great Muslim general. The statue was erected less than a hundred yards from a massive portrait of Asad himself in an apparent attempt to link the two rulers, at least from a propaganda perspective. Saddam Hussein, the cruel dictator of Iraq, referred to himself as the "new Saladin," and liked to draw attention to the fact that they were both born in the same town of Tikrit. In an action designed to link the two men even further, Hussein changed his birthdate to that of Saladin's. It was sadly ironic that Hussein would use biological weapons against the Kurds, who tried in vain to rid Iraq of the despot—since Saladin was ethnically Kurdish. But as with all tyrants, propaganda trumped truth.

Further contributing to the false narrative of the Crusades, and cited as a source by liberal Western intellectuals to validate the myth that the Crusades are the source of the modern tension between Islam and the West, is the book, *The Crusades Through*

Arab Eyes, by the Lebanese-born novelist Amin Maalouf. In it he attempts to provide an Arabic narrative of the Crusades using Islamic sources, an effort made difficult due to the "paucity of contemporary Arab scholarship."[683] In seeking to provide an Islamic narrative of the Crusades, Maalouf merely succeeded in illustrating Islam's reliance on Western research and scholarship of the Crusades.[684] His myth-supporting book ends with an exaggerated statement indicative of the popular false narrative of the Crusades: "[T]here can be no doubt that the schism between these two worlds [Islam and the West] dates from the Crusades, deeply felt by the Arabs, even today, as an act of rape."[685]

The false narrative of the Crusades, created by Europeans and furthered by Arab nationalists, changed in the 1970s. During this time, the Islamic animus against the Crusades was portrayed in religious terms, and was used by *jihadis* who turned their hatred and violence away from secular Muslim regimes and toward the West.

Hijacking the Crusades

The politicization of the Crusades in the Islamic world was greatly amplified by the rise of Al-Qaida and the attacks against the United States on September 11, 2001. Those heinous actions in New York, Washington, D.C., and Shanksville, Pennsylvania thrust the Crusades into the minds of modernity precisely because Osama bin Laden, the leader of Al-Qaida, cited the Crusades as an excuse for his despicable actions.

> The Arabian peninsula has never . . . been stormed by any forces like the Crusader armies, spreading in it like locusts, eating its riches and wiping out its plantations. This is a battle of Muslims against the global Crusaders . . . our goal is for the nation to unite in the face of the Christian Crusade . . . This is a recurring war. The original Crusades were brought by Richard from Britain, Louis from France, and Barbarossa from Germany. Today the Crusading countries rushed as soon as Bush raised the cross. They accepted the rule of the cross.[686]

Despite the propaganda of Osama bin Laden or other terrorists, the Crusades are not to blame for the September 11 attacks, or for the resurgence of militant Islam. Instead we should point to the "artificial memory of the Crusades," fashioned into "an icon for modern agendas that medieval Christians and Muslims could scarcely have understood, let alone condoned."[687] This false presentation of the Crusades has been trumpeted as a convenient rationale for Islamic terrorists in their desire to fulfill Mohammed's command to "fight all men until they say there is no God but Allah."[688]

What if . . . ?

History is replete with examples of "what if" scenarios. The history of the Crusades provides many examples for this question, some of which we have already noted. The question of the resurgence of Islam weighed heavily on the mind of Catholic author Hilaire Belloc, who wrote extensively on this issue in the early twentieth century. Even though he wrote at the time when the major Islamic countries were subservient to European colonial powers and the mighty Ottoman Empire had finally succumbed, Belloc foretold the rise of Islam. He firmly believed that the grandchildren of his generation would witness the rebirth of Islam and its spread throughout the world. In his book *The Crusades*, Belloc posited the quintessential "what if" question on the subject, opining that had the Second Crusade succeeded in capturing Damascus, Christendom would have triumphed, and Islam would have perished:

That story [the Crusades] must not be neglected by any modern, who may think, in error, that the East has finally fallen before the West, that Islam is now enslaved—to our political and economic power at any rate if not to our philosophy. It is not so. Islam essentially survives, and Islam would not have survived had the Crusade made good its hold upon the essential point of Damascus.[689]

Unfortunately, the question is moot. The French and German Crusaders did not succeed at the walls of Damascus in 1149. They were defeated, and although the Crusading movement continued on for another 600 years, the chance to achieve ultimate victory had passed, and the contest between Islam and Christendom persisted and grew.

The Crusades and the Church in the Modern World

The Crusades have always been controversial, but since the Reformation their memory has suffered from the creation of false narratives and mythistory designed to attack the Catholic Church generally and the papacy specifically. Despite the significant work of Crusade historians and scholars over the last generation, the authentic story of the Crusades remains, for the most part, locked within academia. There are many reasons for the sustainment of the myths about the Crusades, since "misconceptions about the past can persist for centuries, despite the diligent work of historians, either because vested interests benefit from the distortions or because the fanciful version is more fun."[690] But the time has arrived to change this narrative and present to the modern world the authentic story of the Crusades.

For that to occur, Catholics must first learn for themselves the authentic story of the movement that was an integral part of the Church's history for six centuries. Too many see the Crusades as an aberration in Church history, a sin that should be forgotten and never discussed, swept into the dustbin of history along with equally misunderstood historical cases such as the Inquisition, Galileo, and Pius XII and the Jews. For many Catholics, "the wars of the cross have become like a lingering bad smell in a lavishly refurbished stately home."[691]

The Crusades were an inherently Catholic undertaking. They were promoted by the papacy, encouraged by the clergy, and fought by Catholic warriors. An authentic understanding of the Crusades, rooted in a contemporary perspective, is best achieved by those who believe today what the Crusaders believed. *Catholics* are uniquely positioned to understand the glory of the Crusades, and to help those outside the Church begin to see it.

The false narratives about the Crusades, so deeply ingrained in the modern world and for too long ignored or blindly accepted by Catholics, can only be overcome by study and knowledge, charity and courage. It is time to reclaim the true story of the Crusades and of the Catholic Faith. The fate of the Church, the West, and the world depends on it.

Timeline of Crusades and Other Major Events

Dates	Crusade	Pope	Christian Warriors
1096–1102	First	Bl. Urban II	Hugh of Vermandois, Raymond of Toulouse, Robert of Normandy, Stephen of Blois, Robert II of Flanders, Godfrey de Bouillon, Bohemond, Bishop Adhemar
1147–1149	Second	Bl. Eugenius III	St. Bernard of Clairvaux, King Louis VII of France, Conrad III of Germany
1187		Urban III	King Guy de Lusignan, Raymond III of Tripoli, Reynald of Châtillon, Balian of Ibelin
1189–1192	Third	Gregory VIII	Frederick Barbarossa, Richard the Lion-Hearted, Philip II Augustus
1201–1205	Fourth	Innocent III	Thibaut III of Champagne, Enrico Dandolo, Boniface of Montferrat, Alexius Angelus
1218–1221	Fifth	Innocent III	King John of Brienne, Cardinal Pelagius, St. Francis of Assisi
1228–1229	Sixth	Gregory IX	Frederick II
1248–1254	1st Crusade of St. Louis IX	Innocent IV	St. Louis IX
1269–1272	2nd Crusade of St. Louis IX	Clement IV	St. Louis IX
1291		Nicholas IV	King Henry II of Jerusalem, Amalric
1453		Nicholas V	Constantine XI
1565		Pius IV	Jean de La Valette
1571		St. Pius V	Don Juan of Austria
1683		Bl. Innocent XI	Emperor Leopold I, Rüdiger Starhemberg, King Jan Sobieski

Opponents	Events	Locations
Kilij Arslan, Kerbogha	Liberation of Nicaea and Antioch. Battle of Dorylaeum, Liberation of Jerusalem, Establishment of Crusader States	Anatolia (modern-day Turkey), Syria, Holy Land
Zengi, Nur-al Din	Siege of Damascus	Damascus
Saladin	Battle of Hattin Fall of Jerusalem	Outrémer
Saladin	Conquest of Cyprus, Siege of Acre, Battle of Arsuf	Cyprus, Anatolia, Syria, Outrémer
Alexius III, Alexius V	Sieges of Zara and Constantinople	Venice, Dalmatia, Constantinople
al-Kamil	Siege of Damietta	Egypt
al-Kamil	Jerusalem	Outrémer
Turan Shah	Siege of Damietta, Mansourah	Egypt, Outrémer
Baybars	Tunis	North Africa
al-Mansur Qalawun, al-Ashraf Khalil	Fall of Acre	Outrémer
Mehmet II	Fall of Constantinople	Constantinople
Suleiman the Magnificent, Mustapha Pasha, Piyale	Siege of Malta	Malta
Selim II, Ali Pasha	Battle of Lepanto	Gulf of Lepanto
Mehmet IV, Kara Mustapha	Siege of Vienna	Austria

Bibliography

- Ali, Daniel and Spencer, Robert. *Inside Islam: A Guide for Catholics*. West Chester, PA: Ascension Press, 2003.
- Barron, Robert. *Catholicism—A Journey to the Heart of the Faith*. New York: Image Books, 2011.
- Beeching, Jack. *The Galleys at Lepanto*. New York: Charles Scribner's Sons, 1982.
- Belloc, Hilaire. *The Crusades—The World's Debate*. Rockford, IL: TAN Books and Publishers, Inc., 1992.
- Benedict XVI. *Holy Men and Women of the Middle Ages and Beyond—General Audiences, 13 January 2010–26 January 2011*. San Francisco: Ignatius Press, 2012.
- Bostom, Andrew G., ed. *The Legacy of Jihad—Islamic Holy War and the Fate of Non-Muslims*. New York: Prometheus Books, 2005.
- Brandmüller, Walter. *Light and Shadows—Church History Amid Faith, Fact and Legend*. trans. Michael J. Miller. San Francisco: Ignatius Press, 2009.
- Carroll, Warren H. *"The Glory of Christendom—Volume III"* in *A History of Christendom*. Front Royal, VA: Christendom Press, 1993.
- Carroll, Warren H. and Carroll, Anne W. *"The Crisis of Christendom—Volume VI"* in *A History of Christendom*. Front Royal, VA: Christendom Press, 2013.
- Chesterton, G.K. *Lepanto—with Explanatory Notes and Commentary*. ed. Dale Ahlquist. San Francisco: Ignatius Press, 2003.
- Clark, Kenneth. *Civilisation—A Personal View*. New York: Harper & Row, Publishers, 1969.
- Comby, Jean. *How to Read Church History, Volume I—From the Beginnings to the Fifteenth Century*. New York: Crossroads, 2001.
- Correggio, Francisco Balbi di. *The Siege of Malta 1565*. Originally published in Ernle Bradford, trans., The Siege of Malta, Spanish Edition of 1568. Rochester, NY: The Boydell Press, 2005.
- Crowley, Roger. *1453—The Holy War for Constantinople and*

the Clash of Islam and the West. New York: Hyperion, 2005.

• _____. Empires of the Sea—The Siege of Malta, the Battle of Lepanto, and the Contest for the Center of the World. New York: Random House, 2009.

• Dickson, Gary. The Children's Crusade—Medieval History, Modern Mythistory. New York: Palgrave Macmillan, 2010.

• Delaney, Carol. Columbus and the Quest for Jerusalem. New York: Free Press, 2011.

• Duffy, Eamon. Ten Popes Who Shook the World. New Haven, CT: Yale University Press, 2011. Kindle edition.

• France, John. Victory in the East—A Military History of the First Crusade. New York: Cambridge University Press, 1996.

• _____. Western Warfare in the Age of the Crusades, 1000—1300. Ithaca, NY: Cornell University Press, 1999.

• Gaposchkin, M. Cecilia. The Making of Saint Louis—Kingship, Sanctity, and Crusade in the Later Middle Ages. Ithaca, NY: Cornell University Press, 2008.

• Grousset, Réne. The Epic of the Crusades. Translated by Noel Lindsay. New York: Orion Press, 1970.

• Hallam, Elizabeth, ed. Chronicles of the Crusades—Nine Crusades and Two Hundred Years of Bitter Conflict for the Holy Land Brought to Life Through the Word of Those Who Were Actually There. New York: Weidenfeld and Nicolson, 1989.

• Hanson, Victor Davis. The Father of Us All—War and History, Ancient and Modern. New York: Bloomsbury Press, 2010.

• Holland, Tom. The Forge of Christendom—the End of Days and the Epic Rise of the West. New York: Doubleday, 2008.

• _____. The Shadow of the Sword—The Birth of Islam and the Rise of the Global Arab Empire. New York: Doubleday, 2012. Kindle edition.

• Housley, Norman. Fighting for the Cross—Crusading to the Holy Land. New Haven, CT: Yale University Press, 2008.

• _____. Contesting the Crusades. Malden, MA: Blackwell Publishing, 2006.

• Hughes, Philip. The Church in Crisis: A History of the General Councils, 325—1870. Garden City, NY: Hanover House, 1961.

• Karsh, Efraim. *Islamic Imperialism—A History*. New Haven, CT: Yale University Press, 2006.
• Le Goff, Jacques. *Saint Louis*. Translated by Gareth Evan Gollrad. Notre Dame, IN: University of Notre Dame Press, 2009.
• Maalouf, Amin. *The Crusades Through Arab Eyes*. New York: Schocken Books, 1984.
• Madden, Thomas F. *The New Concise History of the Crusades— Updated Edition*. New York: Rowman & Littlefield Publishers, Inc., 2005.
• _____. ed., *Crusades—The Illustrated History*. Ann Arbor, MI: The University of Michigan Press, 2004.
• _____. ed., *The Crusades—The Essential Readings*. Malden, MA: Blackwell Publishing, 2002.
• Millar, Simon. *Vienna 1683—Christian Europe Repels the Ottomans*. New York: Osprey Publishing Limited, 2008.
• Moczar, Diane. *Islam at the Gates—How Christendom Defeated the Ottoman Turks*. Manchester, NH: Sophia Institute Press, 2008.
• Möhring, Hannes. Translated by Bachrach, David S. *Saladin—The Sultan and His Times, 1138—1193*. Baltimore, MD: The Johns Hopkins University Press, 2005.
• Mullins, Edwin. *Cluny—In Search of God's Lost Empire*. New York: BlueBridge, 2006.
• Nicolle, David. *The Fourth Crusade, 1202–1204—The Betrayal of Byzantium*. New York: Osprey Publishing Limited, 2011.
• _____. *Poitiers AD 732—Charles Martel Turns the Islamic Tide*. New York: Osprey Publishing Limited, 2008.
• _____. *Acre 1291—Bloody Sunset of the Crusader States*. New York: Osprey Publishing Limited, 2005.
• _____. *The Third Crusade, 1191—Richard the Lionheart, Saladin and the Struggle for Jerusalem*. New York: Osprey Publishing Limited, 2005.
• _____. *The First Crusade, 1096–1099—Conquest of the Holy Land*. New York: Osprey Publishing Limited, 2003.
• _____. *Hattin 1187—Saladin's Greatest Victory*. New York: Osprey Publishing Limited, 1993.
• Pickles, Tim. *Malta 1565—Last Battle of the Crusades*. New

York: Osprey Publishing Limited, 1998.
* Pernoud, Régine. trans. Enid Grant. *The Crusaders—the Struggle for the Holy Land*. San Francisco: Ignatius Press, 2003.
* _____. *The Templars—Knights of Christ*. Translated by Henry Taylor. San Francisco: Ignatius Press, 2009.
* Phillips, Jonathan. *The Second Crusade—Extending the Frontiers of Christendom*. New Haven, CT: Yale University Press, 2007.
* _____. *The Fourth Crusade and the Sack of Constantinople*. New York: Penguin Books, 2004.
* Peters, Edward, ed. *The First Crusade—The Chronicle of Fulcher of Chartres and Other Source Material, Second Edition*. Philadelphia: University of Pennsylvania Press, 1998.
* Powell, James M. ed., *Innocent III—Vicar of Christ or Lord of the World?* Washington, DC: The Catholic University of America Press, 1994.
* Queller, Donald E. and Madden, Thomas F. *The Fourth Crusade—The Conquest of Constantinople, Second Edition*. Philadelphia: University of Pennsylvania Press, 1997.
* Rega, Frank M. *St. Francis of Assisi and the Conversion of the Muslims—with a Concise Biography of the Saint*. Rockford, IL: TAN Books and Publishers, Inc., 2007.
* Riley-Smith, Jonathan. *The First Crusade and the Idea of Crusading*. Philadelphia: University of Pennsylvania Press, 2009.
* _____. *The Crusades, Christianity, and Islam*. New York: Columbia University Press, 2008.
* _____. *The Crusades—A History, Second Edition*. New Haven, CT: Yale University Press, 2005.
* _____. *What Were the Crusades? Third Edition*. San Francisco: Ignatius Press, 2002.
* _____. *The First Crusaders 1095–1131*. New York: Cambridge University Press, 1997.
* _____, ed. *The Oxford Illustrated History of the Crusades*. New York: Oxford University Press, 1995.
* _____, ed. *The Atlas of the Crusades*. New York: Facts on File, Inc., 1991.
* Runciman, Steven. *A History of the Crusades, Volume I—The*

First Crusade and the Foundation of the Kingdom of Jerusalem. London: The Folio Society, 1994.

* _____. *A History of the Crusades, Volume II—The Kingdom of Jerusalem and the Frankish East, 1100–1187.* London: The Folio Society, 1994.

* _____. *A History of the Crusades, Volume III—The Kingdom of Acre and the later Crusades.* London: The Folio Society, 1994.

* Seward, Desmond. *The Monks of War—The Military Religious Orders.* New York: Penguin Books, 1995.

* Society for the Study of the Crusades and the Latin East. *Crusades*—Volume 11, Surrey, England: 2012.

* _____. *Crusades*—Volume 10, Surrey, England: 2011.

* _____. *Crusades*—Volume 9, Surrey, England: 2010.

* _____. *Crusades*—Volume 8, Surrey, England: 2009.

* _____. *Crusades*—Volume 7, Surrey, England: 2008.

* Smail, R.C. *Crusading Warfare, 1097–1193,* New York: Cambridge University Press, 1995.

* Spencer, Robert. *The Truth about Muhammad—Founder of the World's Most Intolerant Religion.* Washington, D.C.: Regnery Publishing, Inc., 2006.

* Stark, Rodney. *God's Battalions—The Case for the Crusades.* New York: HarperCollins, 2009.

* Stoye, John. *The Siege of Vienna—The Last Great Trial between Cross and Crescent.* New York: Pegasus Press, 2006.

* Strayer, Joseph R. *The Albigensian Crusades.* Ann Arbor, MI: The University of Michigan Press, 1992.

* Sumption, Jonathan. *The Age of Pilgrimage—the Medieval Journey to God.* Mahwah, NJ: HiddenSpring, 2003.

* Tyerman, Christopher. *The Debate on the Crusades.* Manchester: Manchester University Press, 2011.

* _____. *God's War—A New History of the Crusades.* Cambridge, MA: The Belknap Press of Harvard University Press, 2006.

* Wilken, Robert Louis. *The Christians as the Romans Saw Them.* Second Edition. New Haven, CT: Yale University Press, 2003.

About the Author

Steve Weidenkopf is a lecturer in Church history at the Notre Dame Graduate School of Christendom College in Alexandria, Virginia. He is the creator and co-author of *Epic: A Journey Through Church History* and the author and presenter of *The Early Church* adult faith formation studies. Steve is a member of the Society for the Study of the Crusades and the Latin East—an international academic group dedicated to the field of Crusading history—and is also a Knight of the Equestrian Order of the Holy Sepulchre of Jerusalem. Steve and his wife live in Northern Virginia with their six children.

Endnotes

1. Rodney Stark, *God's Battalions—The Case for the Crusades* (New York: HarperCollins Publishers, 2009), 6–7.
2. Which usually involves a negative and unhistorical presentation of such events as the Crusades, the Inquisition, the Spanish Armada, and the reign of Queen Mary (falsely known as "Bloody Mary").
3. Charlotte Edwardes, "Ridley Scott's New Crusades films 'panders to Osama bin Laden,'" *The Telegraph*, January 18, 2004, accessed February 2, 2013, http://www.telegraph.co.uk/news/worldnews/northamerica/usa/1452000/Ridley-Scotts-new-Crusades-film-panders-to-Osama-bin-Laden.html.
4. "Kingdom of Heaven," accessed February 2, 2013, http://www.imdb.com/title/tt0320661/?ref_=sr_1.
5. Christopher Tyerman, *The Debate on the Crusades* (New York: Manchester University Press, 2011), 1.
6. Ibid., 5.
7. See Thomas F. Madden, *The New Concise History of the Crusades Updated Edition* (New York: Rowman & Littlefield Publishers, Inc., 2005), 209.
8. Kenneth M. Setton, "Lutheranism and the Turkish Peril," *Balkan Studies* 3 (1962): 142, in Madden, *New Concise*, 209.
9. Madden, *The New Concise History of the Crusades*, 210.
10. Tyerman, *Debate*, 67.
11. This is the true legacy of the Enlightenment in relation to the Crusades. As Christopher Tyerman points out, "The legacy of the Enlightenment had established the Crusades as a reference point for cultural commentary as much on contemporary as on medieval society" (*Debate*, 95).
12. Stark, 6.
13. Tyerman, *Debate*, 67.
14. Jonathan Riley-Smith, *The Crusades—A History*, (New Haven, CT: Yale University Press, 2005), 298.
15. Denis Diderot, *Dictionnaire encyclopedique, Oeuvres complètes* (Paris, 1821), xiv, 496–511, in Tyerman, *Debate*, 78.
16. Tyerman, *Debate*, 81, and Hume, *The History of England*, vol. I, 234, Stark, 6.
17. Edward Gibbon, *The History of the Decline and Fall of the Roman*

Empire, vii, 188, in Tyerman, *Debate*, 85.

18. Gibbon, *Decline and Fall*, book 6, chapter 58.

19. Madden, *The New Concise History of the Crusades*, 215.

20. Jonathan Riley-Smith, "Islam and the Crusades in History and Imagination, 8 November 1898–11 September 2001," Crusades 2 (2003): 158. Quoted in Madden, *The New Concise History*, 215.

21. Published from 1934–1936.

22. Thomas F. Madden, *The Crusades—The Essential Readings* (Malden, MA: Blackwell Publishing, 2002), 1.

23. Erdmann was not a Nazi; in fact he despised the Nazi regime. He was conscripted into the *Wehrmacht* and served as a translator. He contracted typhus in March 1945 and died.

24. Thomas Madden wrote that "Runciman singlehandedly crafted the current popular concept of the Crusades." Madden, *The New Concise History*, 216.

25. Tyerman, *Debate*, 197.

26. Ibid., 192.

27. Stephen Runciman, "Byzantium and the Crusade," in Madden, *The Crusades—The Essential Readings*, 220.

28. Tyerman, *Debate*, 195.

29. Steven Runciman, *A History of the Crusades*, vol. III (London: The Folio Society, 1996), 401.

30. Some of these scholars are faithful Catholics, including Jonathan Riley-Smith, who is a Knight of Malta and began the shift of modern Crusade studies toward a religious-participant view. Another Catholic scholar is Thomas Madden, who teaches at St. Louis University.

31. Robert Barron, *Catholicism—A Journey to the Heart of the Faith* (New York: Image Books, 2011), 162.

32. Ibid.

33. Ibid.

34. Headed at the time by Joseph Cardinal Ratzinger—later Pope Benedict XVI.

35. International Theological Commission, *Memory and Reconciliation: The Church and the Faults of the Past*.

36. The pope's recognition of the importance of historical context and the work of historians was illustrated in his *Discourse to the Participants in the International Symposium of Study on the Inquisition* held on October 31, 1998. He said, "This is the reason why the first step consists in asking the historians . . . to offer help toward a reconstruction, as

precise as possible, of the events, of the customs, of the mentality of the time, in the light of historical context of the epoch." In terms of passing judgment on past Catholics, John Paul II said in his Angelus Address on March 12, 2000: "This is not a judgment on the subjective responsibility of our brothers and sisters who have gone before us: judgment belongs to God alone . . . Today's act is a sincere recognition of the sins committed by the Church's children in the distant and recent past, and a humble plea for God's forgiveness. This will reawaken consciences, enabling Christians to enter the third millennium with greater openness to God and his plan of love."

37. Available online at http://www.vatican.va/holy_father/john_paul_ii/audiences/1999/documents/hf_jp-ii_aud_01091999_en.html. Accessed March 2, 2013.

38. Hilaire Belloc, *The Great Heresies* (Manassas, VA: Trinity Communications, 1987), 127.

39. The full quote is "Reading history from present to past is reading into rather than learning from it." Steven Ozment, *A Mighty Fortress—A New History of the German People* (New York: HarperCollins, 2004), 8.

40. International Theological Commission, *Memory and Reconciliation*, 4.2.

41. Walter Cardinal Brandmülller, trans. Michael J. Miller, *Light and Shadows—Church History amid Faith, Fact and Legend* (San Francisco: Ignatius Press, 2009), 84.

42. Indeed, there are five different schools of historians, each advocating a different definition of the Crusades. The Generalists believe any Christian religious war fought for God was a Crusade. The Popularists think a Crusade was an eschatological expression of the people. The Traditionalists view only those expeditions launched toward Jerusalem or for its recovery as Crusades. The Pluralists posit that the Crusades were not discrete campaigns but rather continuous expeditions throughout the world. Finally, the Traditional-Pluralists believe the eight traditionally numbered Crusades to the Holy Land and Egypt assist in understanding the general movement but also acknowledge the Crusades took on different forms and encompassed many regions.

43. Jonathan Riley-Smith, "The Crusading Movement and Historians," *The Oxford Illustrated History of the Crusades,* ed. Jonathan Riley-Smith, (New York: Oxford University Press, 1995), 8.

44. Tyerman, *Debate*, 77. In the sixteenth through eighteenth centuries the terms "holy war" and "war of the cross" were used to describe the Crusades.

45. The words are from Pope Pius II (r. 1458–1464), the only pope to actually take the Crusader vow. Norman Housley, "Pope Pius II and Crusading," *Crusades*, vol. 11, The Society for the Study of the Crusades and the Latin East, (Burlington, VT: Ashgate Publishing Company, 2012), 221. Other terms used were *iter* (journey), *expeditio* (expedition), and *peregrinatio* (pilgrimage).

46. Riley-Smith, *The Crusades*, xxxi.

47. Ibid., 15.

48. These ingredients are defined in Jonathan Riley-Smith, *What Were the Crusades?*, (San Francisco: Ignatius Press, 2002), 2–3.

49. Jonathan Riley-Smith, *The Crusades*, 15.

50. Jonathan Riley-Smith, *The Crusades, Christianity, and Islam*, 4.

51. Ibid., 5.

52. Tom Holland, *In the Shadow of the Sword—The Birth of Islam and the Rise of Global Arab Empire*, (New York: Doubleday, 2012), loc. 952. Kindle edition.

53. A professor at the University of Münster has recently opined that Mohammed is a figure of myth. See Holland, loc. 764.

54. Ibid., loc. 721. Kindle edition.

55. The opinion of a sixth-century Christian as quoted in Holland, *In the Shadow of the Sword*, loc. 3792. Kindle edition.

56. It was reported that they drank their victims' blood during battle. See Holland, *In the Shadow of the Sword*, loc. 3800. Kindle edition.

57. Holland, *In the Shadow of the Sword*, loc. 3800. Kindle edition.

58. Ibn Ishaq, *The Life of Muhammad: A Translation of Ibn Ishaq's Sirat Rasul Allah*, trans. A. Guillaume (Oxford University Press, 1955), 106. Quoted in Robert Spencer, *The Truth about Muhammad—Founder of the World's Most Intolerant Religion* (Washington, DC: Regnery Publishing, Inc., 2006), 42.

59. Holland, *In the Shadow of the Sword*, loc. 5623. Kindle edition.

60. For the numbers of raids see Ibn Ishaq in Tom Holland, *The Forge of Christendom—The End of Days and the Epic Rise of the West* (New York: Doubleday, 2008), 424. For the name of Mohammed's sword see Holland, *The Forge of Christendom*, 82.

61. Salih Muslim in Holland, *In the Shadow of the Sword*, loc. 64. Kindle edition.

62. Muhammad ibn Umar al-Waqidi, *Kitab al-Maghazi*, vol. 3 (London: Oxford University Press, 1966), 1113. Quoted in Efraim Karsh, *Islamic Imperialism—A History* (New Haven, CT: Yale University

Press, 2006), 19.

63. Qur'an 9.29.

64. See Qur'an quote in Karsh, 19.

65. Holland, *The Forge of Christendom*, 237. The church was rebuilt in 1048 and then renovated and expanded by the Crusaders after the liberation of Jerusalem.

66. Ibid., 235.

67. Ibid., 236.

68. Yahya ibn Said, ed. And trans. Ignati Kratchkovsky and Alexander Vasiliev, in *Patrologia Orientalis*, ed. René Graffin and François Nau (Paris, 1907–), 23:502–12. Quoted in Andrew Jotischky, "The Christians of Jerusalem, the Holy Sepulchre and the Origins of the First Crusade," *Crusades*, vol. 7, The Society for the Study of the Crusades and the Latin East (Burlington, VT: Ashgate Publishing Company, 2008), 45.

69. Jonathan Sumption, *Age of Pilgrimage—The Medieval Journey to God* (Mahwah, NJ: HiddenSpring Books, 2003), 257–258.

70. Hilaire Belloc, *The Crusades—the World's Debate* (Rockford, IL: TAN Books and Publishers, Inc., 1992 reprint), 17. René Grousset considers the loss at Manzikert "one of the worst disasters in European history." See Grousset, *The Epic of the Crusades*, trans. Noel Lindsay (New York: Orion Press, 1970), 3.

71. Jonathan Riley-Smith, *The Oxford Illustrated History of the Crusades*, 1.

72. There are five different accounts of Urban's speech, all written well after the event, although it is probable that most of the authors were present or at least compiled their version of the speech from those who were present. The five authors are Fulcher of Chartres, who was present at Clermont but did not write his account until 1101; Robert the Monk, who wrote his account in 1107 and may have been present; Baldric of Dol, who may have been present, wrote his account c. 1108–1110; Guibert of Nogent, who may have been present, wrote his work in 1109; William of Malmesbury, who was not present at Clermont, wrote his work in 1129.

73. Jonathan Riley-Smith, *The First Crusaders, 1095–1131* (Cambridge University Press, 1997), 33.

74. Robert the Monk, *Historia Hierosolymitana*, in *The First Crusade—The Chronicle of Fulcher of Chartres and Other Source Material*, ed. Edward Peters, (Philadelphia: University of Pennsylvania Press, 1998), 28.

75. Robert the Monk, in Peters, 27.

76. Canon of the Council of Clermont in Peters, 37.

77. Pope Bl. Urban II, *Letter to His Supporters in Bologna* in Peters, 44.

78. Christopher Tyerman, *God's War—A New History of the Crusades* (Cambridge, MA: The Belknap Press of Harvard University Press: 2006), 32–35.

79. Ex. 15:3

80. See 1 Sam. 15:3 and 2 Macc. 15:27–28.

81. John 18:11, Matt. 26:51, and Luke 22:51.

82. For Jesus' acknowledgement of the centurion's faith, Matt. 8:5–13; Luke 7:2–9. For the centurion at the Cross, Matt. 27:54, Mark 15:39, and Luke 23:47.

83. Acts 10.

84. Sts. Sebastian and Mercurius are two examples.

85. Aristotle, *Politics,* Books I & VII.

86. Tyerman, *God's War,* 32.

87. *Catechism of the Catholic Church,* 2309.

88. Tyerman, *God's War,* 35.

89. Jonathan Riley-Smith, *The Crusades,* 13.

90. See Humbert of Romans, "*Sermo I ad peregrinos crucesignatos,*" in *Crusade Propaganda,* ed. Maier, 212 in Jonathan Riley-Smith, *The Crusades, Christianity, and Islam,* 40.

91. Tyerman, *God's War,* 75.

92. John France, "Patronage and the Appeal of the First Crusade" in *The Crusades—The Essential Readings,* ed. Madden, 195–196.

93. Ibid., 196.

94. J.A. Brundage, *Medieval Canon Law and the Crusader* (Madison: University of Wisconsin Press, 1969), 77 in Norman Housley, *Contesting the Crusades* (Malden, MA: Blackwell Publishing, 2006), 15.

95. Jonathan Riley-Smith, *The Crusades,* 20.

96. Housley, *Contesting the Crusades,* 29.

97. Jonathan Riley-Smith, *The First Crusade and the Idea of Crusading* (Philadelphia: University of Pennsylvania Press, 2009), 140.

98. Jonathan Riley-Smith, "Crusading as an Act of Love" in *The Crusades—The Essential Readings,* ed. Madden, 38.

99. Housley, *Fighting for the Cross,* 180.

100. Ibid., 173–176.

101. Ibid., 73

102. Eudes of Châteauroux, "*Sermo V ad invitandam ad crucem,*" in *Crusade Propaganda,* ed. Maier, 170. Quoted in Jonathan Riley-Smith, *The*

Crusades, Christianity, and Islam, 40.
103. James of Vitry, "Sermo II ad crucesignatos vel-signandos," in *Crusade Propaganda*, ed. Maier, 112. Quoted in Jonathan Riley-Smith, *The Crusades, Christianity, and Islam*, 40.
104. *Recueil des chartes de l'abbaye de Cluny*, ed. A. Bruel, v. (Paris: 1894), 51–3, no. 3703; *Cartulaire de l'abbaye de Saint-Victor de Marseille*, ed. M. Guérard (Paris: 1857), I, 167–168, no. 143, Tyerman, *God's War*, 27.
105. Giles Constable, "Medieval Charters as a Source for the History of the Crusades," in *The Crusades—The Essential Readings*, ed. Madden, 148.
106. Riley-Smith, *The First Crusade*, 23.
107. Baldric of Bourgueil, "*Historia Jerosolimitana*," in Jonathan-Riley Smith, *The Crusades, Christianity and Islam*, 17.
108. Jonathan Riley-Smith, *The Crusades, Christianity and Islam*, 40–41.
109. Régine Pernoud, *The Crusaders*, trans. Enid Grant (San Francisco: Ignatius Press, 2003), 23.
110. Madden, *New Concise History of the Crusades*, 13.
111. Ibid.
112. Housley, *Fighting for the Cross*, 236.
113. New American Bible translation.
114. Fulcher, *Chronicle*, Book I, XXX. 1, in Peters, 93.
115. John France, *Western Warfare in the Age of the Crusades 1000–1300* (Ithaca, NY: Cornell University Press, 1999), 210.
116. Thomas F. Madden, *The New Concise History of the Crusades Updated Edition* (New York: Rowan & Littlefield Publishers, Inc., 2005), 10.
117. Urban II, Letter to the Faithful in Flanders, December 1095, in Peters, *The First Crusade*, 42.
118. Steven Runciman, *A History of the Crusades, vol. 1, The First Crusade and the Foundation of the Kingdom of Jerusalem* (London: The Folio Society, 1994), 94.
119. There were reports of exorcised demons, healings, and conversions. Some believed Peter held a letter from heaven wherein God urged Christians to take the cross. Madden, *The New Concise History of the Crusades*, 16.
120. John France, *Victory in the East—A Military History of the First Crusade* (New York: Cambridge University Press, 1994), 136.
121. The phrase "advance guard" is from Tyerman, *God's War*, 94.
122. Tyerman, *God's War*, 97.
123. France, *Victory*, 93.
124. Madden, *The New Concise History of the Crusades*, 17.

125. France, *Victory*, 93.

126. Albert of Aachen in Peters, *The First Crusade*, 149.

127. Salomon bar Simson, *Chronicles of the Crusades—Nine Crusades and Two Hundred Years of Bitter Conflict for the Holy Land Brought to Life Through the Words of Those Who Were Actually There*, ed. Elizabeth Hallam (New York: Weidenfeld and Nicolson, 1989), 69.

128. Anonymous of Mainz in Peters, *The First Crusade*, 114.

129. Pernoud, *The Crusaders*, 126.

130. Tyerman, *God's War*, 101–102.

131. Numbers from Albert of Aachen in Peters, *The First Crusade*, 110.

132. For the numbers of warriors, see France, *Victory*, 142. Raymond d'Aguilers, who was a participant, used the phrase "God's Army" in his chronicle of the First Crusade. Crusaders possessing a special identity, see Tyerman, *God's War*, 105.

133. Tyerman, *God's War*, 119.

134. Henry IV, holy Roman emperor, had been excommunicated because of the Investiture Controversy. King Philip I of France was excommunicated by Urban II at Clermont for his bigamous marriage, and King William II of England had political issues with the Church and St. Anselm of Canterbury.

135. Fulcher of Chartres lists the following nationalities in his *Chronicle*: French, Flemings, Frisians, Gauls, Lotharingians, Allemani, Bavarians, Normans, English, Scots, Aquitanians, Italians, Dacians, Iberians, Bretons, Greeks, and Armenians. Fulcher of Chartres, *Chronicle*, Book I, XIII.4 in Peters, 68.

136. Hilaire Belloc makes this point: "For it was Gaul, between the Rhine, the Atlantic, the Alps, and the Pyrenees, which furnished by far the greater part of the armies which attempted to restore the Christian Roman world and throw back the Mohammedan in the East." *Crusades—The World's Debate* (Rockford, IL: TAN Books and Publishers, Inc., 1992), 22.

137. Tyerman, *God's War*, 117.

138. Ibid., 82.

139. France, *Western Warfare*, 159.

140. His brother Baldwin I and his cousin Baldwin Le Bourcq (II).

141. Tyerman, *God's War*, 114.

142. Warren Carroll, *The Building of Christendom—A History of Christendom, vol. 2* (Front Royal, VA: Christendom College Press, 1987), 538.

143. Ibid.

144. France, *Victory*, 155.

145. Ibid, 157.

146. The clearing of the old Roman road is in France, *Victory*, 122, and the placing of the crosses is mentioned in the *Gesta* in Peters, 180.

147. Tyerman, *God's War*, 124.

148. *Chronicle*, Book I, X.7, in Peters, 64.

149. David Nicolle, *The First Crusade 1096–1099—Conquest of the Holy Land* (New York: Osprey Publishing Ltd., 2003), 33.

150. France, *Victory*, 137.

151. Nicolle, *The First Crusade*, 45.

152. Fulcher of Chartres, *Chronicle* Book I. XIII in Peters, *The First Crusade*, 68.

153. Tyerman, *God's War*, 131.

154. John C. Anderssohn, *The Ancestry & Life of Godfrey of Bouillon* (Bloomington, IN: Indiana University Publications, 1947), 73.

155. France, *Victory*, 222.

156. Ibid., 224.

157. Ibid., 208

158. Albert of Aachen, *Historia Hierosolymitana*, RHC Oc. 4, 372, in France, *Victory*, 230.

159. W. Stubbs, ed., *Itinerarium peregrinorum et Gesta regis Ricardi* (RS, London, 1864), trans. H.J. Nicholson as *Chronicle of the Third Crusade* (Aldershot: 1997), ch. 67, tr. pp. 127–8 quoted in Housley, *Fighting for the Cross*, 153.

160. Fulcher of Chartres, *Chronicle*, Book I, XVI.2, in Peters, 73.

161. France, *Victory*, 241.

162. Ibid., 267.

163. Pope Paschal II in his letter to the clergy in Gaul (1099) wrote: "[W]e decree that those be held in disgrace who left the siege of Antioch through weak or questionable faith; let them remain in excommunication, unless they affirm with certain pledges that they will return." Peters, 297.

164. Some sources indicate Stephen was at Antioch, but deeming the siege a failure left one day before the Crusaders liberated it. Madden believes Stephen was in Alexandretta. Madden, *New Concise History of the Crusades*, 28.

165. France, *Victory*, 279.

166. Tyerman, *God's War*, 144.

167. France, *Victory*, 283.

168. Ibid., 294.
169. *Gesta Francorum* in Peters, *The First Crusade*, 223.
170. France, *Victory*, 197.
171. Ibid., 148.
172. France, *Victory*, 311.
173. Fulcher of Chartres, *Chronicle*, Book I, XXV.2, in Peters, 84.
174. Numbers marching to Jerusalem from Raymond d'Aguilers in France, *Victory*, 3.
175. Raymond d'Aguilers in Peters, 254.
176. Ibid., 255.
177. France, *Western Warfare*, 118.
178. Tyerman, *God's War*, 157.
179. France, *Victory*, 355.
180. Thomas F. Madden, "Inventing the Crusades," review of *The Crusades, Christianity and Islam*, by Jonathan-Riley Smith, First Things, June/July 2009, http://www.firstthings.com/article/2009/05/inventing-the-crusades-1243195699, accessed July 31, 2013.
181. France, *Victory*, 355.
182. Peters, 255.
183. *Chronicle*, Book I, XXVII, 13, in Peters, *The First Crusade*, 91.
184. Peters, 294.
185. Raymond d'Aguiliers, *Historia Francorum qui ceperunt Iherusalem*, RHC Occ, iii, 300, trans. J.H. and L.L. Hill (Philadelphia: 1968), 128. in Tyerman, *God's War*, 31.
186. The linkage of the passages in the various chronicles to Scripture is found in Walter Brandmüller, *Light and Shadows*, 31 & 157.
187. G.K. Beale, *The Book of Revelation—A Commentary on the Greek Text* (Grand Rapids, MI: William B. Eerdmans Publishing Company, 1999), 775.
188. Ibid., 780. Beale also comments: "Perhaps uppermost in John's mind is Joel 4:2, 11–12, 14, which says that God will enter into judgment with the 'surrounding nations' outside Jerusalem"; Ibid., 781.
189. Ibid., 781.
190. Ibid., 782.
191. John Hugh Hill and Laurita L. Hill were the first to recognize the imagery used by Christian sources referenced scripture. Kedar, "The Jerusalem Massacre of 1099 in the Western Historiography of the Crusades," *Crusades*, vol. 3 The Society for the Study of the Crusades and the Latin East (Burlington, VT: Ashgate Publishing

Company, 2004), 65.

192. France, *Victory*, 356.

193. Kedar, "The Jerusalem Massacre of 1099 in the Western Historiography of the Crusades," 25.

194. Ibid.

195. Amin Maalouf, *The Crusades through Arab Eyes*, trans. Jon Rothschild (New York: Shocken Books, 1984), 135.

196. Madden, New Concise history of the Crusades, 182.

197. "[A] position which recognized the claims of the Church while conceding practical power to the lay authority." France, *Victory*, 357.

198. Housley, *Fighting for the Cross*, 7.

199. France, *Victory*, 14.

200. The eleven-percent figure is found in Jonathan Riley-Smith, "Early Crusaders to the East and the Costs of Crusading, 1095–1130" in Madden, *The Crusades—Essential Readings*, 161. Numbers of Western Europeans by 1100 is in Jonathan Riley-Smith, *The Crusades—A History, Second Edition* (New Haven, CT: Yale University Press, 2005), 66.

201. An anonymous trouvère song used for recruitment during the Second Crusade, J. Bédier and P. Aubry, eds., *Les Chansons de Croisade avec Leurs Melodies*, 1909, 8–11; trans. M. Routledge in Jonathan Phillips, *The Second Crusade—Extending the Frontiers of Christendom* (New Haven, CT: Yale University Press, 2007), 283.

202. *Divina dispensation II* in Phillips, *The Second Crusade*, 134.

203. Bernard of Clairvaux, "Epistolae," in *Sancti Bernardi Opera*, 8 vols., eds. J. Leclercq and H. Rohais, (Rome, 1955–1977), no. 247, 140–141 in Phillips, *The Second Crusade*, 65.

204. Outrémer, meaning "overseas," was the French term for the Crusader States.

205. Tyerman, *God's War*, 201.

206. Grousset, *The Epic of the Crusades*, 41.

207. John France, *Western Warfare in the Age of the Crusades 1000–1300* (Ithaca, NY: Cornell University Press, 1999), 214.

208. Benjamin Z. Kedar, "The Subjected Muslims of the Frankish Levant" in Thomas F. Madden, *The Crusades—Essential Readings* (Malden, MA: Blackwell Publishing, 2002), 250.

209. See Riley-Smith, *The Crusades*, 71.

210. Ibid.

211. R.C. Smail, *Crusading Warfare, 1097–1193* (Cambridge, New York:

Cambridge University Press, 1995), 102.
212. Jonathan Riley-Smith, *The First Crusaders*, 161.
213. Pernoud, *The Crusaders*, 104.
214. Riley-Smith, *The Crusades*, 80.
215. Desmond Seward, *The Monks of War—The Military Religious Orders* (New York: Penguin Books, 1995), 19.
216. Riley-Smith, *The Crusades*, 76.
217. Ibid.
218. Seward, *The Monks of War*, 35.
219. Terence Wise, *The Knights of Christ* (London: Osprey Publishing, 1984), 6.
220. Riley-Smith, *The Crusades*, 79.
221. Wise, *The Knights of Christ*, 7.
222. Ibid.
223. Seward, *The Monks of War*, 35.
224. Miriam Rita Tessera, "The Papal Schism of 1130," in *Crusades*, vol. 9 of The Society for the Study of the Crusades and the Latin East (Burlington, VT: Ashgate Publishing Company, 2010), 11.
225. Seward, *The Monks of War*, 17.
226. Wise, *The Knights of Christ*, 26.
227. Seward, *The Monks of War*, 35.
228. Pernoud, *The Crusaders*, 104.
229. Tyerman, *God's War*, 269.
230. Phillips, *The Second Crusade*, xviii.
231. Maalouf, *The Crusades through Arab Eyes*, 135.
232. Madden, *The New Concise History of the Crusades*, 51.
233. *Quantum Praedecessores*, trans. L. & J.S.C. Riley-Smith, *The Crusades: Idea and Reality*, 1095–1274 (London: 1981), 57–59, in Phillips, *The Second Crusade*, 282.
234. Ibid., 281.
235. Phillips, *The Second Crusade*, 50.
236. Warren Carroll, *The Glory of Christendom—A History of Christendom, vol. 3* (Front Royal, VA: Christendom College Press, 1993), 20.
237. Christopher Rengers, O.F.M., Cap., *The 33 Doctors of the Church* (Rockford, IL: TAN Books and Publishers, Inc.), 282.
238. Ibid.
239. Bernard referred to the Crusade as "the business of God, namely the expedition to Jerusalem." Phillips, *The Second Crusade*, 65.
240. Bernard, *"Epistolae,"* in *Sancti Bernardi Opera*, 8 vols., eds J. Leclercq

and H. Rochais, (Rome: Editiones Cistercienses, 1955–77), no. 363, p. 314. Quoted in Phillips, *Second Crusade*, 73.

241. Bernard of Clairvaux, *Letters*, ed. B. Scott James, 2nd ed. (Stroud: 1998), no. 391, 460–463, in Housley, *Fighting for the Cross,* 33.

242. Bernard, *"Epistolae,"* Quoted in *Chronicles of the Crusades,* Hallam, 126.

243. Radulf preached at Cologne, Mainz, Worms, Speyer and Strasbourg.

244. Phillips, *The Second Crusade*, 87.

245. Ibid., 85.

246. Phillips, *The Second Crusade*, 28.

247. *Vita Prima S. Bernardi* in Phillips, *The Second Crusade*, 95.

248. Phillips, *The Second Crusade*, 169.

249. Ibid., 174.

250. Niketas Choniates, *O City of Byzantium—The Annals of Niketas Choniates,* trans. H.J. Magoulias (Detroit: 1984), 39, in Phillips, *The Second Crusade*, 206.

251. Tyerman, *God's War*, 325.

252. Phillips, *The Second Crusade*, 62.

253. Ibid., 63.

254. Ibid.

255. Ibid., 126–127.

256. Grousset, *The Epic of the Crusades,* 118.

257. William of Tyre, *Chronicon*, ed. R.B.C. Huygens, 2 vols., CCCM 63, 63A (Turnhout: 1986), 755, in Phillips, *The Second Crusade*, 211.

258. Ibn Jubayr, *The Travels of Ibn Jubayr*, trans. R.J.C. Broadhurst (London: 1952), 271–272. in Phillips, *The Second Crusade*, 218.

259. Phillips, *The Second Crusade*, 220.

260. *Die Urkunden Konrads III. Und seines Sohns Heinrich*, ed. F. Hausmann, MGH DD 9 (Vienna: 1969), 197, 357 Quoted in Phillips, *The Second Crusade*, 222.

261. Phillips, *The Second Crusade*, 223–224.

262. Tyerman, *God's War*, 335.

263. Ibid.

264. Madden, *The New Concise History of the Crusades*, 61.

265. Ibid.

266. Tyerman, *God's War*, 336.

267. Rengers, *The 33 Doctors of the Church*, 294.

268. Bernard, *De Consideratione*, in Riley-Smith, *The Crusades*, 131.

269. Würzburg, chronicler in *Chronicles of the Crusades,* 147.

270. Phillips, *The Second Crusade*, 278–279.

271. For criticism of Bernard, see Barron, *Catholicism*, 162.

272. Carroll, *The Glory of Christendom*, 75.

273. Ibn Munir of Tripoli was a Palestinian poet in the service of the Muslim ruler Nur al-Din. Ibn Munir of Tripoli, *The Crusades: Islamic Perspectives* trans. C. Hillenbrand, (Edinburgh: 1999), 150, in Tyerman, *God's War,* 344.

274. Opening lines of *Audita Tremendi.*

275. William of Tyre, *A History of Deeds Done Beyond the Sea*, trans. E.A. Babcock and A.C. Krey (New York: 1976, reprint of 1941 ed.), ii, 407–408 in Tyerman, *God's War*, 343.

276. Hannes Möhring, *Saladin—The Sultan and His Times, 1138–1193*, trans. David S. Bachrach, intro and preface Paul M. Cobb (Baltimore: The Johns Hopkins University Press, 2005), xviii.

277. Edward Gibbon, *The Decline and Fall of the Roman Empire*, ch. LIX.

278. Francesco Gabrieli, *Arab Historians of the Crusades* (Routledge: New York, 1969), 100 in Madden, *The New Concise History of the Crusades*, 69.

279. Möhring, *Saladin*, 29.

280. Tyerman, *God's War*, 349.

281. Möhring, *Saladin*, 31.

282. Ibid., 36.

283. Tyerman, *God's War*, 353.

284. David Nicolle, *Hattin 1187—Saladin's Greatest Victory* (Oxford, UK: Osprey Publishing, 1993), 48.

285. Tyerman, *God's War*, 356.

286. The apt description of the effects of Baldwin's leprosy is found in Tyerman, *God's War*, 356. The king, at times, was too sick to even stand, so he marched with his army while being carried on a litter.

287. Madden, *New Concise History of the Crusades*, 72.

288. Marriage was frequently used by medieval nobility as an avenue for power, and although the Church taught the indissolubility of the sacrament, the teaching was not always perfectly lived, especially during dynastic disputes.

289. Tyerman, *God's War*, 365.

290. Nicolle, *Hattin 1187*, 56.

291. Seward, *The Monks of War*, 53.

292. Tyerman indicates Saladin had a 30,000-man army (*God's War*, 368), whereas Seward believes it was 60,000 strong (*The Monks of War*, 53).

293. Tyerman, *God's War*, 368.

294. Nicolle, *Hattin 1187*, 65.

295. Ibid., 64.
296. Ibid., 79.
297. Ibn al-Athir in Seward, *The Monks of War*, 54.
298. Nicolle, *Hattin 1187*, 79.
299. Tyerman, *God's War*, 371.
300. Nicolle, *Hattin 1187*, 88.
301. France, *Western Warfare*, 224.
302. John France, "The Second Crusade—War Cruel and Unremitting", in *Crusades—The Illustrated History*, ed. Thomas F. Madden (Ann Arbor: The University of Michigan Press, 2004), 76.
303. Ibn al-Athir in Maalouf, *The Crusades Through Arab Eyes*, 198. In Ridley Scott's 2005 film, *Kingdom of Heaven*, Balian of Ibelin is the main character and is portrayed by Orlando Bloom. This historical scene of Balian staring down and threatening Saladin is ripe for a great on-screen portrayal. Unfortunately, the reality is watered down to fit the preconceived erroneous notions of the Crusades held by the director, producer, and writer. It was but one great opportunity lost in the film.
304. Grousset, *The Epic of the Crusades*, 173.
305. Möhring indicates 7,000–8,000 were sold (*Saladin*, 66). France in Madden's *Illustrated History of the Crusades* provides a figure of 15,000 (p. 77).
306. Möhring, *Saladin*, 67.
307. Stark, *God's Battalions*, 198.
308. Gregory VIII, *Audita Tremendi* in Riley Smith, *The Crusades*, 137.
309. Tyerman, *God's War*, 374.
310. *Itinerarium Peregrinorum et Gesta Regis Ricardi, The Chronicle of the Third Crusade*, trans. H. Nicholson, (Aldershot: 2001), 48, in Tyerman, *God's War*, 396.
311. Tyerman, *God's War*, 398.
312. David Nicolle, *The Third Crusade 1191—Richard the Lionheart, Saladin and the Struggle for Jerusalem* (Oxford, UK: Osprey Publishing, 2005), 43.
313. There is some debate in academic circles over whether Isaac actually entered into the treaty. Riley-Smith (*The Crusades*, 139) and Madden (*The New Concise History of the Crusades*, 80) agree he did but Savva Neocleous in "The Byzantines and Saladin: Opponents of the Third Crusade?," *Crusades*, vol. 9, The Society for the Study of the Crusades and the Latin East (Burlington, VT: Ashgate Publishing Company, 2010), 87–106, argues differently. Neocleous

believes there was no formal alliance between Isaac and Saladin but rather an informal cooperation due to Isaac's belief that Frederick's real objective was Constantinople not Jerusalem. He writes, "[T]he purported Byzantine-Muslim collusion against the Third Crusade was a myth created by the Latins to make sense of Isaak's efforts to destroy the Germans." Regardless, the facts clearly show Isaac was an active antagonist of the Third Crusade, and his efforts clearly hindered German progress on the march.

314. Estimate of strength from France, *Victory in the East*, 136. For the army's taking three days to pass a single point, Tyerman, *God's War*, 418.
315. Kenneth M. Setton, ed., *A History of the Crusades*, vol. II, eds. Robert L. Wolff and Harry W. Hazard (Philadelphia: 1962), 113, in Carroll, *The Glory of Christendom*, 123.
316. Tyerman, *God's War*, 427.
317. Helen Nicholson, "The Third Crusade—A Campaign of Europe's Elite," in *Crusades—The Illustrated History*, ed. Madden, 84.
318. Ibn al-Athir. *Chronicles of the Crusades—Nine Crusades and Two Hundred Years of Bitter Conflict for the Holy Land Brought to Life Through the Words of Those Who Were Actually There*, ed. Elizabeth Hallam (New York: Weidenfeld and Nicolson, 1989), 174.
319. E.N. Johnson, "The Crusades of Frederick Barbarossa and Henry VI" in K.M. Setton, gen. ed., *A History of the Crusades* (Madison, WI: 1969–1989), vol. 2, 87–122, in Housley, *Fighting for the Cross*, 97.
320. Pernoud, *The Crusaders,* 235.
321. Tyerman, *God's War*, 389–390.
322. Ibid., 451.
323. Ibid., 378.
324. Riley-Smith, *The Crusades*, 141.
325. Ibid., 444.
326. Pernoud, *The Crusaders*, 237.
327. Ibid.
328. Ibid., 446.
329. Baha' al-Din Ibn Shaddad, *The Rare and Excellent History of Saladin*, trans. D.S. Richards (Aldershot: 2001), 143, in Housley, *Fighting for the Cross*, 158.
330. Thomas Gregor Wagner and Piers D. Mitchell, "The Illnesses of King Richard and King Philippe on the Third Crusade: An Understanding of Arnaldia and Leonardie," *Crusades*, vol. 10, The Society for the Study of the Crusades and the Latin East (Burlington,

VT: Ashgate Publishing Company, 2011), 26.

331. Helen Nicholson, "The Third Crusade—A Campaign of Europe's Elite," in *Crusades—The Illustrated History*, ed. Madden, 87.

332. Tyerman, *God's War*, 453.

333. Edbury, *Conquest of Jerusalem*, 179–180, in Tyerman, *God's War*, 456.

334. Tyerman, *God's War*, 457.

335. Ibid., 456.

336. Ibid., 454.

337. Ibid., 455.

338. Nicolle, *The Third Crusade*, 37.

339. Ibid., 38.

340. *Itinerarium* in K, Fenwick, *The Third Crusade* (London: 1958), 247–248, in Nicolle, *The Third Crusade*, 75.

341. Nicolle, *The Third Crusade*, 81.

342. Tyerman, *God's War*, 466.

343. Ibid., 464.

344. Möhring, 87.

345. John Gillingham, *Richard the Lionheart* (New York: 1947), 226–230, 233–239, in Carroll, *The Glory of Christendom*, 140.

346. Ibn Shaddad, *Saladin*, 28–29, in Tyerman, *God's War*, 353.

347. Tyerman, *God's War*, 350.

348. Möhring, 91–92.

349. Paul M. Cobb, "Introduction: The World of Saladin," in Möhring, xxiii.

350. Carroll, *The Glory of Christendom*, 148.

351. J.B. Gillingham, *Richard I* (New Haven: 1999), 323–325, in Jonathan Phillips, *The Fourth Crusade and the Sack of Constantinople* (New York: Penguin Books, 2004), 10.

352. John's legacy was so tainted that no future monarch ever used his name.

353. Raimbaut of Vaqueiras, *The Poems of the Troubadour Raimbaut de Vaqueiras*, ed. and trans. J. Liniskill (The Hague: 1964), 218–220, in Phillips, *The Fourth Crusade*, 88.

354. Spoken to the Crusaders upon arrival in Constantinople. Geoffrey of Villehardouin, "The Conquest of Constantinople," *Chronicles of the Crusades*, trans. M.R.B. Shaw (London: 1963), 59, in Phillips, *The Fourth Crusade*, 159.

355. Albigensianism, or Cartharism, was a heresy that erupted in the south of France in the early part of the eleventh century. Migrating from the East, the heresy was a new manifestation of the ancient

Gnostic and Manichaean heresies that infected the early Church. Pope Innocent III tried to stop the heresy by reforming the clergy in southern France, sending missionaries and urging secular rulers to intervene but to no avail. Frustrated by the lack of success and concerned with the growth of the pernicious heresy, Innocent called a Crusade in 1209. The Crusade, which was really a civil war, lasted twenty years and was exceptionally bloody. It achieved mixed results in combating the heresy, which was eventually eradicated through a new papal creation: the inquisitors.

356. R. Bartlett, *Medieval Panorama* (London: 2001), 12–13, and Phillips, *The Fourth Crusade*, xiv.

357. Innocent III, *Solitae*, in A.J. Andrea, *The Medieval Record: Sources of Medieval History* (Boston: 1997), 9, n.4, in Phillips, *The Fourth Crusade*, 5.

358. Innocent III, *Die Register Innocenz' III*, ed. Othmar Hageneder and Anton Haidacher (Graz-Cologne: Hermann Böhlaus Nachf., 1964), I:II, 18–20, in Donald E. Queller and Thomas F. Madden, *The Fourth Crusade—The Conquest of Constantinople*, (Philadelphia: University of Pennsylvania Press, 1997), 1.

359. Tyerman, *God's War*, 480.

360. His first Crusade (the Fourth) was called less than six months into his pontificate. He called his last Crusade at Perugia in the rain less than ten weeks before his death. (Dickson, *The Children's Crusade*, 30.) Among the Crusades called by Innocent are the major campaigns known as the Fourth and Fifth Crusades as well as the Albigensian Crusade.

361. Riley-Smith, *The Crusades*, 148–149.

362. This was instituted during the Albigensian Crusade and led to great difficulty in the prosecution of the campaign for the commanders of the Crusade, as manpower constantly fluctuated based on time rather than mission requirements.

363. Phillips, *The Fourth Crusade*, xiii.

364. Ibid., 47

365. Queller and Madden, *The Fourth Crusade*, 10.

366. On the life expectancy of the Dandolo family see Thomas Madden, "Enrico Dandolo: His Life, His Family, and His Venice before the Fourth Crusade" (Ph.D diss., University of Illinois at Urbana-Champaign, 1993), 63–65, in Queller and Madden, *The Fourth Crusade*, 9. Mariano Sanudo, a sixteenth-century Venetian chronicler indicates Dandolo was eighty-five when elected doge.

Marino Sanudo, *Vitae ducum venetorum*, ed. Lodovico Antonio Muratori, in *Rerum Italicarum Scriptores* (Milan: 1733), vol. 22, col. 527, in Queller and Madden, *The Fourth Crusade*, 9.

367. Queller and Madden, *The Fourth Crusade*, 12.

368. Phillips, *The Fourth Crusade*, 66. What the Crusaders were asking was daunting: ships for an army of almost 35,000 men. The Crusaders also proposed an installment plan of 15,000 marks due on August 1, 1201; 10,000 marks due on November 1, 1201; 10,000 marks due on February 2, 1202 and the balance of 50,000 marks due at the end of April 1202. The ambassadors paid 5,000 marks up front in order to begin construction of the fleet immediately.

369. Phillips, *The Fourth Crusade*, 61.

370. Ibid.

371. Ibid., 65.

372. Queller and Madden, *The Fourth Crusade*, 17.

373. Robert of Clari, *La conquête de Constantinople*, English trans. Edgar H. McNeal (New York: Columbia University Press, 1936), sec. 7, 8, and sec. 11, 9-10, in Queller and Madden, *The Fourth Crusade*, 17.

374. Tyerman, *God's War*, 513.

375. Queller and Madden, *The Fourth Crusade*, 19.

376. Ibid., 23.

377. Villehardouin, *Conquête de Constantinople*, sec. 56, I: 58. In Queller and Madden, *The Fourth Crusade*, 48.

378. Queller and Madden, *The Fourth Crusade*, 49.

379. Ibid., 51.

380. Vitaliano Brunelli, *Storia della città di Zara* (Venice: Istituto Veneto di Arti Grafiche, 1913) 361, in Queller and Madden, *The Fourth Crusade*, 56.

381. Queller and Madden, *The Fourth Crusade*, 57.

382. Ibid., 74.

383. Villehardouin, *Conquête de Constantinople*, sec. 83, I: 82–84. In Queller and Madden, *The Fourth Crusade*, 75.

384. Ibid.

385. Peter of Les Vaux-de-Cernay, *The History of the Albigensian Crusade*, trans. W.A. and M.D. Sibly (Woodbridge: 1998), 58, in Tyerman, *God's War*, 529.

386. Innocent III, *Register*, 5:160 (161), 316, in Queller and Madden, *The Fourth Crusade*, 77.

387. Queller and Madden, *The Fourth Crusade*, 77.

388. Innocent III, *Contemporary Sources for the Fourth Crusade*, trans. A.J. Andrea (Leiden: 2000), 41, in Phillips, *The Fourth Crusade*, 124.
389. Phillips, *The Fourth Crusade*, 196.
390. Queller and Madden, *The Fourth Crusade*, 90.
391. Ibid., 89.
392. Tyerman, *God's War*, 532.
393. Queller and Madden, *The Fourth Crusade*, 102.
394. Ibid.
395. Innocent III, letter to Crusade leaders in *Chronicles of the Crusades*, ed. Hallam, 211.
396. Tyerman, *God's War*, 543.
397. Queller and Madden, *The Fourth Crusade*, 108.
398. France, *Western Warfare*, 107.
399. Villehardouin, "Conquest," *Chronicles of the Crusades*, 64, in Phillips, *The Fourth Crusade*, 164.
400. Robert of Clari, *The Conquest of Constantinople*, trans. E.H. McNeal (New York: 1966), 67, in Tyerman, *God's War*, 544.
401. Villehardouin, *Conquête de Constantinople*, sec. 165, I:166, in Queller and Madden, *The Fourth Crusade*, 122.
402. Queller and Madden, *The Fourth Crusade*, 123.
403. For the number of acres destroyed see Tyerman, *God's War*, 546. For the number of homeless see Thomas F. Madden, "The Fires of the Fourth Crusade in Constantinople, 1203–1204: A Damage Assessment," *Byzantinische Zeitschrift*, 84/85 (1992): 73–74, 88. In Queller and Madden, *The Fourth Crusade*, 125.
404. Tyerman, *God's War*, 546.
405. David Nicolle, *The Fourth Crusade 1202–1204—The Betrayal of Byzantium* (Oxford, UK: Osprey Publishing, 2011), 64.
406. Casualty figures from Queller and Madden, *The Fourth Crusade*, 146, and Nicolle, *The Fourth Crusade*, 64.
407. Tyerman, *God's War*, 549.
408. Queller and Madden, *The Fourth Crusade*, 151.
409. According to Queller and Madden, *The Fourth Crusade*, 179, the Crusaders suffered 100 killed in action and presumably many wounded.
410. Robert of Clari in Nicolle, *The Fourth Crusade*, 70.
411. Robert of Clari, *Conquest*, 97, in Phillips, *The Fourth Crusade*, 251.
412. Queller and Madden, *The Fourth Crusade*, 183.
413. Ibid.
414. Ibid.

415. Nicolle, *The Fourth Crusade*, 76.

416. Ibid.

417. Geoffrey of Villehardouin, *The Conquest of Constantinople*, trans. M.R.B. Shaw (London: 1963), 93, in Tyerman, *God's War*, 501.

418. Phillips, *The Fourth Crusade*, 258.

419. Queller and Madden, *The Fourth Crusade*, 195.

420. Nicetas Choniates, *Historia*, 573. In Queller and Madden, *The Fourth Crusade*, 194.

421. Geoffrey of Villehardouin, *La Conquête de Constantinople*, ed. and French trans. E. Faral, 2 vols. (Paris: 1973), English trans. M.R.B. Shaw as *Joinville & Villehardouin: Chronicles of the Crusades* (Harmondsworth: 1963), ch. 250, tr. 92, in Housley, *Fighting for the Cross*, 165.

422. The estimate is Villehardouin's in Queller and Madden, *The Fourth Crusade*, 200.

423. Madden, *The New Concise History of the Crusades*, 118.

424. Horace K. Mann, *The Lives of the Popes of the Middle Ages*, vol. XII (London: 1925–1932), 266–267; Mary Purcell, *St. Anthony and His Times* (Dublin: 1960), 26, in Carroll, *The Glory of Christendom*, 158.

425. Steven Runciman, *A History of the Crusades*, iii (Cambridge: 1951–1953), 130, in Tyerman, *God's War*, 495.

426. Tyerman, *God's War*, 553.

427. Phillips, *The Fourth Crusade*, 311.

428. Queller and Madden, *The Fourth Crusade*, 198.

429. John Paul II, "Welcome Address to the Ecumenical Patriarch Bartholomew I," 3. http://www.vatican.va/holy_father/john_paul_ii/speeches/2004/june/documents/hf_jp-ii_spe_20040629_bartholomew-i_en.html. Accessed November 1, 2013.

430. Ibid.

431. 1 Cor 4:5.

432. John Paul II, "Welcome Address to the Ecumenical Patriarch Bartholomew I," 3. http://www.vatican.va/holy_father/john_paul_ii/speeches/2004/june/documents/hf_jp-ii_spe_20040629_bartholomew-i_en.html. Accessed November 1, 2013.

433. Arnaldo Fortini, *Nova Vita di San Francesco* (Roma: Carucci Editore, 1981), 14, in Frank M. Rega, *St. Francis of Assisi and the Conversion of the Muslims With a Concise Biography of the Saint* (Rockford, IL: TAN Books and Publishers, Inc., 2007, 130).

434. Ibn al-Djusi was a contemporary of Frederick II's living in Jerusalem when the emperor visited in 1229. Thomas C. Van Cleve, *The*

Emperor Frederick II of Hohenstaufen (Oxford: 1972), 225. Cited in Carroll, The Glory of Christendom, 214.

435. "Francesco" was a nickname meaning "the Frenchman" since the boy's mother was French and his merchant father spent time in France on business. Rega, St. Francis of Assisi, 3.

436. Thomas of Celano, The Second Life of St. Francis, Book One, trans. Placid Hermann, O.F.M., Chapter 7, no. 12, 372, (included in Omnibus, in Rega, St. Francis of Assisi, 10.)

437. Gary Dickson, The Children's Crusade—Medieval History, Modern Mythistory (New York: Palgrave Macmillian, 2010), xi.

438. Ibid., 127.

439. Tyerman, God's War, 609.

440. Ibid., 610.

441. Dickson, The Children's Crusade, 55.

442. Auctarium Mortui Maris (to 1234) ed. D.L.C. Bethmann, MGH. SS. 6:467, in Dickson, The Children's Crusade, 55.

443. The story of Stephen's receiving a divine mandate and the number of participants (more than likely an exaggerated number; Dickson cites an English chronicler that puts the number at 15,000, which may be closer to the actual number. Dickson, The Children's Crusade, 71) is from the Laon Anonymous chronicle. Chronicon Universal Anonymi Laudunensis 1154–1219, ed. A. Cartellieri and W. Stechele (Leipzig: 1909), 70–71. Translation from J.F.C. Hecker, The Epidemics of the Middle Ages (trans. B.G. Babington) 3rd ed. (Trübner & Co.: London: 1859), 354. Quoted in Dickson, The Children's Crusade, 65.

444. Dickson, The Children's Crusade, 109.

445. Ibid., 124.

446. Annales Marbacenses (to 1220) ed. H. Bloch in MGH. SS. Rerum Germ. In usum scholar. 9:82, in Dickson, The Children's Crusade, 113.

447. Dickson, The Children's Crusade, 118–119.

448. Iacopo da Varagine e la sua chronica di Genova (to 1297) ed. G. Monleone Ist. Stor. Ital., Fonti, 85, 2 (Rome: 1941), 374. J.F.C. Hecker, The Epidemics of the Middle Ages (trans. B.G. Babington) 3rd ed. (Trübner & Co.: London, 1859), 358. Quoted in Dickson, The Children's Crusade, 2.

449. Annales s. Medardi Suessionensibus (to 1249) ed. G. Waitz, MGH. SS. 26: 521. Hecker, 359, in Dickson, The Children's Crusade, 2.

450. Ibid., 165.

451. Ibid., 166.

452. Voltaire, *Le Micromégas avec une historie des croisades*, in Dickson, *The Children's Crusade*, 171.
453. Tyerman, *God's War*, 606.
454. Ibid., 612
455. Ibid., 614.
456. Ibid., 622.
457. Ibid., 621.
458. *Patrologia cursus complètes. Series Latina*, ed. J.P. Migne (Paris: 1844–1864), 216, col. 830, no. xxxv, in Tyerman, *God's War*, 615.
459. Pernoud, *The Crusaders*, 166.
460. René Grousset, *The Epic of the Crusades*, trans. Noel Lindsay (New York: Orion Press, 1970), 207.
461. Tyerman, *God's War*, 629.
462. High number of Crusaders in Tyerman, *God's War*, 637. Numbers of those who marched to Cairo from Oliver of Paderborn, *Capture of Damietta*, trans. E. Peters, *Christian Society and the Crusades 1198–1229* (Philadephia: 1971), 114, in Tyerman, *God's War*, 638.
463. Madden, *The New Concise History of the Crusades*, 148.
464. Tyerman, *God's War*, 626.
465. Madden, *New Concise History of the Crusades*, 150.
466. Oliver of Paderborn, *Capture of Damietta*, 124, in Tyerman, *God's War*, 633.
467. Tyerman, *God's War*, 643.
468. Ibid., 638.
469. Omar Englebert, *St. Francis of Assisi* (Chicago: 1965), 236, in Carroll, *The Glory of Christendom*, 197.
470. Pernoud, *The Crusaders*, 267.
471. Rega, *St. Francis of Assisi*, 61.
472. Englebert, *St. Francis of Assisi*, 236–240 in Carroll, *The Glory of Christendom*, 197.
473. Pernoud, *The Crusaders*, 269.
474. Rega, *St. Francis of Assisi*, chs. 13 & 14.
475. From a total population of 60,000. Madden, *The New Concise History of the Crusades*, 151.
476. Oliver of Paderborn, *The Capture of Damietta*, 94, in Madden, *The New Concise History of the Crusades*, 151.
477. Seward, *The Monks of War*, 66.
478. Tyerman, *God's War*, 649.
479. Ibid., 739.

480. Maalouf, *The Crusades Through Arab Eyes*, 226.
481. Tyerman, *God's War*, 740.
482. Carroll, *The Glory of Christendom*, 210.
483. Tyerman, *God's War*, 756.
484. Carroll, *The Glory of Christendom*, 210.
485. The term is Régine Pernoud's. See *The Crusaders*, 274.
486. Tyerman, *God's War*, 745.
487. Ibid., 747.
488. Van Cleve, *Frederick II*, 217 note 5, in Tyerman, *God's War*, 750.
489. Grousset, *The Epic of the Crusades*, 231.
490. Ibid., 232.
491. Tyerman, *God's War*, 753.
492. Pernoud, *The Crusaders*, 291.
493. Tyerman, *God's War*, 740.
494. To his troops before the amphibious landing at Damietta, Egypt in 1249, in Pernoud, *The Crusaders,* 301.
495. David Nicolle, *Acre 1291—Bloody Sunset of the Crusader States* (New York: Osprey Publishing, 2005), 89.
496. The story is recounted by John of Joinville in his *Histoire de Saint Louis*, 61–63. Jacques Le Goff, *Saint Louis*, trans. Gareth Evan Gollrad (Notre Dame: University of Notre Dame, 2009), 109.
497. The story is from Matthew Paris as quoted in Le Goff, *Saint Louis*, 112.
498. France at the time of St. Louis contained 10 million out of a total 60 million people in Christendom. (R. Fossier, *"Les campagnes au temps de Philippe Auguste: developpement demographique et transformations sociales dans le monde rural,"* in *La France de Philippe Auguste. Le Temps des mutations* (Paris: 1982), 628. In Le Goff, *Saint Louis*, 33.) The royal capital of Paris contained 100,000 inhabitants (Le Goff, *Saint Louis*, 33).
499. The term "perfect Crusader" is Pernoud's. See Pernoud, *The Crusaders*, 294.
500. Le Goff refers to the thirteenth century as the century of St. Louis. Le Goff, *Saint Louis*, xx.
501. Le Goff, *Saint Louis*, xxi.
502. Ibid., 74.
503. Joinville, *Histoire de Saint Louis*, 40–41, in Le Goff, *Saint Louis*, 6.
504. Le Goff, *Saint Louis*, 587.
505. Ibid., 205.
506. The Franciscans, especially the Poor Clares, have a special devotion

to her. She is also one of the "incorruptibles," or saints whose bodies have not decayed or decomposed since death.

507. Le Goff, *Saint Louis*, 204.

508. Ibid., 610.

509. Ibid., 630.

510. William of Saint-Pathus, *Vie de Saint Louis*, ed. Henri-François Delaborde (Paris: 1899), 123, in Le Goff, *Saint Louis*, 622.

511. Le Goff, *Saint Louis*, 625.

512. Previous Crusade historians numbered the two expeditions of Louis as the Seventh and Eighth Crusades but modern Crusade historians refer to them as the First and Second Crusades of St. Louis.

513. Tyerman, *God's War*, 781.

514. Le Goff, *Saint Louis*, 126. According to Le Goff, fifteen of the twenty-eight royal investigators were mendicant friars: eight Dominicans and seven Franciscans. Le Goff, *Saint Louis*, 613.

515. Tyerman, *God's War*, 782.

516. W.C. Jordan, *Louis IX and the Challenge of the Crusade* (Princeton: Princeton University Press, 1979), 65–104, in Tyerman, *God's War*, 777.

517. Louis Sébastien Le Nain de Tillemont, *Vie de Saint Louis* (Société de l'Histoire de France: 1847–1851), 3:177–78, in Le Goff, *Saint Louis*, 132.

518. Le Goff, *Saint Louis*, 66.

519. Tyerman, *God's War*, 784.

520. Ibid., 788.

521. Gabrieli, *Arab Historians of the Crusades* (New York: Routledge, 1969), 90, in Tyerman, *God's War*, 792.

522. John France, *Western Warfare*, 109.

523. Le Goff, *Saint Louis*, 202.

524. Ibid., 225.

525. Tyerman, *God's War*, 793.

526. Ibid., 795.

527. Ibid.

528. Ibid., 796.

529. William of Nangis, *Gesta Ludovici IX, Recueil des historiens des Gaules et de la France*, vol. 20, ed. C.F. Daunou and J. Naudet (Paris: 1840), 381, in Le Goff, *Saint Louis*, 616.

530. Le Goff, *Saint Louis*, 624.

531. William of Saint-Pathus, *Vie de Saint Louis*, 127–128, in Le Goff, *Saint Louis*, 624.

532. David O'Connell, *Les Propos de Saint Louis* (Paris, 1974), 163–172, in

Le Goff, *Saint Louis*, 139.

533. Le Goff, *Saint Louis*, 143.

534. Grousset, *The Epic of the Crusades*, 258.

535. Ibid., 260.

536. Maalouf, *The Crusades Through Arab Eyes*, 248.

537. Tyerman, *God's War*, 807.

538. Francesco Gabrieli, *Arab Historians of the Crusades* (New York: Routledge, 1969), 311, in Madden, *The New Concise History of the Crusades*, 182.

539. Tyerman, *God's War*, 808, 809.

540. *Vita* in *Recueil des historiens des Gaules et de la France*, xx, 20, in Tyerman, *God's War*, 810.

541. Tyerman, *God's War*, 810.

542. Ibid., 812.

543. The hour of mercy is 3 p.m., the time when Jesus died on the Cross. For Louis's death at that time see *Vita* in *Recueil des historiens des Gaules et de la France*, 20:23, in Le Goff, *Saint Louis*, 226. For Louis's last words see William of St. Pathus, *Vie de Saint Louis*, ed. Delaborde (Paris: 1899), 153–155, in Steven Runciman, *A History of the Crusades—vol. III, The Kingdom of Acre and the later Crusades* (London: The Folio Society, 1994), 244.

544. Tyerman, *God's War*, 812.

545. It was not uncommon for women to journey on Crusade. The presence of women can be traced back to the First Crusade. Some were wives of noblemen and took the cross motivated by their faith as well as a desire not to be separated from their spouse. Like the men, most desired to receive the spiritual benefits promised for participation in the holy endeavor.

546. Kenneth M. Setton, *A History of the Crusades, vol. II* (Madison, WI: 1969), 517, in Carroll, *The Glory of Christendom*, 294.

547. Nicolle, *Acre 1291*, 52.

548. Ibid., 53.

549. Ibid.

550. Ibid.

551. Acre was on a thirteenth-century list of Islamic holy sites. Nicolle, *Acre 1291*, 8.

552. For Muslim numbers see Seward, *The Monks of War*, 87. For Christian numbers see Nicolle, *Acre 1291*, 39.

553. Tyerman, *God's War*, 821.

554. Ibid., 818.
555. Ibid., 820.
556. Nicolle, *Acre 1291*, 53.
557. Ibid., 57.
558. Ibid., 65.
559. Ibid.
560. Ibid., 68.
561. Templar of Tyre in Nicolle, *Acre 1291*, 68.
562. Nicolle, *Acre 1291*, 76.
563. Ibid.
564. Ibid.
565. Grousset, *The Epic of the Crusades*, 265.
566. Templar of Tyre in Nicolle, *Acre 1291*, 77.
567. Grousset, *The Epic of the Crusades*, 265.
568. Nicolle, *Acre 1291*, 81.
569. Templar of Tyre in Nicolle, *Acre 1291*, 82.
570. The events in the Templar Tower were recorded by the Templar of Tyre in Pernoud, *The Crusaders*, 330–331.
571. Nicolle, *Acre 1291*, 84.
572. Tyerman, *God's War*, 826.
573. Ibid., 825.
574. A speech at the Congress of Mantua to rally Western warriors to fight the Ottoman Turks after the sack and conquest of Constantinople. Pius II in Franz Babinger, *Mehmet the Conqueror and His Time* 170–171, in Roger Crowley, *1453: The Holy War for Constantinople and the Clash of Islam and the West* (New York: 2005), 242.
575. Jérome Maurand, *Itinénraire de J. Maurand d'Antibes à Constantinople (1544)* (Paris: 1901), 67–69, in Roger Crowley, *Empires of the Sea— The Siege of Malta, the Battle of Lepanto, and the Contest for the Center of the World* (New York: Random House, 2009), 68.
576. 12,000 of the 22,000 inhabitants were killed during the invasion. Crowley, *1453*, 241.
577. Giovanni Laggetto, *Historia della guerra di Otranto del 1480*, in Matthew E. Bunson, "How the 800 Martyrs of Otranto Saved Rome," *This Rock* (Catholic Answers), vol. 19, Number 6, July 2008. http://www.catholic.com/magazine/articles/how-the-800-martyrs-of-otranto-saved-rome. Accessed January 20, 2014.
578. Saverio de Marco, *Compendiosa istoria degli ottocento martiri otrantini*, in Bunson, "How the 800 Martyrs of Otranto Saved Rome."

579. Norman Housley, "Pope Pius II and Crusading," *Crusades*, vol. 11, The Society for the Study of the Crusades and the Latin East (Burlington, VT: Ashgate Publishing Company, 2012), 245.

580. Crowley, *1453*, 44.

581. Ibid., 42.

582. Tyerman, *God's War*, 863.

583. Doukas, *Fragmenta Historicorum Graecorum*, vol. 5 (Paris: 1870), 247–248, in Crowley, *1453*, 90.

584. Crowley, *1453*, 93–94.

585. Ibid., 94

586. Ibid.

587. Ibid., 116.

588. Crowley, *1453*, 67.

589. Ibid., 116.

590. Total number of guns and shots per day from Crowley, *1453*, 112, 118.

591. Nestor-Iskander, *The Tale of Constantinople*, 49, in Crowley, *1453*, 161.

592. The core of the Ottoman army was the fearsome "Janissary" troops who were personally loyal to the sultan. Janissaries were taken from the Ottoman system of "boy tribute," which required Christian parents in the occupied territories of Eastern Europe to hand over their male children between six and twenty years of age to Muslim authorities. These male tributes were sent to the sultan's court where they were forcibly converted to Islam and educated. Some of the tributes were chosen for a civil service career path, and served as government officials throughout the Ottoman Empire. Others became Janissaries and were sent to military schools where they learned the art of personal combat and military science. Originally, the tributes were not allowed to marry or own property because their lives were totally dedicated to the sultan's service. In the history of the Ottoman Empire upwards of a million Christian boys were forcibly removed from their homes and compelled to serve the sultan. The system of "boy tributes" was not officially abolished until 1848. Diane Moczar, *Islam at the Gates—How Christendom Defeated the Ottoman Turks* (Manchester, NH: Sophia Institute Press, 2008), 40.

593. Crowley, *1453*, 211.

594. Leonard of Chios, *De Capta a Mehemethe II Constantinopoli*, 44, in Crowley, *1453*, 177.

595. Crowley, *1453*, 215.

596. Carroll, *The Glory of Christendom*, 568.

597. Ibid.

598. Crowley, *1453*, 220.

599. Although recent reports indicate a movement in Istanbul to return the space to a mosque.

600. Number of killed, see Tyerman, *God's War*, 864. Number seized and enslaved, see Crowley, *1453*, 233, 235.

601. Referred to by the Greeks as *polis* or "the city," and when going to the city they said "*eis tin polin*"; it is possible the Ottomans heard "Istanbul," giving the conquered city its new name. Crowley, *1453*, 30. It is also recorded that Mehmet called the city "Islambol" meaning "full of Islam." Crowley, *1453*, 237.

602. Norman Housley, "Pope Pius II and Crusading," 245.

603. Pius II in Franz Babinger, *Mehmet the Conqueror and His Time,* 170–171, in Crowley, *1453*, 242.

604. Moczar, *Islam at the Gates*, 90.

605. Ludwig von Pastor, *History of the Popes*, vol. III (St. Louis: 1895–1935), 326, in Carroll, *The Glory of Christendom*, 583.

606. *Pii II Orations*, 3:117, in Housley, "Pope Pius II and Crusading," 234.

607. Housley, "Pope Pius II and Crusading," 246.

608. Crowley, *Empires of the* Sea, 4.

609. Ibid., xvi.

610. Tim Pickles, *Malta 1565—Last Battle of the Crusades* (New York: Osprey Publishing, 1998), 14.

611. Crowley, *Empires of the Sea*, 90.

612. Numbers of troops from Pickles, *Malta 1565*, 23. Number of artillery pieces from Crowley, *Empires of the Sea*, 95–96.

613. Crowley, *Empires of the Sea*, 111.

614. Ernle Bradford, *The Great Siege* (New York: 1961), 43, in Warren H. Carroll, *The Cleaving of Christendom—vol. IV in A History of Christendom* (Front Royal, VA: Christendom Press, 2000), 824.

615. Warren H. Carroll and Anne W. Carroll, *The Crisis of Christendom—vol. VI in A History of Christendom* (Front Royal, VA: Christendom Press, 2013), 824.

616. Bradford, *The Great Siege*, 18, in Carroll, *The Crisis of Christendom*, 824.

617. Pickles, *Malta 1565*, 64.

618. Crowley, *Empires of the Sea*, 95.

619. Ibid., 113.

620. Ibid., 123.

621. Ibid., 115.

622. Seward, *The Monks of War*, 283.
623. Ibid.
624. Pickles, *Malta 1565*, 45.
625. Crowley, *Empires of the Sea*, 139.
626. Ibid., 142.
627. Bradford, *The Great Siege*, 123, in Carroll, *The Crisis of Christendom*, 827.
628. Seward, *The Monks of War*, 284; Crowley, *Empires of the Sea*, 140.
629. Seward, *The Monks of War*, 286.
630. Francisco Balbi Di Correggio, *The Siege of Malta, 1565*, trans. Ernle Bradford (Rochester, NY: The Boydell Press, 2005), 144.
631. Vertot, *Histoire des Chevaliers Hospitaliers de S. Jean de Jerusalem*, vol. IV, 51, in Seward, *The Monks of War*, 286.
632. Francisco Balbi, *The Siege of Malta*, 144.
633. Crowley, *Empires of the Sea*, 176.
634. Ibid., 185.
635. Number of knights killed from Moczar, *Islam at the Gates*, 157. Number of Maltese killed from Crowley, *Empires of the Sea*, 185.
636. Balbi, *The Siege of Malta*, 189.
637. Crowley, *Empires of the Sea*, 196.
638. The best image of galley warfare comes from the 1959 movie *Ben Hur*, starring Charlton Heston. Although that movie was set in the time of the Roman Empire, the sixteenth-century Mediterranean oared galley was not much different from the Roman vessels portrayed in the movie.
639. Crowley, *Empires of the Sea*, 77.
640. Ibrahim Pecevi, *Pecevi Tarihi*, vol. 1 (Ankara: 1981), 310–311, in Crowley, *Empires of the Sea*, 234.
641. Crowley, *Empires of the Sea*, 232.
642. Jack Beeching, *The Galleys at Lepanto* (New York: Charles Scribner's Sons, 1982), 216. Cervantes would recall the Battle of Lepanto in his most famous work, *Don Quixote*, when he wrote, "Those Christians who died there were even happier than those who remained alive and victorious." In Victor Davis Hanson, *Carnage and Culture* (New York: Anchor Books, 2001), 253.
643. Crowley, *Empires of the Sea*, 256.
644. P. de Bourdeille de Brantome, *Oeuvres complètes*, vol. 3 ed. L. Lalanne, (Paris: 1864), 125, in Crowley, *Empires of the Sea*, 256.
645. G.K. Chesterton, *Lepanto*, ed. Dale Ahlquist (San Francisco: Ignatius Press, 2003), 62.

646. For the amount of time it took to form up see Crowley, *Empires of the Sea*, 257.

647. Crowley, *Empires of the Sea*, 264.

648. Ibid., 274.

649. Ibid., 260.

650. Ibid., 276.

651. Moczar, *Islam at the Gates*, 192.

652. G.K. Chesterton, *Lepanto*, ed. Dale Ahlquist, 79 & 88.

653. *Lepanto*, 88, ed. Dale Ahlquist—from *On the Place of Chesterton*, 78.

654. John Stoye, *The Siege of Vienna—The Last Great Trial Between the Cross and Crescent* (New York: Pegasus Books, 2006), 27.

655. Ibid., 28.

656. Moczar, *Islam at the Gates*, 200.

657. Ibid.

658. Simon Millar, *Vienna 1683—Christian Europe Repels the Ottomans* (New York: Osprey Publishing, 2008), 44.

659. Stoye, *The Siege of Vienna*, 108.

660. Millar, *Vienna 1683*, 17.

661. Stoye, *The Siege of Vienna*, 131.

662. Ibid., 138.

663. Millar, *Vienna 1683*, 93. These small pastries acquired the name *croissant* for their crescent shape, and are usually associated with France, but their origin stems from the siege of Vienna and so they are rightfully considered Austrian. Legend has it that the French adopted the tasty pastry when Marie Antoinette, who was born in Vienna, brought the item with her to France.

664. Millar, *Vienna 1683*, 89.

665. L. Pukianiec, *Sobieski a Stolica Apostolska na tle wojny z Turcja (1683–1684)* (Vilna: 1937), 1, in Stoye, *The Siege of Vienna*, 174. Charles V's quote was adopted from Julius Caesar's famous phrase, "I came, I saw, I conquered."

666. Moczar, *Islam at the Gates*, 207.

667. Belloc, *The Great Heresies*, 71. It is interesting that two great Ottoman defeats occurred on September 11: Malta in 1565 and Vienna in 1683. I believe that Osama bin Laden was aware of the significance of these dates and specifically choose that day for his attacks on the United States.

668. Stoye, *The Siege of Vienna*, 194.

669. For the Turks' declaring World War I a *jihad*, see Housley, *Contesting*

the Crusades, 157.

670. Prayer from a thirteenth-century knight in Tyerman, *God's War*, 921.

671. Quote from the man who tried to assassinate Pope John Paul II in May 1981. Carole Hillenbrand, "The Legacy of the Crusades," in *Crusades—The Illustrated History*, ed. Thomas F. Madden (Ann Arbor: The University of Michigan Press, 2004), 208.

672. Tyerman, *God's War*, 918.

673. Andrew Curry, "The First Holy War," *U.S. News & World Report*, March 31, 2002. Accessed February 2, 2014.

674. Karen Armstrong, *Holy War: The Crusades and Their Impact on Today's World*, 2nd edition (New York: Random House, 2001), xiv, in Rodney Stark, *God's Battalions*, 245. For Armstrong's self-description as a "freelance monotheist," see "The Freelance Monotheism of Karen Armstrong", transcript of an interview with Krista Tippett on the show "On Being," May 8, 2008. http://www.onbeing.org/program/freelance-monotheism-karen-armstrong/transcript/4487. Accessed February 2, 2014.

675. Madden, *The New Concise History of the Crusades*, 217.

676. Emmanuel Sivan, *Modern Arab Historiography of the Crusades* (Tel Aviv: Tel Aviv University, Shiloah Center for Middle Eastern and African Studies, 1973), 12, in Stark, *God's Battalions*, 247.

677. Tyerman, *The Debate on the Crusades*, 150.

678. Madden, *The New Concise History of the Crusades*, 220.

679. One scholar maintains that Muslims remembered Saladin in the centuries after his death, although the argument is not overwhelmingly convincing. Diana Abouali, "Saladin's Legacy in the Middle East before the Nineteenth Century," *Crusades*, vol. 10, The Society for the Study of the Crusades and the Latin East (Burlington, VT: Ashgate Publishing Company, 2011), 175–189.

680. See Scott's 1825 novel, *The Talisman*.

681. Madden, *The New Concise History of the Crusades*, 219.

682. Ibid.

683. Tyerman, *The Debate on the Crusades*, 239.

684. Ibid.

685. Maalouf, *The Crusades Through Arab Eyes*, 266.

686. Riley-Smith, *The Crusades*, 307.

687. Madden, *The New Concise History of the Crusades*, 222.

688. Muhammad ibn Umar al-Waqidi, *Kitab al-Maghazi*, vol. 3 (London: Oxford University Press, 1966), 1113, in Karsh, *Islamic Imperialism*, 19.

689. Belloc, *The Crusades*, 5.

690. Piers Paul Read, Foreword, in Regine Pernoud's *The Templars—Knights of Christ*, trans. Henry Taylor (San Francisco: Ignatius Press, 2009), 7.

691. Tyerman, *God's War*, 917.